Praise for *The Man Who Mapped the Arctic* by Peter Steele

"The stuff of myth comes from a book like this … George Back's diaries describe a far north so full of wonder that he returned over and over, even after near starvation and the deaths of fellow crew members on previous voyages. His journals record physical hardship beyond what most of us could imagine …

I was most fascinated by the cumulative effect of the enormous quotidian detail author Peter Steele has brought to his subject. His wide-ranging research gives us a thorough sampling not only of Back's journals but of others' writing at the same time, and informative and appealing conjecture on 'what it must have been like,' the dark, cold forts, the starving natives camped outside, the fearsome ice, the intense hope aroused by a single first ray of spring sunshine."
— *The Globe & Mail*

"The history of Arctic exploration is replete with tales of hardship and heroism, but few more so than the epic that is the life of George Back … Steele's book is peppered with snippets that fill in the mundane blanks of Back's life. This detailed research is what makes his book so very readable … A well-researched portrait of one of the Arctic's most remarkable, yet, little-known explorers."
—*Arctic Book Review*

"Peter Steele, who once ran the Grenfell flying doctor service in Labrador, lives in Whitehorse. The author of numerous books on mountaineering, he personally followed Back's progress in Canada's north country by plane, boat and on foot. And he probably had better provisions than Back, who was often reduced to eating his moccasins or *tripe de roches*, a stomach-destroying lichen that helped sustain life for Franklin's followers … [this] well-researched, entertainingly written saga of northern derring-do arrives like fat caribou to a starving reading audience."
— *The Sun-Times*, Owen Sound

Praise for Peter Steele's previous biography, *Eric Shipton: Everest and Beyond:*

"A passionate and sensitive portrait."   — *Literary Review*

"It is strong narrative drive and vivid scene-setting, based on his own authentic experience, that make the whole book so enjoyable."
— *Daily Telegraph*

"The best and most rounded account that I have read on the life of a great mountaineer, explorer, and charismatic man ... A must read."
— *The Explorer's Journal*

Praise for Peter Steele's *Doctor On Everest*:

"An intensely human book which leaves the ordinary reader with a much more vivid idea of what an attempt on Everest must be like ... The drama, tragedy and high adventure are all there, but taken almost casually in the doctor's long stride."
— *Daily Telegraph*

"Of the many books about Everest published during the past fifty years, *Doctor on Everest* is the only one to give the uninitiated the exact feeling of what it is like to be on one of these expeditions."
— *The Sunday Times*, UK

"An invaluable account of men — and one woman — under the extremest pressure in a howling waste and [Steele] makes no bones about the private horror of the experience."
— *The Observer*, UK

The Man who Mapped the Arctic

Also by Peter Steele

Two and Two Halves to Bhutan
Doctor on Everest
Backcountry Medical Guide/Far From Help
Atlin's Gold
Eric Shipton – Everest and Beyond
(Winner of 1998 Boardman Tasker prize for mountain literature)

The Man who Mapped the Arctic

Peter Steele

RAINCOAST BOOKS

Vancouver

Published in Canada in hardcover in 2003 by Raincoast Books
9050 Shaughnessy Street
Vancouver, British Columbia
Canada, v6p 6e5
www.raincoast.com

Raincoast Books acknowledges the ongoing financial support of the
Government of Canada through The Canada Council for the Arts and the Book Publishing
Industry Development Program (BPIDP); and the Government of
British Columbia through the BC Arts Council.

Maps by Peter Steele

NATIONAL LIBRARY OF CANADA CATALOGUING IN PUBLICATION

Steele, Peter, 1935-
The man who mapped the Arctic : the intrepid life of George Back, Franklin's lieutenant / Peter Steele.

Includes index.
ISBN 1-55192-648-2 (bound.) — ISBN 1-55192-648-2 (pbk.)

1. Back, George, Sir, 1796-1878. 2. Back, George, Sir, 1796-1878—Journeys–Arctic Regions. 3.
Arctic Regions—Discovery and exploration—British. 4. Back River (Nunavut)—Discovery and
exploration—British 5. Explorers—England—Biography. 6. Explorers—Arctic
Regions–Biography. 1. Title.
FC3961.1.B32S73 2003   917.1904'1'092   C2003-910392-7

F1090.5.B32.S7 2003

10 9 8 7 6 5 4 3 2 1 0

At Raincoast Books we are committed to protecting the environment and to the responsible
use of natural resources. We are acting on this committment by working with suppliers and
printers to phase out our use of paper produced from ancient forest. This book is one step
towards thatgoal. It is printed on 100% ancient-forest-free paper (100% post-consumer
recycled), processed chlorine-and acid-free, and supplied by New Leaf Paper. It is printed
with vegetable-based inks. For further information, visit our website at www.raincoast.com.
We are working with Markets Initiative (www.oldgrowthfree.com) on this project.

Printed and bound in Canada by Friesens

To Jan and Elizabeth Morris,
and for Tim, Ben and Sasha

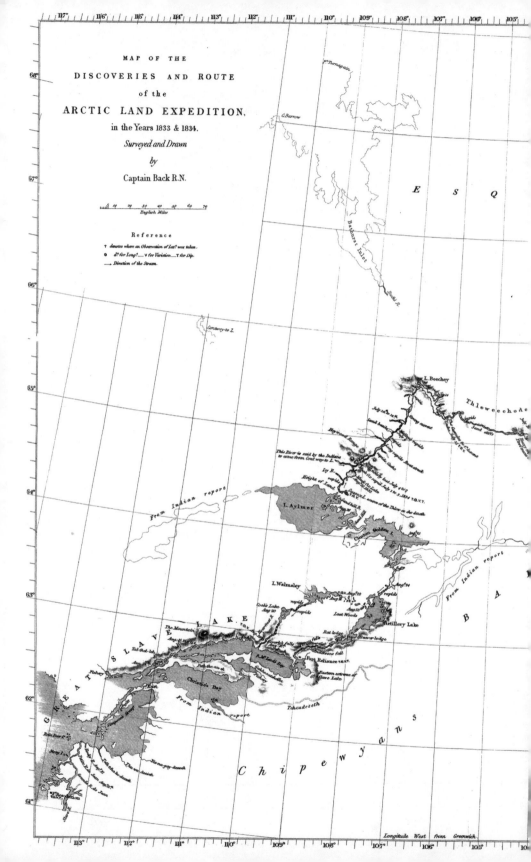

MAP OF THE

DISCOVERIES AND ROUTE

of the

ARCTIC LAND EXPEDITION,

in the Years 1833 & 1834.

Surveyed and Drawn

by

Captain Back R.N.

English Miles

Reference

† denotes where an Observation of Lat.? was taken.
⊙ d.? for Long? ⊻ for Variation ⊤ for Dip.
→ Direction of the Stream.

Contents

Illustrations

Preface

Biographers of nineteenth-century Royal Navy officers have to overcome a fundamental problem: the tight lips of their subjects, the upper one being stiff as well. Partly this is the style of an era when such people did not wear their hearts on their sleeves; partly because most service writing took the form of official journals or reports ultimately for the eyes of their employer, the Admiralty; partly because when they did write letters – even love letters – these were couched in circuitous prose that allowed scant expression of personal feelings. Sensing the character of one's subject, therefore, often relies on interpreting snippets, either in their own writings or in the comments of others. In George Back's case, one of the most distinguished yet least written about Arctic explorers, my quest has left me constantly in awe of his strengths and surprised at his weaknesses.

My researches have taken me to George Back's birthplace in Stockport, Cheshire; across France from the Pyrenees to his Napoleonic prison in Verdun; and along his stagecoach route from Great Yarmouth to the northern tip of Scotland when he was obliged to chase after his first expedition ship. I have followed his Arctic journeys by floatplane throughout Canada's Northwest Territories and Nunavut; on foot through the Richardson Mountains and by canoe to the Mackenzie Delta; overland to the shores of Prudhoe Bay, Alaska; by boat to the northern tip of Labrador.

I am grateful to various companions on these Canadian Arctic journeys which, while tough for us, left me with an increased respect for the stamina of a man who travelled with none of our foreknowledge of the land or survival techniques, and whose equipment was greatly inferior. John Faulkner, judge perforce, pilot for pleasure, in the summer of 2000 flew me in his single-engine floatplane over some of George Back's remote routes in Canada's north and kept his cool when the plane's generator quit over the Barrens near the Arctic Ocean. My thanks too to the nameless Quebecois pilot/mechanic who by chance was in the area photo-mapping the tundra when we needed help. Monty Alford and David Young shared with me several long traverses on foot across the wildest parts of the Yukon, most notably the Richardson Mountains. Alan Dennis was my canoeing partner on the Ogilvie-Peel River.

Edmund Clerihew Bentley made a pertinent distinction:

> The art of Biography
> Is different from Geography.
> Geography is about maps
> But Biography is about chaps.

However, the chaps in this narrative were much exercised about maps. Mapping was why they were there. So the aim in my sketch maps has been for readers to know at all times where that is. The indigenous peoples appear to have given few names to prominent geographical features, certainly not the plethora that sprang from visits by Europeans. Franklin, Back, and other explorers could, and did, walk in and map a continent. Then by way of recognizing their patrons and sponsors these 'first white men' sprinkled the maps they drew with the names of luminaries, major and minor, who are now recorded in perpetuity to the total denial of native culture. In our more politically enlightened time several places across the north have acquired, or reverted to, Indian or Inuit usage. However, the maps in this book follow Back and Franklin's nomenclature and, by the same token, the currently unacceptable term Eskimo is used throughout for consistency because that is how the journals of the period refer to the Inuit.

Authors get their names on the title page of their books; but biography is necessarily a collaborative effort. I have leaned shame-lessly on friendly readers, critics, librarians, and experts in their own special fields.

Researching from the Yukon, far away from major libraries,

would have been impossible without the superb service of Inter Library Loan, coordinated by Joy Wicket at Whitehorse Public Library, which supplied me with several dozen books from every corner of Canada and photocopied articles mentioned in my bibliography.

The Canada Council for the Arts awarded me a very generous fellowship. A Northern Research Institute Endowment Fellowship of Yukon College and the Advanced Artist Award funded by Lotteries Yukon together financed the fly-over of most of George Back's routes.

Those who read this book in typescript have widely disparate expertise and viewpoints. Their red-inked corrections, which may have saved me from some critics' jaws, made my intended final draft look like a bad case of measles. Philippa Foster-Back has unstintingly supported my quest of her great-great-great-great-Uncle George, as did her perceptive husband, Simon, bilingual in French. Stuart and Mary Houston transcribed, annotated, and published the journals of Franklin's three fellow officers on the first Arctic Land Expedition. Not only did this labour save me countless hours of deciphering spidery copperplate handwriting, but Stuart read my near final draft and in an amiable headmasterly way corrected and deservedly chastised me. Ian MacLaren, the Houstons' scholarly colleague gave me encouragement and advice. Robert Stacey, University of Toronto, provided access to and wise commentaries on J. Russell Harper's transcript of Back's journal written on Franklin's Second Land Expedition.

I also owe heartfelt thanks to: Peter Hopkirk, my mentor, whose friendship I treasure and pearls I heed; William Mills of the Scott Polar Research Institute for sowing the seed of an idea to write about George Back in the first place; Louise Crossley, polar historian from Tasmania, happily met at dinner in Somerset, England; Richard Gregory, who showed me the workings of camera lucida and obscura on original instruments from his own collection; Guy Crowden and Alec Dennis (retired Royal Navy) and Andy Williams and Rod Tuck (ex-Royal Marines) who brought naval expertise to my research; Jamie Zeppa, talented author and astute critic with scant previous knowledge of Arctic explorers, now I hope remedied; Kathy Weltzin and Beatrice Franklin of Alaska

and Pat Paton of Colorado who offered an American perspective;
Wayne Grady, Yukon Writer-in-Residence at Whitehorse Public
Library; Maureen Long, teacher, Arctic student, and Franklin
aficionado.

I was further helped with interviews, letters, and phone calls by:
Doug LeMond, traditional boat-builder and hunting guide; Jim
Raffan, canoeist and elegant writer on canoeing; Colonel Philippe
Truttman of Vittel, France, historian of Verdun Citadel; Don
Johnson, researcher into Old Montreal in the Back era; Ian Brodo,
lichenologist; Kenn Back, curator of the museum on South
Georgia, distant nephew of George Back; Adam Steele who
arranged our visit to the rare book collection at the Urbana-
Champaign campus of the University of Illinois; Horst Mueller,
Afan Jones, Owen Williams, and Gary Hewitt who advised me on
mapping; Carol O'Brien and Anna Williamson of Constable &
Robinson and Scott Steedman of Raincoast Books, my UK and
Canadian publishers, and Maggie Body, at whose kitchen table in
Llangennith the final editing was painlessly concluded between
Gower walks.

Finally, my thanks go to the librarians and archivists of the
Arctic Institute of North America, Calgary; McCord Museum,
Montreal; National Archives of Canada, Ottawa; National Mari-
time Museum, Greenwich; Peterborough Canoe Museum; Royal
Geographical Society, London; Public Records Office, Kew; Scott
Polar Research Institute, Cambridge; Stockport Public Libraries;
University of Illinois, Urbana-Champaign rare book collection;
HMS *Victory*, Portsmouth; Whipple Museum, Cambridge; Yukon
College Library and Yukon Archives.

PS
Whitehorse, Yukon, October 2002

Maps

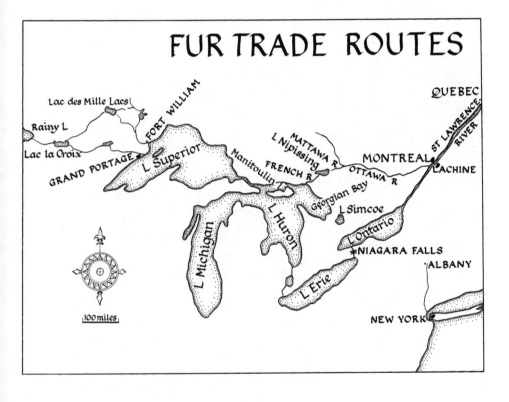

FUR TRADE ROUTES

Lac des Mille Lacs
Rainy L
Lac la Croix
GRAND PORTAGE
FORT WILLIAM
L Superior
Manitoulin
L Nipissing
MATTAWA R
FRENCH R
OTTAWA R
Georgian Bay
L Simcoe
L Michigan
L Huron
L Ontario
NIAGARA FALLS
L Erie
QUEBEC
ST LAWRENCE RIVER
MONTREAL
LACHINE
ALBANY
NEW YORK
100 miles

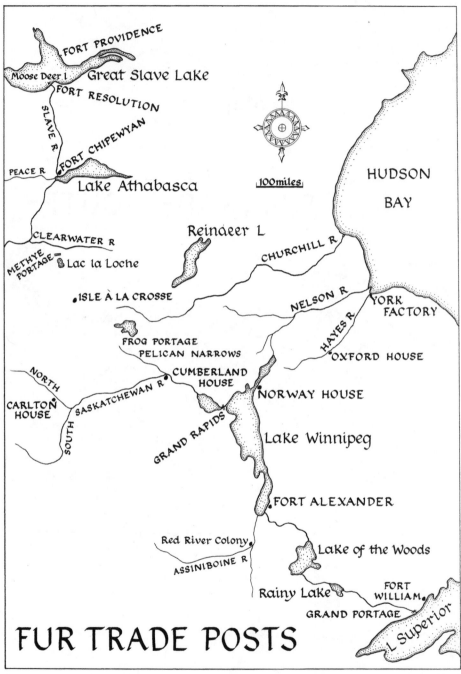

FORT PROVIDENCE
Moose Deer I.   Great Slave Lake
FORT RESOLUTION
SLAVE R.
FORT CHIPEWYAN
PEACE R.
Lake Athabasca

100 miles

HUDSON BAY

CLEARWATER R
METHYE PORTAGE   Lac la Loche
Reindeer L
CHURCHILL R
ISLE À LA CROSSE
NELSON R
YORK FACTORY
FROG PORTAGE
PELICAN NARROWS
HAYES R.
OXFORD HOUSE
NORTH
CUMBERLAND HOUSE
CARLTON HOUSE
SASKATCHEWAN R.
NORWAY HOUSE
SOUTH
GRAND RAPIDS
Lake Winnipeg
FORT ALEXANDER
Red River Colony
Lake of the Woods
ASSINIBOINE R
Rainy Lake
FORT WILLIAM
GRAND PORTAGE
L. Superior

FUR TRADE POSTS

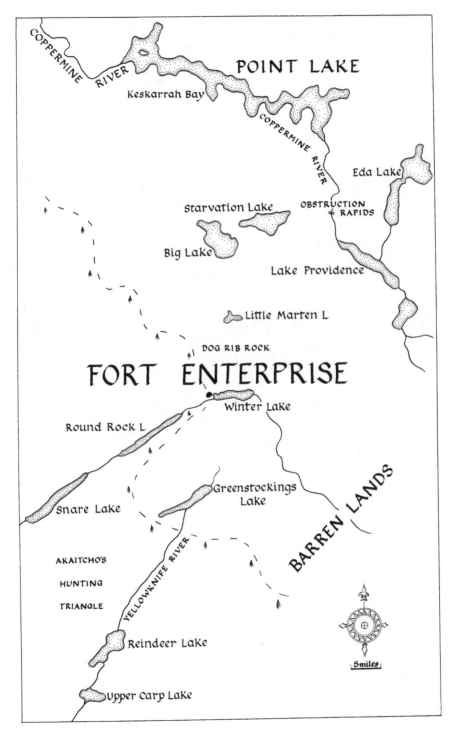

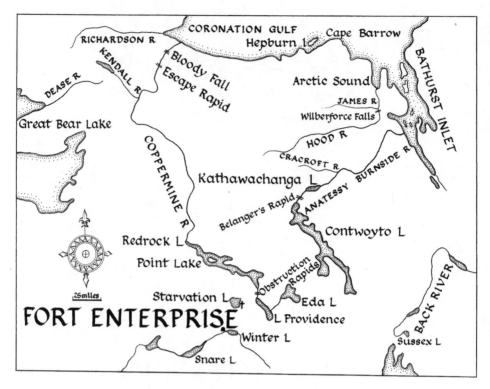

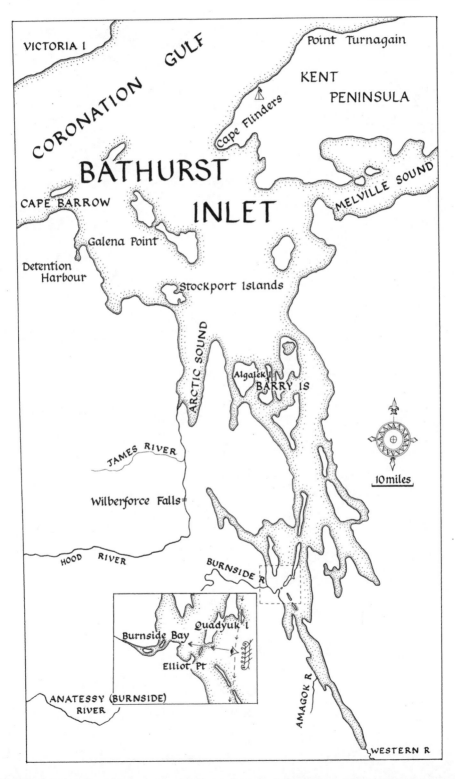

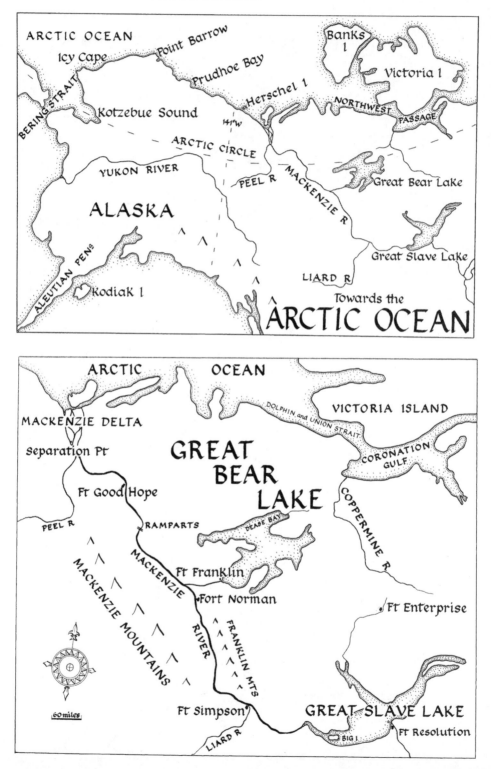

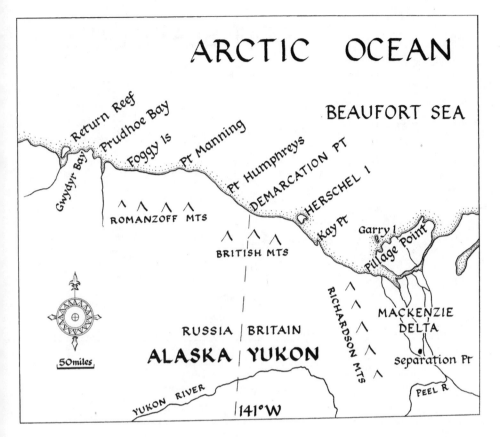

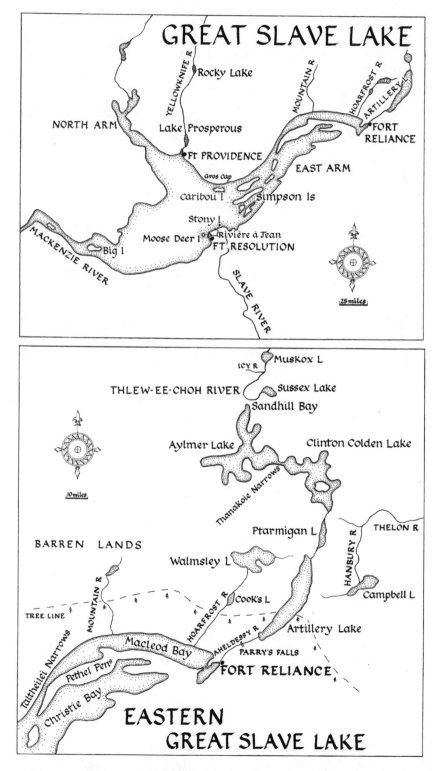

GREAT SLAVE LAKE

Rocky Lake

YELLOWKNIFE R.

MOUNTAIN R.

HOARFROST R.

ARTILLERY L.

NORTH ARM

Lake Prosperous

FORT
RELIANCE

Ft PROVIDENCE

EAST ARM

Gros Cap

Caribou I

Simpson Is

Stony I

MACKENZIE RIVER

Big I

Moose Deer I

Rivière à Jean

FT RESOLUTION

SLAVE RIVER

25 miles

Muskox L

ICY R

THLEW-EE-CHOH RIVER

Sussex Lake

Sandhill Bay

Aylmer Lake

Clinton Colden Lake

10 miles

Thanakoie Narrows

Ptarmigan L

HANBURY R.

THELON R.

BARREN   LANDS

Walmsley L

Cook's L

Campbell L

TREE LINE

MOUNTAIN R.

HOARFROST R.

AHELDESSY R.

Artillery Lake

Taltheilei Narrows

Macleod Bay

PARRY'S FALLS

Pethei Pene

FORT RELIANCE

Christie Bay

EASTERN
GREAT SLAVE LAKE

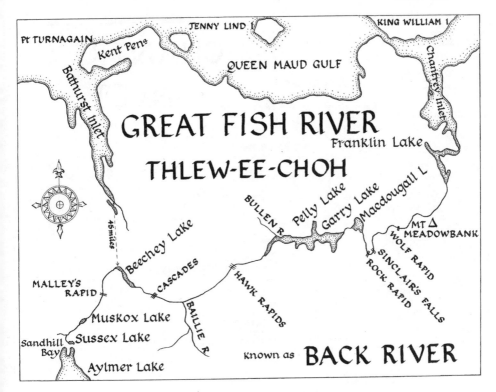

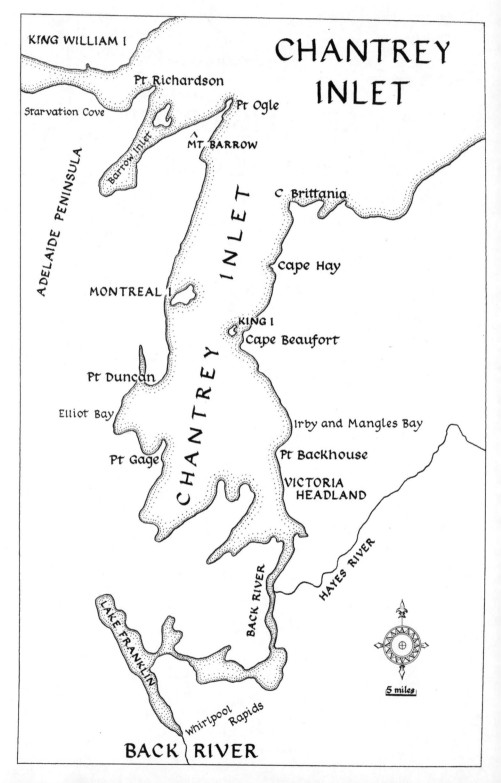

KING WILLIAM I

CHANTREY INLET

Pt Richardson

Starvation Cove

Pt Ogle

Barrow Inlet

MT BARROW

ADELAIDE PENINSULA

C. Brittania

Cape Hay

INLET

MONTREAL I

KING I

Cape Beaufort

Pt Duncan

Elliot Bay

CHANTREY

Irby and Mangles Bay

Pt Gage

Pt Backhouse

VICTORIA HEADLAND

HAYES RIVER

BACK RIVER

LAKE FRANKLIN

Whirlpool Rapids

BACK RIVER

5 miles

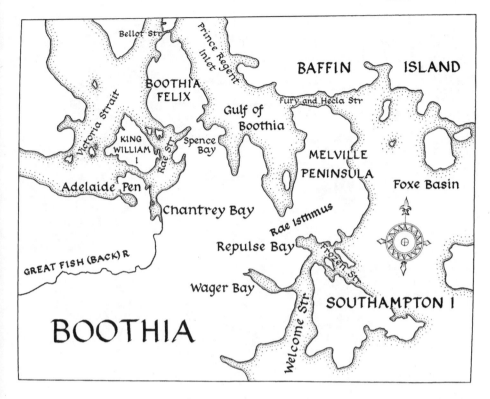

SOUTHAMPTON ISLAND

PART ONE

APPRENTICE TO HARDSHIP

CHAPTER 1

King's Letter Boy

1796–1809

The Flying Dutchman; or, Vanderdecken's Message Home.

To a boy like George Back Britain's Royal Navy held glamour. In those heady days, town criers roamed the streets blowing horns shaped like mammoth tusks to extol a galaxy of recent British naval battle successes – Camperdown, the Nile, Copenhagen, Trafalgar. In pubs of English ports men sang eulogies of courageous captains and their crews' gallant deeds. Horatio Nelson – legendary in life and tragic in death – inspired many boys (George Back among them) to become sailors. He remained their icon during the nascent nineteenth century and long thereafter.

George Back was born in England on 6 November 1796. His parents, John and Ann Back, lived in a half-timbered house in respectable Holly Vale, Stockport, which lies to the south of Greater Manchester, in the county of Cheshire. He shared middle-class origins with his hero, Horatio Nelson, son of a Norfolk country parson.

Young George caught his first whiff of the sea in 1807 during a visit with his father to Liverpool docks. There he saw several men-of-war being re-fitted for action, and others lying 'in ordinary', or in reserve. John Back entrusted his eleven-year-old son to the care of two Liverpudlian watermen whom he instructed to sail round *Princess Royal*, lying at anchor. As Back notes in his unfinished memoir, *A Long Yarn*, his father told the men to 'throw a spray or two' over the lad's face by luffing the boat's head up to wind against the waves. This outing, however, did nothing to dampen George's yearning for the excitement of life at sea.

The fifteenth-century halls of Shaw's (or Shaa's) Grammar School in Stockport must have seemed to Back musty and lifeless com-pared with his dreams of adventure. Although he did well at school, particularly in French and drawing, he quit before it could turn him into a scholar. John Back applied to a leading navy agent, Messrs C & L, to secure a posting for his son. A navy agent would advance funds to a commissioned admiral or captain in order to finance fitting out his ship. For a paltry five per cent interest the agent also handled a captain's prize, money which came from the sale of a captured ship and its cargo, shared proportionately among officers and crew.

Captain Sir Robert Mends entered Back on the books of his 38-gun frigate, HMS *Arethusa* as a 'volunteer of the first class'. Boy volunteers, also known as king's letter boys, were appointed by royal order. Boys under fifteen years – the minimum age for a midshipman – went to sea as servant to an admiral or captain, who was often a relative or family friend. Boys might number fifty in a crew of 750–900 manning a 2,000-ton ship-of-the-line which carried 90–120 guns.

Early in the nineteenth century a man, or boy, did not 'join the navy' as such, rather he joined a particular ship for the duration of its commission, known as 'entering for the ship'. At the end of a voyage officers and men (excluding permanent career warrant officers) were paid off. Each man then dispersed to fend for himself until he found another commission. Aspiring officers persuaded important relatives to write letters on their behalf to people of influence, or they hung about the halls of the Admiralty hoping to be noticed.

For a seaman, meeting a ship's lieutenant in a recruiting station at a seaport inn rendezvous often led to a commission. If unlucky, a sailor might be grabbed by a press gang. Warships anchored near the mouth of the River Thames – especially off the Nore, a sandbank lying near the mouth of the River Medway – lay in wait to board any likely merchant ship, plunder it for crew, and impress them to sail against their will. Also a company of Royal Marines stationed in the market house at Harwich would drag men from their homes and imprison them until they could be transferred to a suitable ship. Carpenters and skilled tradesmen capable of ship-building were at a premium, as well as 'able Seamen who gain their living by the Salt water'.

Regulations stated that officers' sons younger than eleven could not enter the navy. This rule was often ignored. Some boys as young as six went to sea and moved from ship to ship with their patron. Edward Hamilton joined his father's ship, HMS *Surprise*, at the age of seven, and saw action a year later. Older boys, aged eleven or twelve, if not officer material, were rated as able seamen. Since seniority in the navy was counted from the time of signing on, the younger a boy got his name on the books the quicker he rose in the service. Some unscrupulous skippers listed a name but did not carry the lad.

Many sons of the nobility and gentry went to sea for the same reasons as remittance men went to the colonies. Remittance men were second and subsequent sons of landed families paid a remittance to disappear abroad – most often to Canada or Australia – in order to keep intact the family estate which was destined to be inherited by the eldest son. Professional openings at home were few. Entering politics, or the royal court, required aristocratic connections; an army commission demanded cash up front, and also some academic inclination. Medicine and surgery were generally for barbers, not for respectable citizens. Thus a viable option for a remittance man was life in an outpost of the expanding British

Empire, whose red blotches on a map of the world became yearly more ubiquitous.

The navy offered a lad like Back an appealing alternative: good prospects on the lower deck where life was snug, albeit airless and rank. He received hot food every day, free clothes and medical attention (of a sort). Furthermore he had the chance of lifetime employment with possible prize money and, finally, a pension. Young naval entrants aspiring to become officers came from all strata of society. A father, keen to launch his son into the naval world needed no financial investment, unlike the army where private means were essential just to sign on.

For the poor of the Industrial Revolution misery was often absolute. To enter the navy young compared favourably with life ashore, where boys of Back's age often had to crawl on all fours in harness hauling carts down damp, dark coal mines. In Scotland, miners were virtually bonded serfs and no inquests were held into deaths. Children swept chimneys or picked pockets. Pauper orphans from workhouses were often apprenticed to villainous tradesmen like Peter Grimes, who worked them to death. Young girls were bound to cotton mills and clothing factories. Only in 1833 did the first Factory Act impose legal limits on working hours for children, the same year as an act was passed abolishing slavery in the British Empire.

The earlier the navy could get its hands on a young apprentice, the more easily could it mould him to life at sea. Considering the alternatives, Back's career outlook at sea seemed bright and relatively comfortable.

So in September 1808, two months shy of his twelfth birthday, Back bade a tearful farewell to his mother and father and took the mail coach from Stockport to London to join the navy, as had Nelson at the same age. Back would not see his family again for five years.

Back was a handsome lad with curly black hair and prominent eyebrows who looked even younger than his actual years, especially since he was only five feet tall. As he notes, he boarded *Arethusa* with some apprehension, despite the captain assigning him to the supervision of the first lieutenant. Straightaway some rambunctious midshipmen pushed him into their mess – a 'very dingy and unsavoury den'. One jovial fellow announced to the company, 'Gentlemen, our new messmate, Mr Back.'

The midshipmen harassed Back with horseplay. They let down his hammock during the night, rattled his boots over his face as he was falling asleep and, while dowsing him with water to make him think he was drowning, cried, 'Throw a rope – man overboard.' He survived this hazing ritual with good humour, so his tormentors soon left him alone. Before long he would turn the tables himself and torment innocent unfledged newly arrived boys and midshipmen.

After her refit, *Arethusa* lay at anchor off the Nore. Each afternoon while in harbour the bo'sun gave classes in knotting and splicing to midshipmen and volunteer boys like Back. The master, or his mates, taught them seamanship, navigation, and log-keeping. The yeoman instructed signalling, a Royal Marine sergeant gave them practice in small arms, and the gunner led gun drill.

Admiralty orders demanded daily training aloft to teach young sailors to handle the ropes. It also taught discipline. During action at sea their very survival depended on understanding how the ship functioned. Sure-footedness aloft, while she pitched and rolled through an arc of ninety degrees or more, could be lifesaving for a boy furling and unfurling sails out on a yardarm spar. Falling from the rigging was a common cause of death aboard ship, second only to dying of a tropical disease like yellow fever, and more frequent by far than being killed in battle.

Life was not all work for Back and the other boys, who had plenty of time to play. Attending divine service on Sunday, however, was obligatory. Boys also received classes from the schoolmaster, a lowly figure in the ship's hierarchy, on a par with chaplains and surgeons. All of these were considered drunkards, eccentrics, or madmen unsuitable for a job ashore, and consequently paid at the same rate as the youngest midshipman.

Within two months of enlisting, in November 1808, Back was at sea in *Arethusa* cruising the English Channel off Cherbourg in search of French ships as potential prizes. Constant tacking, which required frequent making and shortening sail, was good practice for raw recruits. In a large sailing ship topmen worked aloft, high above the deck, furling and loosening topsails; the youngest and lightest topmen – upper yardmen – mere boys like Back, worked the topgallants and royals. They would run barefoot along the yards like gymnasts on a balancing bar, then drop on their stomachs to lie athwart the yard with their feet on loose footlines suspended on stirrups. Sprawled there they handled the gaskets – plaited ropes that secured sail to yard when furled, or hung free when the sail was loose. On the larger ships topmen could fall as much as 130 feet.

Nonetheless Back thrived on these challenges. However, like the dozy teenager he nearly was, more than once he was caught asleep on watch. As punishment he was soused with water and sent to the masthead. This was a good lesson to learn early because on a ship in action sleeping on duty was a heinous, even a capital, crime.

Back was impressed by the nautical skill of Captain Mends in saving *Arethusa* from being wrecked on the Casquettes in a gale. Because she was drifting onto the rocks the captain ordered the

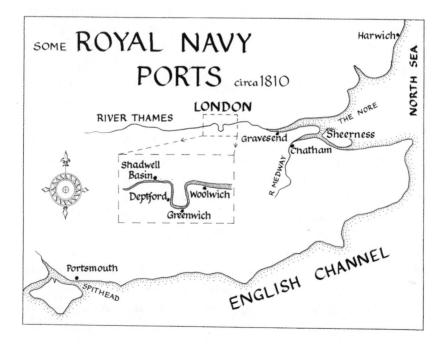

close-reefed topsails to be shaken out in order to get maximum power from extra mainsail canvas – a risky manoeuvre for a ship on a lee shore. He pushed *Arethusa* up into the wind by luffing hard, so she heeled over in the heavy sea, sending spume and spray over the quarterdeck. As the ship finally rounded out, almost grazing the jagged reef, the relief on board was palpable.

This was Back's first experience of a large sailing ship working in the tight confines of coastal waters. After it was over, he asked the deck officer what he thought of their narrow escape.

'Think of it, youngster?' replied the lieutenant. 'Why, that in a quarter of an hour the ship will be in splinters on those confounded rocks to leeward, that's what I think of it. And I expect my promotion on our return.'

The lieutenant was not promoted, but he and the rest of the crew did get a share of prize money for capturing a 16-gun French privateer, *General Enouf*, between Guernsey and the Isle of Wight. This bonus was surprising since *Arethusa* was at least twice as heavy as the privateer, which had been stripped to its bare bones for speed.

March 1809 saw *Arethusa* rolling through the Bay of Biscay heading for the coast of Spain with Back aboard. As he confides to his memoir: 'the time passed cheerfully enough either in chasing vessels or in cutting out parties.' Cutting out involved sending a small raiding party into an enemy harbour under cover of darkness, and stealthily overpowering a ship's crew. Armed parties were regularly dispatched to cut out enemy vessels, seize small craft, or destroy forts by cooperating with the British army on shore. Just after high water, the cutting out party would sever the mooring cables and use the ebb tide to sail downriver with their prize, out to sea and home.

Great prestige accrued to the captain of a Royal Navy ship who took a French privateer in a single action at sea – one of the few ways he could draw attention to himself and increase his chances of promotion. When in full chase the skipper would order all canvas raised. The best helmsmen took the wheel by turns, and the crew moved weighty cargo aft and slung a cask of water from the mainstay to tighten the rigging. In cramped spaces with little sea room to turn, captains had to skilfully manoeuvre their heavy square-rigged sailing vessels, which headed sluggishly into wind and drifted hard to leeward. To be first aboard an enemy privateer – known as gaining a commission – was dangerous work, but was worth the risks.

During battle life became serious for ships' boys. Those, like Back, with quarterdeck officer potential, carried messages between officers. Less fortunate lads from the fo'c's'le were powder monkeys, who fetched gunpowder for gun crews from magazines on the lowest, orlop, deck. Drummer boys had the job of sounding orders by 'beating to quarters'.

The Royal Navy had recently changed for the better. Just eleven years before, in 1797, the fleets at Spithead (off Portsmouth) and the Nore had mutinied against harsh shipboard conditions, poor food and lack of shore leave. Wages had not risen for more than a century and conditions for sick and injured sailors were abysmal. Other grievances were delay in sharing prize money and unscrupulous ships' pursers extracting their 'eighth' – the share which they pocketed of all stores issued.

Following the mutinies Admiral John Jervis overhauled an ailing navy and turned it into a formidable fighting force through strict discipline and disregard of social rank. By the next year it had trounced Napoleon's fleet at the Battle of the Nile. Manpower numbers speak for themselves: in 1792 the navy had 15,000 men; in 1797 – 120,000; in 1813 – 150,000. When all else failed press gangs would coerce unemployed seamen into service.

Jervis expanded the navy by offering promises of prize money and a bounty to merchant seamen and privateers, who were already trained to 'hand, reef, and steer' a ship.

A British privateer skipper was virtually an authorized pirate who carried out hit-and-run raids on slow, undefended French merchantmen. He needed only a licence issued from a post office, indicating his stated aim was 'to prey upon his country's enemies'. Frigate skippers, like swashbuckling Captain Pellew, became rich folk heroes. A privateer's crew were maritime highwaymen dredged from the scum of seaports, and often composed of navy deserters with lax discipline and few morals.

On land the British army was in poor shape to take on Napoleon rampaging hungrily across Europe, gobbling up countries, and building a massive empire that stretched east to Poland and south to the Balkans and Italy. Spain was his ally; India and the Orient his next goals. By contrast, Back was in a Royal Navy riding the crest of a wave. Equipped with well-built ships, the navy relied on superior, more practised seamanship to blockade French ports. Because the British had more ships, they were able to separate the French Atlantic fleets in Brest and Rochefort from their Mediterranean fleet in Toulon. Not only did this tie up French export trade, but it also kept Napoleon's fighting force landlocked in Europe with his ships confined to harbour.

The Royal Navy was the only force that could foil Napoleon's plan to invade England with a quarter of a million men using a fleet of flat-bottomed barges drawn up on the beaches of Boulogne – a strange reversal of events that would be played out on the same shore a century and a half later on D-Day.

While *Arethusa* hove to, becalmed near Baignio off the north coast of Spain, Back, in poetic mood, records: 'One of those lovely days that goes to fill up the enjoyment of life. The rocks stood boldly out from the coast relieved by the foliage and woods of the sloping uplands, while the Pyrenees, broken in blue ridges, raised their tall heads till their snowy peaks mingled with the cloudless sky. Not a breath of wind was stirring.'

Unexpectedly, a tall swarthy Spaniard rowed out to the ship and sprang aboard heavily armed. He immediately pulled from under his capacious black cloak a packet which he handed to Captain Mends, who escorted him below decks to his cabin. Two hours later both men reappeared, looking sombre. The captain took leave of his mysterious visitor, calling him Antonio.

Antonio soon returned in a boat manned by fourteen tough, determined Spaniards, who exuded vitriol towards the French. The perplexed and curious midshipmen only learned two weeks later that Antonio was a disaffected Spanish priest who had been working as a spy for the French. As Back noted, '[a] Guerilla or a Pilot as circumstances required'. But he had fallen out with a senior officer and turned his coat, vowing to drive every Frenchman back over the Pyrenees.

Gossip now spread around the ship that volunteers were needed for a cutting out expedition. Soon ten times the required number of men had gathered on the quarterdeck, all itching to get their hands on some prize money. Captain Mends ordered a lieutenant to prepare a party consisting of forty men in a launch, to be followed by gigs with crews of twenty men each, and a small jolly boat in charge of a midshipman.

The first lieutenant had previously always refused Back's request to join a cutting out expedition because of his age – he was just twelve years old. This time, however, Back bypassed him, and applied directly to the master, Mr Rodmel, who was in command of the raiding party. He said he would turn a blind eye if young Back crept into the jolly boat, but warned him that the French would 'eat him' if he was caught.

At nightfall the sailors assembled on deck for final orders. They then loaded a week's provisions and several 12-pounder carronades into boats lying alongside. Under a full moon Back watched the first lieutenant go to the opposite side of *Arethusa*. When he was out of sight he ran down the main deck, scrambled through a porthole, lowered himself into a jolly boat, and stowed away under a pile of headsheets.

With a rough sea running, the boats sailed close-reefed towards the enemy port of Deba. One huge favourable wave lifted them clean over the harbour bar into a sheltered bay. Antonio, wrapped in his black cloak, was put ashore to post scouts. Two anxious hours later he reappeared with news that a French three-masted coastal lugger suitable for the taking was anchored in the inner harbour.

Just before dawn the ship's boats prepared to slip up the River Andero into the harbour of Deba. The cutting out party rowed with muffled oars, in two lines towards the enemy ship. One launch passed to starboard, the other to port, ready to scale the enemy quarterdeck from both sides simultaneously. Each man, with pistol at half cock and cutlass handy, was able to climb aboard easily because the enemy had not set their nets, which hung from the yardarms and were secured to the hull, to repel boarders.

The jolly boat went straight towards the enemy ship's bow to secure the fo'c's'le. A nimble crew of boys, including Back, climbed the anchor cables, and scrambled up the ratlines and futtock shrouds, making for the topmasts. The most tricky and dangerous part was sliding in bare feet along footlines, which hung from the main topsail yard. Once they had loosened the gaskets that bound the sail they threw a sheet rope down to the deck for a sailor to cleat.

The British sailors boarded the enemy ship, cut its cables with ease, and locked the enemy seamen up below decks. A midshipman remained in charge and the men all kept strict silence to avoid alerting shore batteries who were defending the harbour. Launches towed the ship downriver, while sailors on board navigated her carefully around shoals.

The wind came up and *Arethusa*, standing offshore, hoisted a signal to recall the landing party. However the officer in charge of the launch found the seas too heavy to comply, so, following the recent example of Lord Nelson, he turned a blind eye to the recall flags and put to shore to await better weather.

Meanwhile the cutting out party, having tasted piracy, determined to carry on with that business. They set out again for Deba fort after a hearty meal of ham and eggs washed down with wine. Among them was Back, armed with a pistol and a cutlass, which dragged on the ground because he was so short. His group climbed to the fort, scaled the crenellated battlements, and spiked the 12-pounder guns, which they then threw over the ramparts. Another party, in an action that took most of the day, captured a haul of arms and ammunition which they took out to sea and dumped overboard. Suddenly, a large body of French troops appeared on the other side of Deba town, so the British crews took to their boats, pulled over the harbour bar and put out to sea with their looted treasures.

Subsequently the boats spent four nights roaming along the coast capturing and destroying cargo-laden French *chasse-marées* — fast trading sloops. 'We were becoming rich and comfortable in our new vocation,' Back confided to his memoir after the crews captured another fine lugger, 'our valuable coadjutor, Antonio . . . invariably brought us bags of dollars and doubloons, which, after some ceremony, to me incomprehensible, the Master put safely by.' Back was thoroughly enjoying this novel way of spending his time and wished, like any teenager, that it would never stop as they were having so much fun. He continued, 'we rather hoped she [*Arethusa*] would obligingly keep away a little longer.'

The wind got up so they crept along the rocky coast in pitch darkness and put in to a nearby harbour where they could not resist attacking another fort. Antonio led a raiding party of the strongest men up some cliffs, with Back tagging along behind. They came out under the gates of the fort on which they proceeded to launch a surprise attack which left the fort severely damaged. Back's contribution was to help disable the guns.

Back tells how the bo'sun's mate of *Arethusa*, stinking drunk, led a party to storm Deba. The mate ran out ahead of his men hurling abuse at French soldiers inside and ordering them to surrender. Then three or four British sailors, totally lost, turned up at the rear gate of the fort, causing the French to think they were surrounded, so the terrified soldiers fled into the woods, leaving the fort empty. The British sailors hauled down the French flag and stood on the parapet waiting for their officers to arrive. Luckily an officer noticed a self-timing fuse, which he disarmed just before it could blow them all to pieces.

When the action was over, the British crew took to their boat. However they were caught by a flood tide that swept like a millrace, carrying their unwieldy launch with it. Some French soldiers gathered on the riverbank and let off a volley of musket fire at the British sailors who, together with Antonio and his men, exchanged fire for a quarter of an hour. Several on both sides were wounded or killed.

The British boat grounded and became a target for the enemy, who pounded it with shot, while Antonio and his surviving Spaniards suddenly threw off their jackets, jumped overboard, and swam for the opposite bank. Back crouched on the stern sheets lying on a skin of wine. A musket ball punctured it and the red wine spilled, looking like blood, so he thought he had been wounded. But he had the presence of mind to pick up two doubloons that Antonio had dropped in his flight, and pocket them in his waistcoat.

About sixty Frenchmen rushed the stranded boat, firing pistols and shouting, '*Vive l'Empereur.*' One huge man aimed a blow at Back, but a French naval officer parried it. He patted Back on the head saying, 'Never mind, no you afraid little Midshipman.' The officer then threw off his coat, jumped into the water with his sword held between his teeth, and swam after Antonio and his cohorts who were captured as soon as they waded ashore.

Back and his three British companions – the sole survivors of the original party of fifteen – were captured and marched to a temporary guardhouse. On 20 March 1809 Back, aged twelve years and four months, became a prisoner of war of Napoleon. So began the next chapter of his life, one that would fill his teenage years.

CHAPTER 2

Prisoner of Napoleon

1809–14

The Fortress of Verdun, from Telegraph Hill: showing the
semaphore for reporting escapes of prisoners to neighbouring
garrisons. From a sketch by James Forbes, a British prisoner.

After his capture, George Back was locked up in a chateau built
into the town walls of Deba. There he met his surviving shipmates,
who had been captured separately, and they started a vociferous
argument about why their foray had failed. The sailors claimed that
they had surrendered too hastily and so were now languishing
behind bars instead of safe in the bosom of their mother ship.

In notes for his memoir, Back records one sailor's growling:

Sea or no sea, I'm damned if we ought not to have thrashed
those French devils, and I'd fight any six of them now —
myself. I means no offense to nobody, but if Bill Smith the
coxswain had had his way, I'm blowed if we shouldn't have
fought our way out and then knocked this bit of a place about

their ears with our two carronades – aye, for that matter, that 'ere young gentleman Mr Back would have helped us.

Some soldiers who brought food to the prisoners narrowly averted fisticuffs arising from this outburst, and the hubbub slowly subsided.

Antonio was also locked up in the chateau in a semicircular tower facing the sea. As he lay on a bed of sour and mouldy straw, he feebly whispered that he was dying. He asked for a priest to give him the last rites, so the guards sent for a Capuchin monk. On seeing the purportedly moribund pilot, the monk said he must immediately collect from his monastery some holy emblems necessary for administering extreme unction. He soon returned, along with another old Capuchin brother, and they performed the solemn rites, their low chants mingling with the gusty night. When the guards went into the cell to check on the dying prisoner, they found instead a pile of Antonio's clothes stuffed with straw. From the stump of a sawn-out bar hung a rope down which Antonio had slid to freedom.

Soon afterwards Back and his shipmates were marched between two lines of soldiers armed with fixed bayonets towards San Sebastian, the nearest large town which overlooked the sea twenty-five miles away. They spent their first night at Zumaya in the common gaol, which was filthy and alive with fleas. Back reports one sailor saying, 'I'm blowed if them Spanish fleas ain't worse than bull terriers, my starboard quarter is regularly stove in.' To this a fellow bedmate retorted, 'Then go on to the other tack.'

From Zumaya they were put aboard a boat, which sailed towards San Sebastian. During the passage the prisoners hatched a plot whereby each man would try to overpower the soldier next to him and throw him overboard. But this was scotched by the officer in charge, who understood enough English to sense mischief afoot, and warned them that he would shoot any prisoner who moved from his seat.

At San Sebastian a guard marched the prisoners into town and put them up in an hotel. The commandant allowed his wards to roam the streets freely until he received orders from Paris instructing him to send them on across France. He took kindly to Back and even promised to release him should an English ship appear off the port, saying, '*Je vous enverrai à votre papa et votre mama* – I'll send you back to your papa and mama.' The small stature of the young prisoner also conjured sympathy among bystanders, who persuaded the officer to spare his charge walking on the rough and muddy roads towards Bayonne, their next destination. The officer agreed, and allowed Back to ride in the empty pannier of a pack mule, the opposite basket being laden with provisions for the prisoners. Once beyond the Pyrenees he was transferred to an open bullock cart.

In Bayonne, the British crewmen were marched to a common prison in the citadel, and put in yet another filthy, flea- and vermin-infested cell. The gaoler suddenly became lenient when Back pulled from his waistcoat one of the doubloons that Antonio had dropped in the boat. The gaoler pocketed the coin and showed the prisoners into an upper room with a wide view over the town and surrounding gently rolling country. He spread a grubby tablecloth on a rough wooden table where he placed bread, wine, soup, and a main dish called *bouillie*.

A merchant of Bayonne visited the prisoners, having recognized *Arethusa*'s master as a brother Freemason. After asking for their word of honour that they would not try to escape, he got permission from the commandant to take them to an hotel on parole. Next day the merchant endorsed their bills of exchange, procured £30 for each of them, and invited them to dinner at his country house. There Back met his pretty daughter, Clotilde, with whom he says he became 'marvellously intimate', while she in turn called him her brother. The merchant and his wife wanted to adopt Back and to continue his education until the end of the war. This news evidently delighted Clotilde, who threw her arms around the neck of her new-found friend, and implored him 'with girlish innocence' to agree to stay with them. However, one of Back's shipmates persuaded him that they should all stay together, so he reluctantly tore himself away from Clotilde, who promptly burst into tears.

Before long they marched to Bordeaux where they stayed in an hotel together with the captain of an American clipper schooner who tried to encourage Back to break parole and stow away on his ship. True to his word to Clotilde's father, however, Back refused.

While strolling through Bordeaux the prisoners met some French naval officers, who said they had been on the ship that got away from *Arethusa* in the gale when she was chasing them along the Spanish coast.

'What a prize you would have had,' said one of them. '*Mais au lieu de çela, vous voici* – but instead of that, you are here.'

The British prisoners were deeply chagrined at the thought of

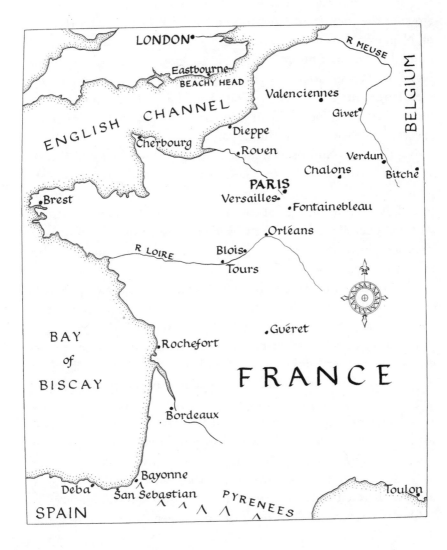

what they had missed, because the French ship was reportedly loaded with treasure.

In his characteristic fashion, Back laconically dismisses the arduous two-month journey diagonally across France to the citadel prison of Verdun as 'nothing of any moment and unattended by any incident worth mentioning'. Verdun lay on the Belgian border, 500 miles away as the crow flies, but more distant via their meandering route along rural byways.

The France through which Back and his fellow prisoners were forced to march was in a maelstrom. Throngs of soldiers were criss-crossing the country in order to join their regiments under the flag of Napoleon Bonaparte, who was busy expropriating Europe to build his Grand Empire. With his superior manpower on land, Napoleon did not attempt to exchange British prisoners for his own men languishing in English gaols. Especially did he not want to return British sailors to their own navy because they were more expert than their French counterparts.

Napoleon also imprisoned most British civilians living in France as civilian hostages – *détenus*. These were a mix of English travellers on holiday, businessmen working in France, army officers returning from Egypt on leave, officials on furlough from India, and invalids who had gone abroad to take the waters at health spas. Most *détenus* were loosely attached to a major prison like Verdun and were let out on parole.

Among this massive continental migration was a ragtag bunch of prisoners of war heading for their various gaols. Nevertheless, amid the apparent chaos a surprising degree of order prevailed. Back's party travelled in charge of several mounted gendarmes (*gens d'armes* or men at arms) and foot soldiers, who changed shifts at stages along the way. Sometimes his fellow prisoners were hand-cuffed in pairs, at other times roped together. Their treatment along the road depended entirely on the mood of the gendarmes, who, Back notes, were callous and brutal fellows. Generally they were more kindly treated by the locals who lived farther inland, well away from the seaboard where they were roughly handled because those citizens had scores to settle with the British navy.

On arriving at the day's destination the gendarmes received the next day's marching orders – *une feuille de route*. Usually the distance was about fifteen to twenty miles. Considering the rutted, muddy country roads, this was quite a long foot-slog for sailors, unused to marching. Officer prisoners, like Back, rode on horseback accompanied by baggage wagons which were also used to carry sick, injured, or exhausted men.

At their destination the senior gendarme would hand over his dossier of prisoners to a local government official – a military commander, mayor, or prefect – who endorsed his *feuille de route*. The gendarmes also arranged victualling and billeting, usually in the town prison. If the prisoners were lucky they were lodged in a barracks, warehouse, or church. Exceptionally, they were put in a farmer's barn where, Back notes, they 'lived like little kings on the fat of the land'. Ordinary soldiers and sailors tried to find bed and breakfast with a family, who got their expenses reimbursed by the government and could enjoy catching up with the countrywide bush telegraph of news and gossip. The following morning Back and his fellow prisoners would set off on the day's stage with leftover food for their midday snack, and with 'marching money' to pay their travelling expenses.

John Wetherell, who went to sea as an apprentice in the British merchant navy, wrote about his capture and journey across France to prison at Givet, sixty miles north of Verdun, and of his subsequent eleven years imprisonment. His experiences as a prisoner of Napoleon were remarkably similar to those of George Back, though Wetherell was earlier, of lower rank and in a different prison. His first-hand account enhances our picture of Back's eventful prisoner life, even though the two never met. While in hospital after being shipwrecked off Brest, Wetherell remarks: 'humane and heavenly treatment we found in the midst of our most inveterate enemies; although prisoners of war, our foes treated us with so much more humanity than we found in the service of our own nation.' Nevertheless, once imprisoned, Wetherell had to pay a fee to the chief of a gang of bullies in charge of the gaol. He complains that they were put in among 'a lousy hurd of murderers thieves pickpockets forgers traitors deserters spys encendiaries lawyers and taylors'.

Back took between two and three months to traverse France from the Pyrenees in the extreme southwest corner to Verdun on the northeast border near Belgium and Luxembourg. The medieval town nestles into a bend of the River Meuse, which flows through wooded rolling hills that rise from flat champagne country to the west. The town is much the same now as when Back was there; formerly walled, today only two of the main fortified gates still stand. The fortress citadel lies a stone's throw from the cathedral which commands the crown of a hill down which radiate streets of elegant merchants' houses.

The citadel was connected to the lawn of the bishop's palace by a drawbridge set across a deep moat. Watchtower turrets jut out over the moat from several angles of the sixty-foot-high walls built round the top of an adjoining hillock. In the centre of the prison compound stood the round, two-storey-high Tour d'Angoulême (now destroyed). Its punishment cells had five-feet-thick walls, iron-plated, barred and double-locked doors, and iron-grated windows. The citadel was originally planned – along with a line of other forts including Vincennes, Givet, and Bitche – to defend the eastern frontier of France. But with the steady extension of Napoleon's Empire, it came to be nearer to the centre than on its border.

Verdun was a prison for 12,000 officers and 500 *détenus*; ordinary seamen were confined to Vincennes and Givet. Escapees and naughty boys went to Bitche – a place they preferred to forget. Little more than a decade later Back would entertain a Christmas concert at Fort Franklin on Great Slave Lake in the wilds of northern Canada with the poem, 'The Fortress of Bitche', which he described as 'a horrid abode of some unfortunate Prisoners whose cells were 60 feet beneath the surface of the pure element in which we breathe – these brave men were treated in the severest manner and generally loaded with irons – these punishments were inflicted by the French for no other reason than an Englishman's attempt to gain that which was born with him – his liberty.' The actual poem in fact lamented the fate of 'a poor captive of Erin'.

I endeavour to scratch my surname on the wall
Oh! where is my mother that nourish'd my childhood
Her counsels too late to my mind I recall . . .

and much more in the same vein. Life was not as dire for either
Back at Verdun or Wetherell at Givet.

Soon after arriving at Verdun every prisoner had a medical
examination, and was given a passport which allowed him to
wander two leagues (six miles) from town. Their hours of freedom
were limited by having to appear twice a day for roll-call, and to
sign their name at the hotel de ville. At 9 p.m. the great bell of the
cathedral tolled, after which prisoners were under curfew in their
lodgings.

Captain Sir Thomas Lane, the senior British naval officer at
Verdun, introduced the new arrivals to the depot. He sent Back,
the youngest prisoner in the citadel, to the midshipmen's mess
situated in a large house within the walls. In order to curb the

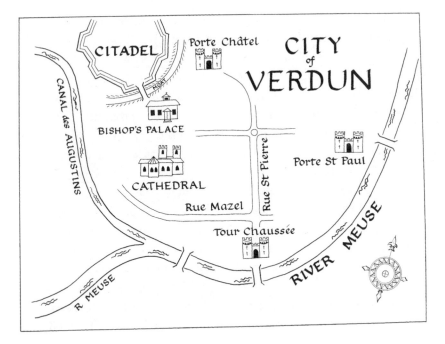

midshipmen's favourite sport of escaping, they had to attend three roll-calls daily and were under restricted parole.

At nearby Givet, Wetherell records, after sweeping the stairs and emptying all the tubs of night-soil, prisoners mustered in the yard. If they missed any of the thrice daily roll-calls they forfeited their liberty and the privilege of exercising on the town ramparts. Every morning country farmers would set up stalls outside the prison gates to sell potatoes, apples, pears and other fresh produce. Among the peasants, Wetherell tells us, 'were some blooming girls and they were verry free with us, several became constant companions, and in the whole I may say lovers.' When scouring the town for local girls, the prisoners' general rule was to leave their gendarme escort drinking in a tavern, take a turn around the town with their dates, and return to the citadel in time to answer roll-call.

Back often rambled along the banks of the River Meuse where, under the tuition of some old fishermen, he became adept at casting a hook. Every fine morning the midshipmen bathed in the river, competed in swimming races and horsed around for hours on end playing practical jokes on each other. A decade later being able to swim saved Back from drowning during a gale en route to the Bahamas while he was serving on the West Indies station.

The prisoners built model sailing boats and organized a regatta with the first prize of a silver cup, won by a boat steered by clockwork. They indulged in other pastimes such as cockfighting, outdoor picnics, duck hunting, and games of cricket and racquets. A certain Captain Molyneux designed a sail-propelled carriage, which got up to speeds of seven or eight miles an hour. After several crashes into farm carts, however, angry farmers stoned him. He also built an ice boat and sailed it on the frozen River Meuse.

Some prisoners acquired riding ponies. Back, being a light-weight and strong for his size, became a jockey at impromptu race meetings held, he notes, 'in the Newmarket spirit'. Nevertheless he took several bad falls. During one race his hard-mouthed, camel-necked horse bolted, stopped suddenly on the riverbank, and tossed him into his favourite swimming spot. The prisoners also acquired a pack of beagles and hunted three times a week, limited by the authorities to cantering within two leagues of Verdun. They chased a midshipman on horseback who dragged a herring behind him on a string. Sometimes the field sported forty riders.

Prisoners gambled in dens such as the Café Caron Club where the 120 members bet on horses, and played hazard and *rouge et noir*. Every Monday evening the Bishop's Palace Club – which had just fifty members, all married men – held either a ball, or an assembly for playing cards. Many midshipmen, usually when drunk, were decoyed into insalubrious gambling halls by 'girls of pleasure'. Jealous quarrels often ended in fatal duels, to which the authorities turned a blind eye.

The French and English governments paid prisoners an allowance of 35 francs each month. The Reverend Gordon, chaplain to the depot, organized a committee to collect funds from England for dispensing to the more needy prisoners, like masters of merchantmen who had no extra pocket money to supplement their meagre monthly living allowance.

The Treasury paid part of a navy prisoner's wages owing to him into the London bank of Messrs Coutts & Co., who remitted the money to a bank in Paris. Back and his fellow midshipmen drew any money they wanted from the bank and, he admits, 'we opened heavy bills on our Parents and began a course of extravagances altogether unwarrantable.' As a result they had spare cash to buy food and luxuries in town. The Rue du Moselle (now Mazel) was known to prisoners as Bond Street; its plentiful shops were run by London *détenus* – for example, 'Anderson's, grocer and tea dealer', and 'Stuckey, tailor and ladies habit-maker' – where the lads could spend money on their girlfriends.

One of the midshipmen who shared a house with Back kept a mistress who apparently 'sat daily with him and his riotous friends at table'. A notebook kept by a prisoner in Verdun contains the entry: 'We have a little Marine Officer who was so lewdly given that he kept a fine Mulatto girl to appease his libidinous desires – she was a frail sister and having many admirers – it is said that she took a special pleasure in discussing one Fundamental Point.' Many courtesans, however, were spies who informed the authorities of goings-on in the prison.

In England, meanwhile, Back's parents remained anxious for their boy. On 27 February 1812, John Back wrote to the Treasury

Board 'representing that [my] son Geo Back was taken Prisoner while serving as a Volunteer Boy on board the Arethusa, and requesting that he may be rated Midshipman; and to be informed whether the time he may continue in Prison will be allowed.' The Admiralty Index and Digest (ADM 12) in the Public Records Office notes tersely: 'acd [acquainted] with the regulations'. At that time much Treasury Board correspondence concerned men requesting back pay for time spent as prisoners of war, or for overdue promotion by which their pay would otherwise have risen commensurately.

Back confides to his memoir that the morals of the prison deteriorated inexorably to unremitting debauchery, and 'there were few things as practised there unknown to me. Excess, no matter in what, produces exhaustion and becomes the very instrument of its own cure.' This was hardly a healthy environment for a fifteen-year-old to grow up in. He eventually tired of the constant revelry, and rented another room in town where he had easy access to the library. The prisoners themselves eventually held a general meeting to try to clean up the moral tone of the citadel.

Several prisoners, including Back, attended day school run by two senior naval officers, Captains Brenton and Otten. This helped relieve boredom and keep them out of mischief from idleness, and prepared them for promotion exams when they might eventually be released. Back studied mathematics, navigation, and theoretical seamanship. He also became fluent in French, which would later prove invaluable for communicating with voyageur canoemen during the Canadian land and river expeditions into the Arctic which he joined under John Franklin. He also had plenty of time to become proficient at drawing, which became his other passport to adventure – and later to a certain fame.

The prison schoolteacher was supported with money and books, mailed from England along with about a hundred letters delivered daily. The prison's ersatz university became known locally as 'The Verdun Repository of Arts and Sciences'. As well as teaching academic studies, the schoolmaster simulated shipboard training for boys of Back's age. In the Citadel grounds he had three masts erected and rigged with yardarms so the boys could learn to strip and rig a ship, send yards up and down, bend and unbend sails, splice ropes, and heave the lead – all useful skills for their return to naval service.

Amateur theatricals became popular in Verdun. Some prisoners bought musical instruments captured in Spain, and formed a musical society with a band of over twenty musicians. In nearby Givet, John Wetherell reported enjoying 'music to which I devoted the greatest part of my time this winter by the side of a good stove. We began to think that it was mere folly to [dream] of ever being released; therefore we might make ourselves as happy as our situation would allow.'

Other prisoners were tailors, button-makers and chair-bottomers, barbers and wooden clog-makers; some made model ships and straw hats. A clique of Jews sold old clothes, watches, and books. These activities helped time pass more quickly towards their release.

In spite of Back's earlier scholastic efforts he again slipped into bad company and associated with 'dissolute characters'. He admits that 'every description of irregularity was openly committed without shame and without reproach.' Eventually the French government, scandalized at repeated reports of depravity within the prison, set up a court of enquiry into the conduct of the universally unpopular commandant, General Wirion. There was, Back admits, 'nothing too bad that the Verdun prisoners can say about [Wirion]'. He gate-crashed private dinner parties and gambling sessions, where the prisoners allowed him to win for fear of being sent – on his mere caprice – to the dreaded fortress of Bitche.

Wirion, knowing he was under investigation for incompetence, and worse, backed off temporarily but, when found guilty, he went into the Bois de Boulogne, put a pistol in his mouth, and pulled the trigger. Back tells how one of Wirion's subordinates, Lieutenant Masson of the gendarmerie, 'followed the example of his chief and blew out his brains with a pistol ball only a few yards from me as I was going across a field to fish'.

Unfortunately Wirion's successor, Colonel Courcelles, was not much better. Back described him as 'a creature who trod in the vile steps of his predecessor' in victimizing junior officers. He was replaced by Baron de Beauchesne and Major Meulan – 'an angel presiding where a fiend had ruled before'.

At this low point in Back's downward spiral, two men helped to turn the young vagabond around. One, the Reverend Gordon, encouraged him to attend diligently to his education. The other was an old Scheldt skipper whom Back met in a merchantmen's boozing parlour and who, he admits, chided him for his drinking.

'With all your cleverness,' said the skipper, 'take one from twenty and tell me how many remain.'

'Nineteen,' replied Back.

'That's just what I expected,' said the skipper, taking a piece of chalk and writing the Roman numeral XIX. 'Now take one from that! You'd better be at school than be drinking amongst men and idling away your time.'

This exchange had a profound effect on young Back who, once out in the street, burst into tears of wounded pride. He cried his eyes out all night, regretting his misspent life, and vowed to turn himself around and embark on a new course – no easy task when surrounded by so much sin.

'To that old skipper,' Back confides to his journal, 'I am indebted for a reformation that has lasted.' Thenceforth he pledged to dissociate himself from 'the dissolute, degraded and disgusting characters whose intemperate and vicious habits had done their worst [in] vice and roguery'. He broke away from his wayward companions and, as he had done previously, set himself to work six to eight hours a day at English, French, mathematics, and drawing.

Prison was hard on the health of inmates. During the first winter of Back's internment, nearly one third of Verdun's 3,000 inmates died of 'putrid fever', as typhus was then known. The disease was thought to arise from spending too much time in bed in cold, damp, crowded dormitories, and from poor food and lack of exercise. A doctor who specialized in infectious diseases was summoned from Paris; he ordered a hole to be cut through the floor under each bed to admit fresh air. In January a heavy frost inexplicably seemed to gain an upper hand over the fever and by February the prison, as if by magic, was free of disease. Typhus is actually caused by a rickettsial parasite, transmitted to humans by lice. The sufferer has intense headache and fever, as well as skin irritation, enough to send him mad and even to contemplate suicide. Scratching perpetuates the cycle by rubbing louse faeces into broken skin. Epidemics occur in three year cycles; during the first two years the infection spreads, mounting to a crisis during which many patients die. In the third year the epidemic tapers off rapidly because most people have become immune. This clinical course, rather than air holes under the beds, probably accounts for the sudden disappearance of the disease in Verdun.

Much coveted newspapers were occasionally smuggled in from England, and newly-arrived prisoners brought news of what was happening in Europe. However it was the arrival of English prisoners from Spain that opened the eyes of Back and his fellows to how badly the war was going for Napoleon. Many men were tempted to escape and desert, so the authorities rescinded prisoners' parole and confined them to the cathedral cloisters. A semaphore telegraph standing on a hill above Verdun reported any escapes. Prisoners would take bets on which way the arms were pointing, but as the semaphore was invisible from inside the high citadel walls, having laid their bets, they blanket-tossed 'Little Back', so he could see to settle the bets.

Midshipmen and some lieutenants were kept together and, as usual, got up to mischief. They staged mock courts martial for minor misdemeanours, and, according to the seriousness of the case, tossed the culprit in a blanket either alone or along with two dogs. Back did not mind being tossed in the blanket with a mongrel called Mouche, but when they added a sharp-clawed greyhound it scratched him painfully. In order to escape his tormentors, Back climbed onto the cathedral roof and lay hidden alongside one of the gargoyles. One of his friends on a search party, heard Back having a fit of the giggles, spied him, and successfully chased him over the roofs.

On one occasion the midshipmen held a serious court martial on the master of a gun brig whom they accused of informing on his fellows. A kangaroo court passed sentence of death, but immediately commuted it to a dozen lashes on bare shoulders. The judicial bench dressed outrageously and disguised themselves using burned cork and flour. They shaved the head of the accused spy and bandaged his eyes. They led him, dressed in a black cloak, in solemn procession to a spot far removed from view of the guards. However, just as they were about to inflict a flogging, a French lieutenant got wind of the gathering and sent half a dozen gendarmes with fixed bayonets to break it up. As Back noted, 'It stopped espionage and no one misconducted himself for the future.'

In 1812 the British prisoners learned that Napoleon's armies were moving east towards the Russian front, together with his élite Old Guard, who stopped for the day in Verdun. 'Finer men have I never seen,' wrote Back. 'Alas! how few of them returned.' Forced marches kept the troops moving day and night, and carts and baggage wagons were used to rest those who were sick, exhausted, or just plain footsore.

Empress Marie Louise, accompanying her seigneur, passed through Verdun in an open carriage with the horses slowed to walking pace. Napoleon Bonaparte followed two weeks later. The prisoners all crowded round their captors hoping to catch their notice, and thereby possibly a reprieve. But no luck.

The River Meuse at Givet joined two halves of the town by a temporary bridge of barges chained together. Flood waters caused by recent incessant rain had washed away the pontoons so the regal entourage was unable to cross. Napoleon ordered the directeur de fortifications to send for thirty English sailors to transport his party across the river. A willing crew of old salts, John Wetherell among them, ferried the imperial party to the other side by rowing a pontoon barge.

To reward their enterprise and skill, Napoleon made the sailors his personal guard of honour for the day, sent some brandy to prevent them catching cold, and promised that they would be sent home early to their native country. But later he changed his mind because, as John Wetherell tells, 'it would cause great discontent in the prisons in England when the Frenchmen there confined heard the newse . . . but every liberty and favour that could be given [to us] in France should be granted.' This was not much solace for some, like Wetherell, who had been imprisoned on foreign soil for more than a decade.

Concerning Napoleon's army, the Russian Ambassador in London prophesied:

We can win by persistent defence and retreat. If the enemy begins to pursue us it is all up with him; for the farther he advances from his bases of supply into the trackless and foodless country, starved and encircled by an army of Cossacks, his position will become more and more dangerous. He will end by being decimated by the winter, which has always been our most faithful ally.

And so it was. Before long, Back and his fellow Verdun prisoners watched the pathetic depleted remnants of the once Grande Armée straggling back in rout from Moscow. Winter had taken a terrible toll of Napoleon's so recently confident troops. Returning were only a fraction of the quarter of a million men, drawn from all the states of Europe, who had started out with such high hopes of conquering Russia and then moving on to Asia. The rest lay dead on the battlefield, or frozen by the wayside during an ignominious retreat.

Their fleeing commander-in-chief passed through Verdun silently at night without his usual fanfare. Hoisted on the shoulders of a sailor, Back called out 'Vivre l'Empereur', hoping he would be noticed by the Emperor. But this availed him nothing since Napoleon remained hidden in his carriage, and soon took off for Paris leaving his marshals to salvage what they could of his failed grand imperial adventure.

Back describes the scene:

Then followed the first installment of wretched wounded soon to be succeeded by numbers of common waggons full, whose creaking axles and wailing burthens chilled the many hearers to the heart. Oh! it was piteous, beyond description to listen to the agonizing cries of those brave soldiers who disturbed what ought to have been the stillness of the night with the racking torture of their undressed wounds, as every jolt of their rude vehicle shook them. The sight was too revolting by day and the authorities forced them to come at night – making it hideous.

Churches were converted into hospitals, and surgeons among the English prisoners volunteered to help. Symptoms of bubonic plague appeared, and several tough master merchantmen died overnight. Every night large carts were filled with dead bodies which were dumped outside town. To prevent the plague spreading, prisoners received strict orders to sponge themselves every morning with a mixture of garlic and vinegar, and to wear bags of camphor under their clothes to scare away infection. They were also told to smoke cigars to fumigate noxious vapours that hung around the town from rotting corpses. As with the earlier outbreaks of typhus, a sharp frost slowed the spread of the epidemic.

It soon became obvious to Verdun prisoners that things were also going badly for Napoleon on other fronts. In October 1813 he lost the battle of Leipzig. The Duke of Wellington was advancing on Paris from the south, having won the Peninsular War in Spain. His victory came partly through better tactics, partly because Napoleon had so reduced his troops there in order to boost the numbers needed in Russia and Germany, and partly from so many French defectors joining the British army.

That conditions for prisoners of war would change radically was still a far-off dream. Late the next year, anticipating the arrival of the Allied armies, orders came from the Commissaire de Guerre in Paris for all British prisoners to be ready to march at an hour's notice – each man to possess a shirt, shoes and stockings. Handbills were posted all over Verdun informing the English that next day they were to leave for Blois. The first division comprised over 2,000 men. With a new *feuille de route* in hand, bugles announced the start of each day's march, and a ragged brass and drum band brought up the rear to encourage marchers. The French government ordered British prisoners to head west immediately to prevent them falling into the hands of the Allies, and thereby boosting their numbers.

Back travelled with a companion, a *détenu* called Mr Richard, 'a most worthy man', with whose family for several months he had been living happily as a paying guest. With their pooled meagre money they bought a 'pretty strong horse and covered light cart' for Richard's wife and two children to travel in. The two men walked alongside. Their route followed in reverse that of the latter part of Back's journey from Spain to Verdun five years before.

Each night the prisoners were billeted; latecomers, encumbered by wagons, got poor pickings and often ended up – as did the Richard/Back party – sleeping outside in their cart wrapped in a greatcoat. Of one night when the river beside them froze over, Back wrote a note: 'I have often thought since that it was a mild fore-hardening of what I was doomed to experience in after life, and truly I learned many useful manipulations which were turned to good account even in the icy North.'

There were no stories of atrocities on the way. Marching prisoners received many kindnesses from villagers as they passed by. As Wetherell recorded: 'we have lived in paradise upwards of 6 weeks where we have become robust healthy looking men, different from when we arrived. In the evening I visited my happy retreat and passed part of the night in the charming embraces of one that proved faithful and true.' Presumably he had previously dallied with her on his northward journey.

Their route passed south of Paris, through Fontainebleau to Orléans, finally reaching Blois where they found lodgings. The journey was especially hard on women and children since the roads were deep in mud, and broken wagon axles were common. Richard's wife fell seriously ill of unknown cause, and soon died. Back stayed with his friend to help with the two children, Sally, aged five, and George, three. Of them Back wrote: 'I found myself at the age of 16 in charge of two little creatures who looked upon me as their brother.' Every Saturday night he bathed the children, lathering them liberally with yellow soap. Prayers followed. Poor Richard, who appears to have given up the struggle and was sliding into melancholy, stayed in a neighbouring house.

To prevent prisoners from being impressed by Wellington's invading Allied armies, they were ordered to march south towards Guéret, in the *département* of Creuse. There Back indulged his lifelong passion of trout fishing, and astonished the locals with his skill in making rough artificial flies. They were now 124 miles south of Blois, and still heading away from England – where they wanted urgently to go. The farther they went, the more vocally the country people proclaimed Louis XVIII as King of France. They gave each Englishman a white-ribboned cockade for his hat, declaring, 'You are no longer prisoners. Napoleon is dethroned.'

Soon, however, they were ordered to turn around and head north again – but this time as free men.

Back still felt obliged to stay the course with Richard and the children, although doing so delayed him getting home to England. They spent a night at Versailles near the camp of a detachment of Cossacks, who had taken care to remove Napoleon's imperial eagle from their uniforms. They toasted their respective commanders, Wellington and Platoff, and got wildly drunk on bumpers of bad brandy mixed with pepper. 'Strange it was to me,' Back remarks, 'to watch these wild denizens of the Steppes shouting and rejoicing around their camp fires, scarcely two dressed alike and all without exception wearing the stript spoils of the conquered.' After a quick visit to Paris, Back, together with Richard and the children, marched north to Rouen and Dieppe.

At last, early in 1814, after five years imprisonment, which had occupied the greater slice of his teenage years, Back celebrated with fellow sailors. 'Now, my boys,' he said, 'we once more behold Salt water and Vessels, being arrived on the Sea coast after all our land travails.' The next morning at Dieppe forty-seven people boarded a chartered fishing boat. While crossing the English Channel they sang and told stories all night. They cheered wildly when they eventually saw Beachy Head, and 'cried like children' as they leapt onto the shingle beach at Eastbourne. Back does not record whether or not they kissed the ground but, at the first pub they reached, everyone ordered porter beer and beef steaks.

And so Back took leave of his friend Richard, and of his two wards who he had grown to love deeply – an empathy with children that he showed repeatedly throughout his life. Then he set off hotfoot for London to meet his adoring parents, brothers and sisters, who were all staying at 15 Princess Street, Spittalfields. Home, sweet home, at last!

CHAPTER 3

Franklin's Midshipman

1815–18

The *Trent* taking the pack.

After a five-year absence George Back barely had time to greet his mother, who was anxiously awaiting his return, and to become 'thrice happy in the comforts of home and the indulgent fondness of family', before he was off again. In this he was fortunate. He had not yet been caught in the upheaval caused after the peace of 1815, when many young officers were laid off and ships decommissioned. Promotion was stagnant since there was no retirement age, and senior jobs (mostly sinecures) were often carefully guarded by men in their seventies. This time Back was to take up his first appointment as midshipman in HMS *Akbar*, a teak-built, 54-gun frigate anchored at Spithead, flagship of Sir Thomas Byam Martin, going overseas to join the North American station. Sir Thomas selected Back on the strength of his recent experience as a prison survivor in France, and also for his knowledge of French. Although Back's family tried hard to persuade him to consider other jobs for his future, but he was still steadfastly in love with the navy. John Back wrote a letter to his son on 14 October 1815, advising him to take advantage of any promotion offered to ex-prisoners of war:

> I hope to recommend to you every attention to perfect yourself in making a good Seaman, & good officer & that your conduct in every respect is that of a Gentleman. If it should be from your own ability & qualifications with the Interest that will be made for you so fortunate as to get you rated Lieutenant – I shall be most Happy. I dont know any thing in my concerns that I more anxiously hope for – Harry Cook [a family friend] have known many Instances of young men having been confined as prisoner for some years have helped them towards passing to the desirable rank of Lieut., that is, provided they possess the proper qualifications.

Midshipman Back reported to Sir Thomas in full dress uniform which he had stored for travel in his sea chest. The rest of his outfit had gone astray because a fellow midshipman prankster had labelled it 'Mr Backbone' and hidden it deep in a basket belonging to the captain. The standup collar of Back's single-breasted navy blue dress coat had small white 'turnback' patches on each lapel. Set at the back edge was a brass button known by midshipmen themselves as 'the mark of the beast'. The front of the coat bore nine brass buttons embossed with a fouled anchor; the back had a split bum-freezer skirt. He wore a buttoned white waistcoat, knee breeches with white stockings, and black buckled shoes. The insignia of a midshipman was his cocked tricorne, or sometimes a floppy top hat, and a dirk that hung from a black leather cross-belt. Later Back carried a sword, which dragged on the ground behind him because he was still so short. On his cuffs were three brass buttons, ostensibly to discourage homesick snivelling midshipmen from wiping their runny noses, or tears, on their sleeves. (The later midshipman's eponym 'snotty' was possibly first applied to Prince William – later King William IV – the Sailor King.)

Akbar sailed into the English Channel, in convoy with ten other ships, straight into the teeth of a gale, which so stretched the newly replaced rigging that the topmasts were in danger of breaking. As a result, Sir Thomas put in to Plymouth Sound to check the ship for damage. There the captain received orders to proceed to Halifax, Nova Scotia, headquarters of the North American station. Midshipman Back, happy to be at sea again, made friends with an old mate named Leworthy with whom he swapped yarns of their strange five years imprisonment together in France. In Halifax, Back came under the command of Sir Edward Colpoys, whose charge was to blockade the east coast of America in the fag end of the Anglo-American war which had developed out of American resentment at British treatment of neutrals in their war with Napoleon. This also involved renewed forays against the French – as if Back hadn't seen enough of them to risk another spell in a French gaol.

On the ship Back was appointed aide to the lieutenant of his division. A lieutenant's job was to manage day-to-day control over the crew, look after their welfare, and supervise young midshipmen's nautical training. He would send them aloft to reef and furl the mizzen topsail, and make them rig a model ship according to Darcy Lever's 1808 handbook, *The Young Sea Officer's Sheet Anchor – a Key to the Leading of Rigging and to Practical Seamanship*. He also made sure midshipmen kept their daily journals up-to-date – a routine procedure for officers in the Royal Navy which explains how there are so many vivid and detailed descriptions of their voyages and adventures. A lieutenant, together with a Royal Marine warrant officer, drilled their wards on the big guns and carronades, and with small arms – musket, pistol and cutlass.

Back was then seventeen and a half years old, well above the lowest age limit for rating as a midshipman. He was determined to show his mettle, and a compliment passed down to him from the second lieutenant boosted his confidence. His sleeping quarters were on the orlop deck, an airless cockpit in the bowels of the ship just one deck above the hold and the bilges. There he stowed his sea chest containing his personal belongings and his shore-going kit. He bundled his sea clothes into a fourteen-inch-wide hammock and slung it from hooks set in the deckhead beams, the regulation twenty-one inches apart that allowed just seven inches between smelly bodies. Although hammock space was meagre despite topping-and-tailing, in fact there was usually an empty spot on either side because midshipmen alternately vacated their position according to starboard and larboard watches. The stench was ghastly because, being below the waterline, they always needed light from candles which consumed any available oxygen.

Midshipmen, like Back, could occasionally relax in the gunroom

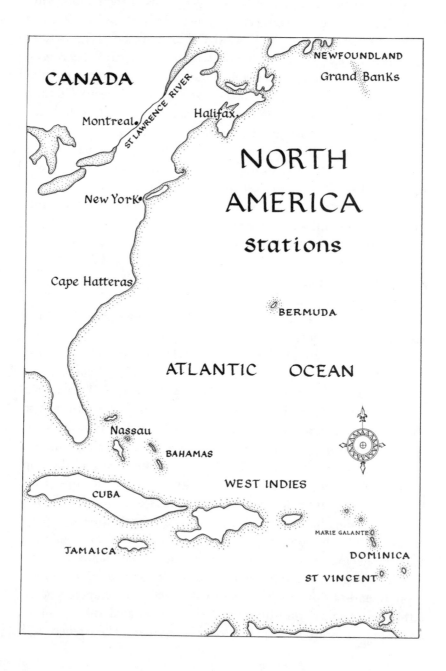

under the watchful eye of the gunner, who kept order according to Navy Regulations and Instructions. The Gunner's wife, one of the few women on board, mothered the youngest boys by proxy. A senior midshipman was responsible to the gunner for discipline over the 'crabs' or 'warts', as his juniors were known.

In their mess on the gun deck midshipmen ate off the amputation tables. Food for growing boys was scant both in amount and quality, especially when at sea on active service. A young volunteer, at the blockade of Brest in 1802, wrote: 'We live on beef which has been ten or eleven years in a cask, and on biscuit which makes your throat cold when eating it owing to the maggots. We drink water the colour of the bark of a pear tree with plenty of little maggots and weevils in it, and wine which is exactly like bullock's blood and sawdust mixed together.' Hunting rats with handmade harpoons was a favourite sport of midshipmen.

Night watch midshipmen often stole food on what they called buccaneering, or cutting out, raids into the steward's wardroom pantry. A standby at sea was 'portable soup', a kind of dried beef stock made into broth with vegetables, and issued by the Sick & Hurt Board of the Admiralty to naval surgeons for the use of their patients. Back would eat much portable soup in the years ahead, since it was also staple expedition fare.

Although the career on which young Back had embarked seemed hard, it was often preferable to civilian life of those days. It was then legal to flog boys and put them in stocks for minor misdemeanours; sheep stealing was at least a transportable, if not a capital, offence. But the discipline and toughness, both mental and physical, imposed on Back in his teens was to prove valuable a few years later in Arctic Canada. Discipline was necessary for the smooth daily working of a ship. In *The Wooden World*, N. A. M. Rodger writes:

Once the anchor tripped and the last libertymen sobered up, they became a different breed of man, alert, intelligent and obedient. This was not because the officers suddenly recollected their duty, it was because the prospect of drowning concentrates a mind wonderfully . . . living, and still more sailing, in the crowded and dangerous environment of a ship required a high degree of self-discipline, and those who had not learnt it, or would not learn, were a burden on their shipmates.

The bo'sun was responsible for discipline aboard ship, backed by a posse of bo'sun's mates, or captain's enforcers. Only men below the rank of petty officer could be flogged. Captains generally tried to avoid ordering a flogging because it required the formality of a court martial. Flogging – 'an elaborate and time-consuming spectacle' – usually entailed twelve lashes, and rarely exceeded forty-eight; the crime and number of lashes were supposed to be logged by the captain in a Punishment Book. During a flogging uniformed marines and a drummer were marshalled on the quarterdeck, and officers stood by to witness the punishment performed in front of the assembled crew. The bo'sun used a cat-o'-nine-tails on the back of a miscreant, who was stripped to the waist and lashed to a wooden frame. Sometimes an offender had to run the gauntlet when, after a dozen or so warm-up lashes, he was wheeled in a seat around the upper deck while the crew struck him with knotted ropes as he passed by. Back witnessed several floggings and John Wetherell described his own: 'after cutting my flesh in a dreadful manner I was cast loose . . . we were so cut and our backs so stiff and sore we sat still and did not go to our quarter.' Sometimes the malefactor had to 'kiss the gunner's daughter', whereby, as John Wetherell records, he was ordered 'to strip down his pantaloons and then lash'd to a gun and had six dozen lashes on my bare posteriors, a pump bolt having been introduced into my jaws and tied back of my head.' This was to stop him screaming. An errant midshipman might be sent to the masthead to stay there in any weather at risk of hypothermia; or he might meet his doom by being put in irons or 'going in the Brig'. One drunken seaman, Wetherell notes, was lashed up in the forerigging and salt water was poured down his throat through a funnel. After repeating this several times he was left spread-eagled in the rigging.

Stealing from a fellow crewman was treated more severely than either mutiny or desertion. Under the Articles of War of 1749 the death sentence was mandatory for the following crimes: corresponding with the enemy, cowardice, neglect of duty, taking a ship over to the enemy, burning a ship or magazine, murder, and buggery. Of these only the last two were actually punished by death.

One might expect homosexual offences to have been common among a large company of men confined in enforced celibacy, and surrounded by boys of Back's age. But this was not so, either from lack of opportunity due to crowded conditions, or because discovery brought harsh penalties – hanging, or up to a thousand lashes. During the Seven Years' War, out of only eleven courts martial for sodomy, four were acquitted; seven were convicted on the lesser charge of indecency, or uncleanliness.

In December 1816 *Akbar*, with Back aboard, returned to Portsmouth loaded with prisoners of war. The crew were disgusted at being sent home following the war with America, only to be ordered back to Halifax again. Approaching the Grand Banks off Newfoundland, Back, for the first time, saw and sketched some icebergs 'with which in aftertimes I was doomed to be very closely acquainted'.

Akbar encountered a fleet of French fishing boats off the coast of America. Back was summoned by the new captain, Sir Charles Bullen, and ordered to act as interpreter for some sailors taken prisoner. He mentions quite casually, 'My knowledge of French [from] my residence in French prisons in the society of persons much older than myself had sharpened my faculties of observation and taught me self-dependence and quickness, so that in worldly knowledge I felt superior to many of my shipmates who sometimes tested me severely and were never tired of questioning me.' Modesty was never Back's weakness.

Back was nearly killed when *Akbar* was dismasted and almost foundered in a hurricane off Cape Hatteras – 'an evil name associated with storm and wreck'. Under a close-reefed main topsail and trysail, a leeward jerk carried away the forward main shroud. The unsupported mainmast broke three feet above the deck, taking mizzen topmasts, rigging and sails with it 'into the yeasty sea'.

Swinging spars injured thirty men and killed two young midshipmen; Back himself narrowly escaped being flailed by loose rigging. Several sharks followed the ship closely when the dead men were committed to the deep 'after the usual solemn ceremony', and bloodstains soon appeared in the wake.

Under makeshift rigging *Akbar* reached Halifax and underwent a complete refit. She then sailed for Bermuda under command of Admiral Edward Griffiths and, in a light breeze, again lost her mainmast which had rotted at its base after a botched repair job. At the dockyard in Nassau, Back learned of his father's death. In order to be alone he wandered off and found some stalactite caves where he notes: 'soft beams of light glanced through the small entrance and brightened up the hundreds of columns glittering like stars . . .'. Nevertheless, overcoming the constraints of a stiff upper lip, he admits: 'I gave full vent to my youthful grief, the first great one of my life.' His senior officers were surprisingly understanding and, to keep him busy, sent him off on long boating duties when he had the chance to observe coral beds and rainbow-coloured tropical fishes.

The West Indies station was a magnet for pirates because of abundant small harbours and bolt-holes. There was also a good chance of booty from precious trade in cotton, indigo, tobacco, ginger, spices, cocoa, coffee, molasses, rum and sugar. In the Mediterranean and West Indies *lettres de marque* obtained from the government might just protect French privateers, if they were lucky, from hanging. Five per cent of the crews on duty there could be expected to die from noxious tropical diseases, especially yellow fever, which was always a death sentence. Another five per cent died in falls from the rigging, or exhaustion at the bilge pumps. Some sailors – mostly British, French, and Spanish – considered that deserting to the many pirate privateers sailing those waters was worth the risk.

Many sea-going sailors died of scurvy, the most prevalent shipboard disease, caused by lack of vitamin C (ascorbic acid). As early as 1593 Sir Richard Hawkins traded cloth for oranges and lemons with the Portuguese, and noted great joy among his ship's scorbutic company who, at the sight of the fresh fruit, 'seemed to recover heart . . . a wonderful secret of the power and wisdom of God, that hath hidden so great and unknown virtue in this fruit, to be a certain remedy for this infirmity'. Sixty years later, a Royal Navy surgeon, James Lind, carried out the pioneering original controlled trial in clinical medicine. In 1753 he published his results in *A Treatise on the Scurvy*. For two weeks he kept twelve scorbutic sailors on the same diet but with different supplements for each of six pairs: elixir vitriol, vinegar, a bizarre medicinal paste, sea water, cider, and oranges and lemons. Those receiving the citrus fruits improved clinically after six days; the next most effective, after two weeks treatment, was cider. Many sea captains, notably James Cook, subsequently studied Lind's conclusions and followed his advice. English sailors became known as 'limeys' because some ships substituted limes for lemons – a mistake, however, because the vitamin C content of limes is considerably less than that of lemons. But Back's ship, *Akbar*, had lemons aboard and no cases of scurvy were reported.

While in Halifax *Akbar*'s crew grew moody and refused to come on deck for harbour duty. The captain quickly quashed this brief mutiny without punishment or loss of face (although he had taken the precaution of having two armed frigates standing by on each quarter in case of trouble). Then when everyone had settled down, *Akbar* set off for Portsmouth. There the midshipmen were paid off and, after playing their usual high jinks on the customs house officers, like schoolboys celebrating the end of term, they dispersed homewards to every point of the compass.

Back spent six weeks with his recently widowed mother at her new home in Hampstead before deciding to sit his exams for lieutenant, for which he had now put in the required time. He passed seamanship with credit, and immediately thereafter took another exam at Greenwich Royal Naval College, this time in navigation, which included calculation of latitude by sextant, and of longitude by lunar observation and by the use of chronometers. After some coaching by 'a well known grinder of dull intellects' the Admiralty Board passed Back for lieutenant with flying colours, and raised him to the rank of admiralty mate. In order to rise to full lieutenant, he then had to wait for a vacancy in the list – as men often did for many years.

By the following March, of 1817, he was appointed to a new commission as admiralty mate in HMS *Bulwark*, a 74-gun guard-ship lying at anchor off Chatham in the River Medway. The ship flew the flag of Rear-Admiral Sir Charles Rowley; in command was Captain McKinley, whose kindness became deeply engraved on Back's memory.

Time hung heavy on Back's hands after so much recent action at sea, so he filled his days with drawing, reading, and studying while awaiting promotion, which never seemed to come. He now started taking his education seriously, having long since given up the dissolute living of his prisoner of war days. He even complained how difficult it was to study in 'the constant bustle and uproar of a midshipman's mess', and was grateful to a friend who offered him a quiet place to read in the privacy of a cabin in the gunroom.

As well as studying, Back taught his messmates French. He worked at drawing and watercolour painting, and became involved in amateur dramatics. Life on board a guardship was monotonous. So the captain, keen to keep his men from getting up to mischief through idleness, asked Back to manage an amateur theatre produc-tion. He was sent up to London to buy supplies for stage scenery, which he painted on board *Hussar* in the storerooms of a Mr Trent, who had lost a leg at the battle of Trafalgar.

Back held auditions to sort out 'certain petty jealousies as to who should perform certain characters'. Then he began rehearsals in earnest, but met some difficulty in teaching his sailors to walk on stage with ladylike steps and to curtsey gracefully. He had invita-tion cards printed in blue ink, and distributed them widely. The play was performed on the main deck, which was decorated with evergreens, flags, and mirrors. The show was a sell-out, and the supper and the ball which followed were such resounding successes that guests demanded an encore.

In the midst of all these hectic theatricals, Back received via the flag lieutenant an urgent summons from Admiral Rowley. In trepidation – since he had no time to change out of his painting clothes – he waited outside the admiral's cabin, believing he could be in trouble over the play. Alternatively, he thought it might be because Rivers, one of his fellow midshipmen, during a recent dinner party with the admiral, winked at Back and tried to kick him under the table, but instead had booted the admiral's shin. Back was hardly in the frame of mind to receive a career challenge which would reset the whole course of his life.

Rowley told him that the government was fitting out a scientific expedition to seek a route to the Orient across the North Pole. His Royal Highness the Prince Regent, in the Official Instructions to the Commissioners for executing the Office of Lord High Admiral of the United Kingdom etc., commanded, 'that an attempt should be made to discover a northern passage, by sea, from the Atlantic to the Pacific Ocean'.

In fact, this was not as silly as it has been branded. For two centuries whalers had suspected the existence of a North West Passage. They knew that a vast area of ocean – the northern waters between Greenland and Ellesmere Island – remained free of ice year-round. If this open ocean extended farther west it was reasonable to suppose that therein lay a route which might lead north of the Americas, linking the Atlantic and Pacific Oceans on a shorter and less arduous route to the Orient.

William Scoresby, an outstanding whaler, submitted to Sir Joseph Banks, President of the Royal Society, a plan suggesting that the Admiralty might explore the North West Passage. John Barrow, second secretary at the Admiralty, upstaged Scoresby by publishing the plan – as his own – in the *Quarterly Review*. He then got permission for two Royal Navy expeditions in 1818.

John Barrow was a powerful bureaucrat, who had earlier travelled in China and South America. He developed a grandiose two-pronged plan to reach the Orient: John Ross and Edward Parry were to be the respective captains of *Isabella* and *Alexander*, charged to proceed north west through Davis Strait and Baffin Bay in order to find a route through the North West Passage. *Dorothea* and *Trent* were to try to pass northward between Spitzbergen and Greenland, then across the North Pole to reach the Bering Strait. Each ship would carry the ice mate of a Greenland fleet whaling vessel, 'much acquainted with the navigation of an icy sea'.

In overall command of the expedition was Captain David Buchan, sailing in *Dorothea*, a sloop of 370 tons. Back was commissioned as admiralty midshipman under Lieutenant John Franklin in *Trent*, a brig of 250 tons. There was strong incentive for both expeditions to succeed since parliament had offered a prize of £20,000 for the first complete navigation of the North West Passage, and £500 to the first ship to reach within one degree of the North Pole.

Admiral Rowley had been asked to select one midshipman for service on each of the two merchant navy ships chartered by the government. He grilled Back for half an hour on all a midshipman needed to know for such an undertaking and, satisfied with the answers, told him that he would recommend him for the post. But he suggested Back mull it over for the night and make a decision by next morning. Back, however, needed no second thoughts, as he wrote in his memoir: 'to one who like me had been nursed in some degree of hardship the very idea of adventure or discovery was captivating beyond language to express.'

The North West Passage beckoned those who believed that endless bounty lay in the crock of gold, brocades, and spices which lay where the rainbow ended in the Orient. Back was one of the beckoned.

Both HMS *Dorothea* and HMS *Trent* had been put into dry dock in Shadwell where, Back tells us, they were 'rendered as strong as wood and iron could make them'. On 25 April 1818, when the Lords of the Admiralty and multitudes of well-wishers had gone ashore after roaming the ships' decks, the vessels set off down the River Thames to Deptford. They called at Woolwich to take on ammunition for firing at icebergs in order to explode them should they obstruct their northerly path.

The brig *Trent* carried a crew of thirty-eight, under command of Lieutenant John Franklin, already an experienced naval officer. Three weeks after entering the Royal Navy at age fourteen, Franklin was at the battle of Copenhagen; as a midshipman under his cousin Captain Matthew Flinders he was shipwrecked off the coast of Australia; at Trafalgar he served in HMS *Bellerophon* where reports from cannons permanently damaged his hearing; while on the navy's North America station he fought at the battle of New Orleans. Then he returned to Britain looking for another command to advance his career. What better than a voyage of exploration to the Arctic?

As it happened, two men appointed as junior officers in *Trent* were in the future to make names for themselves in the Arctic: Frederick Beechey and George Back.

Once out at sea, *Trent* proved to be a 'dull sailer'. As Back notes in his memoir: 'Scarcely had we got well clear of the river before we had the mortification to find that a leak which had not shown itself [until] then had now broken out, and increased to an extent that caused much uneasiness.' The leak was severe enough to keep sailors at the pumps for at least half of each watch. The flow worsened after passing Yarmouth but, instead of turning round and fixing the problem then and there, they sailed up to the Shetlands and put in to Lerwick on 1 May. After high water the crew, using the retreating tide, laid *Trent* on shore on her beam ends so the officers could examine her bottom thoroughly. They found only a few spots that needed caulking, however, certainly not enough, they said, 'to endanger the safety of the vessel'. This was a cavalier attitude to take before setting off into uncharted Arctic waters. Only much later, when she was again laid aground between tides in South Gat, Spitzbergen, did the crew discover the cause of the leak.

The hands Franklin hoped to pick up in Lerwick had heard rumours of the still leaky *Trent* and, with justification as it turned out, sensibly stayed home. Nevertheless, *Trent* pressed on. Stubbornness superseding common sense and lack of humility in listening to locals presaged unhappy events that were soon to dog Franklin's Arctic travels.

A fair wind carried *Trent* across the Arctic Circle toward the midnight sun. Round-the-clock daylight bothered Back and his mates, as he says: '[It] deprived us of many hours of rest and when we returned to the deck to keep our night watch and still saw the sun gilding the sky, it seemed as if the day would never end.' Evidently he did not know the trick of sleeping with a pillow tucked closely round his eyes.

Trent passed Cherie (or Bear) Island, which lies about halfway between Norway and Spitzbergen. This desolate lump of snow-mantled rock is dominated by Mount Misery, evidently named with feeling in 1603 by Stephen Bent, a seaman hunting whales and walrus nearby. Soon afterwards *Trent* entered pack ice, and large icebergs became more numerous. For most of the crew this was their first experience of navigating in ice. On 26 May, a month after leaving the Thames, they sighted Spitzbergen's jagged mountains rising from glaciers surrounding their bases.

A gale blew up, causing ice to amass around the brig and to encase the planks of the hull and the bowsprit with several tons weight of ice. Sailors beat the rigging with sticks to loosen encrusted ice, and used axes to chip it off spars and the hull. No sooner had the gale abated than the ship became shrouded in fog. When it cleared *Trent* cruised along the west coast of Spitzbergen and put in to Magdalena Fjord for a rendezvous with *Dorothea*, from whom she had got separated by the gale and fog. To the north the crew could see a great barrier of permanent ice, which had always previously been the limit of discovery for ships trying to cross the Arctic Ocean to the Orient. Nonetheless, they still hoped they might breach a passage.

While snugly at anchor in Magdalena Fjord some strange Russian boats appeared. Sailors came aboard *Trent* and exchanged half a fresh deer carcass for grog. Their camp nearby, 'probably the most northern and most desolate habitation of our globe', as Back puts it, was one of the few remaining stations of the Merchants of Archangelsk of the Muscovy Company operating on the Russian Arctic shores. They were on their annual hunt for pelts of the numerous walrus and seals, and for walrus tusks.

On 7 June both ships ventured out into the ocean and found pack ice in the same position as before. Large floes, agitated by a huge swell of slushy brash ice, were being turned on end in a great jumble. The leak continued troublesome, but Back says it 'diverted the attention of the crew from reflecting on their situation by compelling them to work constantly at the pump to clear the ship of water'. This presupposes that the men would be more content in dark bilges than on deck surrounded by growling ice.

Trent tried to sail round the northern tip of Spitzbergen, above latitude 80° North, but ice pushed her dangerously close to the isolated Cloven Cliff which explorers Baffin, Hudson, Poole, Barents, and Phipps had all noted before. Using warps, *Dorothea*'s crew anchored her to a floe, which luckily revolved and carried her away from a dangerous lee shore. *Trent* was less fortunate and had to

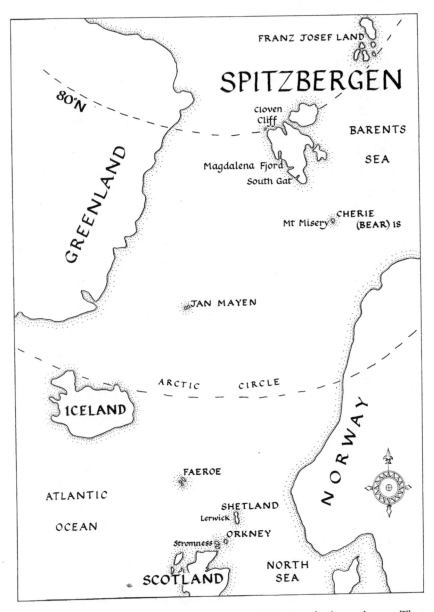

*Back's spelling of Spitzbergen with a 'z' is used throughout. The modern spelling is with an 's'.

struggle to get herself clear into open water. When the ships came together again they both set anchors in large floes whose whims they had to follow willy-nilly.

Water continued to pour into *Trent* through the leak. The assistant surgeon, on hearing a rushing sound below his bunk, discovered a four-foot-high spout of gushing water. On inspection it became clear that some sloppy Bermondsey shipwright had left an open bolt-hole in the ship's bottom and merely covered it over with pitch. Naturally, the pitch washed away as soon as the ship was at sea, and a regular fountain of water had poured in.

A gale blowing from the southwest roared like thunder, and piled up such a sea that pack ice pressed hard against *Trent*. A huge floe forced itself under the keel, raising the ship four feet so with every timber creaking she heeled on to her side. *Dorothea* was not much better off, since a pyramidal piece of upturned floe, imprinted with the planks and bolts of the ship's hull, towered forty feet above her. After three weeks stuck in the ice, drifting southward opposite where they wanted to go, the ships were now spat out into the sea.

Back noted that 'the ice is as fickle as the wind which it obeys', an observation that was to haunt him eighteen years later during his voyage in *Terror*, when he spent months stuck in ice off Southampton Island, north of Hudson Bay, being tossed aimlessly hither and thither. *Dorothea* and *Trent* could not advance beyond 80° 37′ North, despite the crew cutting a path through the ice with huge saws in order to reach open lanes ahead, windlassing and warping on anchors dug into floes, and using full sail to try to force a passage through wayward southerly-flowing ice. Back describes how: 'Vast portions of floes became crumbled and crushed, half acres slided on the mass nearest, immense hummocks toppled over, and cyclopean fragments were piled thirty or forty feet high.'

The officers abandoned their unrealistic hope of reaching the North Pole and turned the ships to run along the edge of the pack towards Greenland. A furious storm hit the fleet on 30 July. *Trent* raised every stitch of sail to stave off drifting on to icebergs to leeward, but even under full canvas she took some mighty blows. *Dorothea* was less fortunate. As a last resort to avoid shipwreck, she took to the pack in the hope that being jammed in the ice might be better than repeatedly bouncing off it. While trying to find her consort, *Trent* was hurled against the pack. Masts bent and hull timbers creaked ominously, so the officers feared she might be stove in. Added to this turmoil, the crew could hardly stand up on the sloping deck, where Back tripped, severely injuring his left foot. He was ordered below to send up on deck all the sailors who were huddling round the galley stove. During this chaos the ship's bell tolled mournfully until muffled by one of the officers.

Back then writes: 'For ten minutes the rising and sinking or see-sawing motion of ice and Brig was something awful and no language can describe our sensations as we beheld the cold blue walls threatening to engulf us.' Suddenly the fury subsided, as though Heaven had intervened, and both ships broke free of the ice in which they had been imprisoned for thirteen successive days.

Twenty-five years later, Frederick Beechey embellished his recall of a lifetime at sea in *Voyage of Discovery towards the North Pole in the Dorothea and Trent under Captain David Buchan 1818*. He describes:

> The sea violently agitated, and rolling its mountainous waves against an opposing body, is at all times a sublime and awful sight; but when, in addition, it encounters immense masses of ice which it has set in motion with a violence equal to its own, its effect is prodigiously increased. At one moment it bursts upon these icy fragments, and buries them many feet beneath the wave, and the next, as the buoyancy of the depressed body struggles for reascendancy, the water rushes in foaming cataracts over its edges, while every individual mass, rocking and labouring in its bed, grinds against the contents with its opponents until one is either split with the shock upheaved upon the surface of the other.

Back noted a strange contrast between a furious gale raging outside the pack ice and the calm on board ship where the masthead wind vane hardly moved: 'Stormy and dark looking clouds enveloped the one while the zenith of the other was blue and serene.' This phenomenon of iceblink is caused by a luminous white haze on the horizon radiated by large masses of distant ice. Iceblink allows a mariner to judge the nature and position of pack ice at some distance from his ship.

The two ships, now both in need of repairs, immediately made for the shelter of South Gat, Spitzbergen. While approaching the anchorage under full sail *Trent* struck a hidden reef, which did her damaged hull no good. When shipwrights examined *Dorothea* they discovered cracks in most of her timbers, and several of her beams had sprung.

As the carpenters set to work, some of the crew went ashore and saw herds of reindeer in a lush valley near by. While hunting a young buck one of Back's friends, Seaman Robert Sparks (who would later, in 1824, accompany him on Franklin's second land expedition as coxswain in *Reliance*) climbed a hill from where he saw a signal flag from the ship recalling the men. So Sparks, 'a strong and jolly joker', tobogganed on his backside off the hilltop, digging his heels into the snow to try to brake. Sparks's stunned shipmates watched him gather speed, totally out of control, and they were sure he would be dashed to pieces on the glacier below. Luckily he catapulted over a cliff and landed in a bank of soft snow from which he emerged, very bruised and sore, with the two pairs of tough worsted trousers he was wearing in shreds.

Some midshipmen took a boat to try hunting birds along the 200-foot face of a glacier, which reached down into the sea. One of them shot at a flock of ducks and the report from his gun loosened a huge piece of glacier face, which broke off – or calved – with the sound of a volley of gunfire and sank into the sea. Calving sets up a tidal wave that stirs up plankton on the seabed. Immediately seals and narwhals basking on floes of previous calvings abandon the bronco-bucking ice and dive down to feed. When the commotion has settled they return to the floes to await the next explosive calving. This one threw the boat ninety-six feet up a shingle beach and damaged its planks. Some angry walruses, barking and snorting, tried to sink the boats by pulling down on the gunwales with their tusks, but a sailor thrust his musket down the throat of one beast and fired. Back never mentions killing seals for fresh meat, which would have been a powerful antidote to scurvy – a fact that eluded him both on the Arctic Ocean with Franklin, and on the *Terror* expedition when many of his men became scorbutic.

One night a polar bear, attracted by the smell of blubber from which the crew were making oil, came close to the ship. They shot the bear and found among its stomach contents a Greenland whaler's stocking garter – but no sign of the owner. One bright midnight Back stumbled upon a deserted camp with several human skeletons nearby, 'one with the stockings still on the shin bones'. He makes no mention of the danger of eating polar bear liver which, being loaded with vitamin A, is deadly poisonous, a fact well known to Inuit (or Eskimos, as he calls them, and will continue to do so). Many years earlier, a fourteen-year-old midshipman, sailing in *Racehorse* under Captain Phipps, had chased a polar bear nearby. His name was Horatio Nelson, and – luckily for Britain and the Royal Navy – he killed it before it killed him; neither did he eat the liver.

While at anchor in South Gat, sailors under Captain Buchan's orders took soundings in the bay and brought up from the bottom, Back notes, 'several species of living zoophytes, a starfish, a lobster, a piece of sponge and a branch of dead coral'. He poses the question whether these Arctic waters were once semi-tropical.

After their icy imprisonment, in spite of repairs to both boats, *Trent* was still leaking; *Dorothea* was in even worse shape. Nevertheless, Lieutenant Franklin asked Captain Buchan's permission to sail round the eastern side of Spitzbergen into the Barents Sea. Buchan considered *Trent* unseaworthy and refused. Even though it was 'dreadfully against [everyone's] inclinations', Back, keen young midshipman that he was, remarks that it was 'proper not to be allowed to be judge of conduct of superior officers'. By not using capitals for 'superior officers', Back suggests his displeasure at their turning for home so soon, before they had accomplished any useful exploration.

Reluctantly, therefore, they headed south – passing Jan Mayen Island, Iceland and the Faroes – and docked in Deptford on 22 October 1818. As they were being paid off Back remarked laconically, '*Point d'argent, point de success* – no money, no success.' More accurately, this should read, 'No success, no promotion.'

For his first sea voyage bearing responsibility aboard ship, Back had gained good experience, especially of Arctic conditions. Little was achieved by the expedition, yet Back made an impression on John Franklin, his commanding officer, which would shortly alter the course of his life. In Back's midshipman's report, Franklin noted that his junior 'uniformly conducted himself as a correct, zealous and attentive officer, and was assiduously anxious to promote every aspect of the voyage . . . I consider Mr Back to be much entitled to my approbation.'

In the meantime, however, he was again appointed admiralty midshipman to HMS *Bulwark*.

PART TWO

FRANKLIN'S FIRST ARCTIC LAND EXPEDITION

CHAPTER 4

To Hudson Bay

1819

John Franklin

Things were slack in the Royal Navy in 1819. Four years earlier the Duke of Wellington had defeated Napoleon Bonaparte at Waterloo, bringing to an end both the Peninsular War and Boney's attempted Hundred Day resurrection on escape from exile on Elba. The erstwhile emperor was now languishing in prison on St Helena.

In the slump that followed war many naval officers went on half pay, and crews were disbanded when their ships were laid up 'in ordinary'. At the height of the Napoleonic wars the British navy numbered 150,000 men; afterwards it was reduced to 20,000, with one officer to every three men. Of the 700 commanders only forty-six had active jobs. The Admiralty's second secretary, John Barrow, planned to concentrate the navy's energy on exploration – specifically the North West Passage, as a viable commercial route to potential riches in the Orient.

The previous year, 1818, coinciding with the Spitzbergen expedition, Captain John Ross in *Isabella* had reached the head of Baffin Bay and poked his nose into Lancaster Sound. Ross claimed that he could see in the distance the 'Croker Mountains' barring his way – they turned out to be a figment of his imagination. Lancaster Sound was, in fact, the very portal of the North West Passage. Ross's failure to push on caused him to fall out with both his keen young second-in-command, William Edward Parry in *Alexander*, and more importantly with Barrow, his ultimate boss.

In 1820 Barrow appointed Parry to lead a sea expedition of two sister ships, *Hecla* and *Griper*. His instructions were clear: to pass through Lancaster Sound, winter over, and then follow the Arctic coastline westwards in search of a North West Passage that might lead to China, with no diversions on the way for mapping or science. Parry chose to hibernate on Melville Island, in what he named Winter Harbour, as far west as anyone had penetrated so far. Next season, however, his way south was barred by choking ice. But that did not diminish his achievement in showing that, with adequate thoughtful preparation, wintering over in the Arctic was possible – even in reasonable health, and marginal comfort.

At the same time, the Admiralty decided on 'sending an Expedition from the shores of Hudson's Bay by land to explore the North Coast of America from the mouth of the Coppermine River to the eastward'. Barrow chose Lieutenant John Franklin to lead the venture. If Franklin could link up with Parry, all well and good because he might be able to guide Parry westwards along the Arctic coast towards Russian Alaska. Nonetheless, the sole stated object of the expedition was to complete the North West Passage, and (unstated) to pre-empt those damnable Russians from being first to find a way from Alaska through the passage eastwards for trade with Europe.

The whole concept, planning, and execution of Franklin's expedition was a mishmash from start to finish. Barrow launched his scheme in February of 1819, and appointed the officers two months later. Franklin's projected departure in May left him just one month to seek advice, gather information, and buy stores and equipment for an expedition across thousands of miles of mostly uncharted northern Canada.

Franklin was a charming, if bombastic, navy man who loved children, and whose men loved and admired him. He was deeply – even excessively – religious. He was plump, unfit, and unused to hard exercise, with no experience of travelling on foot, or running rivers in canoes, or hunting for food – as neither did any of his chosen officers. No competent modern traveller/explorer, equipped with the best gear, using sophisticated technology, and with all the inestimable benefits of hindsight would contemplate allowing less than a year to embark on such a major journey, even over already known and mapped country.

As Franklin was to learn, planning an expedition in the comfort of his drawing room was very different from sorting out adverse problems in wild places with a harsh climate. Yet he was about to launch his party into the virtual *terra incognita* of the Canadian far north bordering the Arctic Ocean. The only non-indigenous person to have crossed some of that country was Samuel Hearne, together with his Chipewyan Indian guide, Matonabbee. Nearly fifty years before, in 1771, they had reached the mouth of the Coppermine River, on a four-year-long journey by foot and canoe in a futile search for copper. From afar Hearne had seen the Arctic Ocean, no part of which was mapped.

Franklin's appointed officers for this expedition were Doctor John Richardson, surgeon and naturalist; and two midshipmen, George Back and Robert Hood, both artists. Richardson was a gentle, scholarly, diversely talented Renaissance man. Nevertheless, over the coming years he would show repeatedly his admirable stamina and pluck. He got on well with his companions and was especially empathetic to native people among whom they travelled, and on whom the expedition relied so heavily. He had studied medicine in Edinburgh and joined the navy as an assistant surgeon, serving during the Napoleonic wars off Denmark, Portugal, Africa, Quebec, and the Mediterranean. In the American war of 1812–14 he was surgeon to the Royal Marines. Returning to Edinburgh, he studied natural history, wrote his MD degree thesis on yellow fever, and went into general practice in Leith, the port of Edinburgh. There he heard that Franklin was looking for a naturalist to go to the Canadian Arctic – and that was that. Certainly Franklin's selection was wise, since Richardson turned out to be the greatest of all contemporary surgeon-naturalists sent around the world by the British. He was always utterly loyal to Franklin, with whom he remained lasting friends. That Franklin retained Richardson's trust over so many arduous years endorses the qualities of both men.

Hood, like Back, was a young midshipman chosen at a time, before the days of photography, when artists were sent with expeditions primarily to survey their routes, make maps, and chart and compile the scientific findings; their secondary task was to record scenery, flora and fauna. Although lacking Back's robust constitution, Hood was nonetheless a hard worker and a meticulous meteorological observer and surveyor in mapping their northward route. Of the two artists, Hood was better with people and animals, Back excelled in scenery and action. Hood's career was short and he left few paintings, while Back's several and scattered sketchbooks display his talent well. The complement of the expedition's British members was made up with two seamen, John Hepburn and Samuel Wilks.

Franklin had read Samuel Hearne's account of his journey of half a century before. However neither Franklin nor his officers had any idea of the scale and distance of the wilderness through which he was planning to travel, nor of the complex and intricate system of linking rivers and lakes that made such travel possible.

Two recent northern travellers offered advice. First, Alexander Mackenzie wrote saying that in the first season they would be unlikely to reach farther than Isle à la Crosse before the onset of winter. At that point the hitherto westward route takes a northerly turn. Mackenzie suggested that during winter some of Franklin's party should go on foot with guides to Fort Chipewyan on the Athabasca River to prepare for their onward journey the following spring.

Second, John Pritchard, on the strength of his 2,000-mile

journey from Hudson Bay to the Red River Settlement (in present-day Manitoba), advocated bacon as their main source of meat – in a land teeming with herds of thousands of buffalo and caribou. As a result, Franklin, who was unfamiliar with pemmican, took seven hundredweight of salted pig, to the exclusion of other meat. As it turned out, he had to leave all the bacon at York Factory because it was too bulky and heavy and was already mouldy. Franklin's blind obedience was to lead him into more than one mortal catastrophe. Nevertheless, in Britain, his heroic reputation – something always enhanced by the drama of a death (or several) – stood high.

For local advice Franklin consulted the London headquarters of both the Hudson's Bay Company and the North West Company, who each assured him of their support. Simon McGillivray of the NWC requested his men 'to provide [the expedition] such conveyance and supplies as may be deemed the fittest for the purpose', and 'to afford every facility and assistance in your power for the prosecution of the undertaking on which they are engaged'. Despite their goodwill, however, from the moment of Franklin's arrival at York Factory on Hudson Bay the companies failed to tell him about their own internecine squabbles which were causing serious supply shortages at their inland posts. In blissful cloud-cuckoo-land, he believed that his route towards the North West Passage would be paved with helpful, co-operative company factors falling over themselves to provide his every request from their bountiful storerooms, and to find unlimited manpower to propel his expedition northwards. He knew nothing of the rival fur companies' years of bitter forest skirmishes, sniping from riverbanks at each others' canoes, occasionally taking prisoners, and resorting *in extremis* to arson and theft, kidnapping and murder – tantamount to open warfare. All this in the quest for territory and power for greater profit. Neither did he understand the cultural differences that might arise between himself and a disparate group of French Canadian voyageur canoemen, Indian hunters, and Eskimo guides, who he expected would guide them through the most barren and inhospitable land anyone could imagine, among people utterly ignorant of intrusive Westerners and their strange ways.

On Sunday, 23 May 1819, Franklin's Arctic Land Expedition

embarked at Gravesend on board the HBC's 342-ton, three-masted supply ship *Prince of Wales*. In the light of inter-company rivalry, travelling on a HBC vessel was a diplomatic error. They sailed in convoy with the 245-ton *Eddystone*, and a two-masted brig *Wear*. After a week of beating against shifting easterly winds in unsettled weather, the captain of *Prince of Wales* put into Yarmouth Roads. This delay allowed the officers time to check their pocket chronometers against the longitude of Yarmouth church, which was known from the trigonometric ordnance survey. Several officers and passengers, looking at the stormy sky, expected their departure to be delayed, so they went ashore for a few hours to do some last-minute shopping.

Back went two or three miles up the coast to visit a 'much respected friend' at Caistor (modern Caister) Castle. During dinner his host ordered a servant to watch the weathercock for a change of wind and for signs of the ship preparing to sail. When the wind suddenly veered favourably to the southwest the captain fired guns to summon everyone aboard and, in order to clear treacherous Cockle Gat before dark, promptly weighed anchor. On hearing the servant's warning, Back's friend drove him at a gallop down to Caistor beach, where they arrived just as *Prince of Wales* was passing 300 yards offshore. Back asked some boatmen to row him out to the ship, but they demanded an exorbitant fee of 20 guineas which he was too short of ready cash – and stingy – to pay. So they refused to help him.

Meanwhile Franklin sent a note, via a midshipman from the survey ship *Protector*, telling Back to hotfoot it to Stromness in the Orkneys, their next port of call. The journey entailed taking the Northern Mail coach to Scotland via Norwich and Newcastle. His fellow passengers took pity on him and lent him some coats and blankets since he was wearing only his blue uniform dress coat with bright brass gilt buttons.

In Edinburgh he hired a gig for the journey to Thurso, which was interrupted at Bonar Bridge beyond Inverness when he met two bibulous Scots looking for a boozing companion. One of them, The Laird, soon drank himself under the table, whereupon the other, The Major, invited Back to his home before continuing north. As Back noted, 'I have a vivid recollection of the plentiful Highland breakfast enjoyed in his company and that of his very pretty daughter, whose regular and intelligent features haunted me for many a long month afterwards in the cheerless forests of America.'

Nonetheless, he reached Thurso after travelling for nine success-ive, crazy, sleepless days and nights. Considering his present discomfort the exorbitant ransom of the Caistor boatmen must have seemed paltry. A gale was blowing so hard in the Pentland Firth that the ferry to Stromness was not running. Back chartered a notorious local smuggler, Old Andrew, to sail him across. On hearing the bagpipes of a crowd giving them a send-off, two 'fine young girls' implored Back to let them accompany him; so, 'with a lassie on each side of me, the one having dark hair, the other light red, we hoisted the close reefed sail and were soon beyond the merry sounds that cheered us.' They had a wild ride across the Pentland Firth, throughout which, Back confided to his journal, 'the helpless girls, completely subdued by sickness, clung to me in their agony with a tenacity quite irresistible.'

Just before dark, Old Andrew drew alongside *Prince of Wales*, at anchor in Stromness harbour. Franklin notes in his *Narrative*: 'we had the gratification of welcoming our absent companion, Mr Back . . . he could not be prevailed upon to withdraw from the agreeable scene of a ball-room, in which he joined us, until a late hour.' This says much about the tenacity and toughness that were Back's hallmark in the years ahead.

While waiting in Stromness, *Prince of Wales* moored beside the brig *Harmony*, belonging to the Moravian Missionary Society, bound for Nain on the northern coast of Labrador. The missionaries invited the expedition officers aboard and taught them a few Eskimo words and phrases that might come in useful in the Arctic.

Franklin tried to recruit boatmen for his expedition in Stromness because he was worried that, with the arrival at York Factory of the HBC's spring fleet, all available company men might be employed ferrying supplies to the company's various inland posts. Mr Geddes, the HBC agent, put notices calling for volunteers on church doors of different parishes as 'the surest and most direct channel for the conveyance of information to the lower classes of these islands, as they inevitably attend divine service there every Sunday'.

Because it was the height of the herring fishery season, Franklin could persuade just four boatmen to join the expedition. The canny Orkneymen signed an agreement stating that they would go only as far as Fort Chipewyan, and no farther. Franklin lugubriously notes: 'they minutely scanned our intentions, weighed every circumstance, looked narrowly into the plan of our route, and still more circumspectly to the prospect of return. Such caution on the part of the northern mariners forms a singular contrast with the ready and thoughtless manner in which an English seaman enters upon an enterprise, however hazardous, without inquiring, or desiring to know, where he is going, or what he is going about.'

In fact, about three-quarters of all the 500 men recruited by the HBC for their various posts came from the Orkneys, where they were accustomed to labouring under rigorous conditions. The company was run like a feudal Scots fiefdom where the laird was the boss – often absentee at that. He would leave a gillie – or factor, in the case of the HBC – in Canada to run the estate, while raking in the profits and banking them in Britain.

A century before, the London committee of the HBC had, for convenience, tried recruiting Englishmen. But they were so dissolute that the governor, John Nixon, recommended they hire 'country lads that are not acquainted with strong drink . . . and are not debauched with the voluptwousness of the city'. He especially liked Scotsmen: 'for that countrie is a hard country to live in, and poor men's wages is cheap, they are hardy people both to endure hunger and cold, and are subject to obedience . . . and better content with their dyet than Englishmen.' He advised sending lads aged fourteen to eighteen for seven-year terms so they might become 'lusty young men, fit for service both at sea and land, and at small wages'.

On the Atlantic crossing Back noted only continual foul weather, and meeting the Greenland whaling fleet. Things became more exciting when *Prince of Wales* came abreast of Resolution Island at the very mouth of Hudson Strait. In dense fog, heavy swell, and an ebb tide she ran below a cliff which towered so close over the mastheads that the crew prepared poles to fend her off. She struck violently against some smooth rocks which lifted the rudder off its pintles and nearly crushed a lifeboat that had been prepared for launching. Without wind or steerage they headed for another cliff and shipwreck seemed inevitable. By some fluke the rudder grazed the rocks and was lifted back into place.

Prince of Wales cleared the point with the help of a light breeze and a tow line from the ship's boat – accompanied by many prayers. She was taking on water fast, so carpenters tried to stop the leaks by forcing oakum (made of loose fibres picked from old ropes) between the timbers. Passengers, in terror for their lives, worked the pumps and carried water buckets in relays. Some women and children, of Selkirk settlers heading for the Red River Settlement, rushed on deck in panic. Crewmen promptly chased them off because of danger from falling spars.

The ship was also in peril from a rising gale that split the sails, and from heavy surrounding sea ice. *Eddystone*, which they believed lost, suddenly appeared out of the fog, and sent a carpenter and some seamen to take her companion ship in tow. They had long since lost touch with *Wear*. Again *Prince of Wales* was driven ashore, this time against a large grounded iceberg which nearly carried away her masts. When it was calm enough, most of the women and children transferred to *Eddystone*, together with one man who was 'dastard enough to conceal himself among them'.

Back, now a hardened midshipman with plenty of sea miles under his belt, wrote in his journal that he was deeply touched by 'these poor creatures . . . unused to such spectacles as they had just witnessed, uttered the most piteous exclamations, fearing the torments of sudden death or the more horrible state of certain starvation, the screams of the children and the agonizing looks of despair of the fathers, with the bustle and confusion of the seamen added an awfulness to the scene which will never be obliterated from my memory.'

Leaking seawater continued to gain on the pumps. Soon there was a five-foot pool of water in the hold, into which one of the seamen fell and had to swim for his life. The flood only started to recede when carpenters successfully caulked the cracks with felt and oakum, and nailed a plank over their flimsy repair. Then they hauled a sail smeared with oakum under the belly of the ship and secured it with ropes. The remaining young women passengers set an example to the men by assiduously working the pumps. Once out of danger, Franklin offered devout prayers of thanks for their deliverance, as was his wont after moments of crisis; one hopes he also thanked the carpenters and crew.

Near Middle Savage Islands off Cape Saddleback, at the mouth of Hudson Bay, the crew heard voices drifting through the mist. Forty single kayaks paddled by Eskimo men appeared, followed by half a dozen sealskin-covered umiaks each holding about twenty women with their children. On arrival of the annual HBC ships, bartering with the crew was a long-established Eskimo custom. In exchange for any metal objects – needles, nails, knives, saws, and kettles – they offered oil, walrus teeth, whalebone, various clothes made from seal and caribou skin, and even their wives (temporarily). They closed every deal by ceremoniously licking each newly acquired article.

On 30 August 1819, after a voyage of three months and seven days from Gravesend, *Prince of Wales* anchored in Five Fathom Hole off the flats in front of York Factory and met William Williams, the governor of the HBC. The British officers then got a firsthand inkling of the squabbles between the two companies when they met four NWC partners recently captured at Grand Rapids on the Saskatchewan River by Governor Williams's force of a dozen constables and twenty Selkirk soldier-settlers of the de Meuron regiment. The NWC men – George McTavish of Fort Chipewyan and three colleagues – had apparently committed 'some violences' against the HBC, and were imprisoned at York Factory awaiting deportation to England. They warned Franklin to expect shortages of supplies at the northern trading posts because of constant hostilities between the companies.

Franklin discussed with Governor Williams various routes into the interior of the country, and chose the one via Cumberland House, which turns north through a chain of company posts to Great Slave Lake. Most of this geographical detail, however, must have eluded them. An anomalous situation now existed: a small band of enthusiastic Royal Navy men with no experience of river travel were about to embark on a vast journey into the Canadian wilderness, depending totally on the help and cooperation of two warring companies who were not beyond murdering each other to further their own trade. It was not a good portent for newcomers to the north country.

CHAPTER 5

A York Boat West

1819–20

Rock with tripe de roche, by Back.

The nation of Canada was built on beaver pelts. During the seventeenth and eighteenth centuries beaver fur was in demand in Europe for coats, for fashionable wide-brimmed felt hats, and for making parchment. Furs were sent to ports that linked Canada with Europe – Montreal for the North West Company and York Factory for the Hudson's Bay Company. Goods for trade with Indian hunters moved inland in the opposite direction.

Before considering the role of the rival trading companies in the commercial opening of Canada, we must look at how the indigenous people of the land viewed these intruders. The earliest record of people having crossed the Bering Strait from Asia was about 20,000 years ago. These were traditionally nomadic hunter-gatherers, who subsisted mostly on bison, moose, caribou, seals, fish, and berries. For countless generations they had lived in small tribal bands with their own informal organization based on strong ties of kinship. They had a profound respect for the land and all creatures that lived in it – on which their very survival depended.

This is still reflected in strong oral history that pervades native culture.

All that changed with the arrival of white men – fur traders, missionaries and explorers. Suddenly these interlopers took control of the natives' lives by the lure of trade goods that ostensibly eased their harsh nomadic existence. It also encouraged native migration towards, and dependence on, the forts, trading posts and settlements that Europeans built after the fashion of their own culture. Aboriginal trappers abandoned their traditioanl traps, nets, and bows and arrows in exchange for modern hunting equipment – guns, ammunition, flints, traps, knives, axes and ice chisels. Their women got a liking for metal cooking pots, blankets, beads, awls, and needles and thread.

Not only did aboriginal ways change, but their very lives were threatened, and frequently decimated, by diseases imported from Europe – smallpox, tuberculosis, measles, whooping cough, and influenza – to which they had no immunity. Traders exploited natives by underpaying them for furs, and plying them liberally with tobacco and 'firewater' spirits, to their perpetual harm. The overbearing and patronizing ways of the interlopers were a puzzlement for naturally polite and compassionate aboriginal people. The newcomers, however, had the power – especially through gunpowder and alcohol – to encourage the natives to abandon their healthy, if arduous, way of life that they had always espoused.

Since the early 1500s, a fur trade had operated as an offshoot to the flourishing cod fishing industry off the Grand Banks of Newfoundland. After the British conquest of New France (Old Quebec) in 1763, the Canadian fur trade opened to upstart NWC entrepreneurs who pushed farther and farther inland in search of untrapped sources of prime beaver to supply Europe's constant demand for pelts. Religious persecution in France had driven the doyens of hatters – Huguenot French Protestants of Rouen – to London where they opened a factory in Wandsworth. There they produced a soft durable felt by shaving the fine, downy beaver underhair (*duvet*), and beating it until its tiny barbs matted together. Lead fumes from shellac, which gave hats a glossy finish, poisoned many workers – hence the saying 'mad as a hatter'.

Milliners also wanted other furs — bear and wolf, fox and lynx, marten, mink and ermine — to make exotic clothing.

Canada appeared to have a boundless supply of fur, especially beaver, which Indians, who were passionately keen to trade for European goods, hunted for little pay. However, this cornucopia lasted only until the 1830s when over-hunting nearly wiped out beavers. Later on the industry was further impoverished when silk replaced felt in hatmaking.

In 1670, King Charles II of England granted a Royal Charter to the 'Company of Adventurers of England Tradeing into Hudson's Bay . . . at their owne great cost and charge undertaken an expedicion for Hudson's Bay . . . for the discovery of a new Passage into the South Sea and for the finding some Trade for Furrs, Mineralls and other considerable Commodityes'. The Hudson's Bay Company standard of currency was the Made-Beaver, a prime quality adult beaver pelt, or its equivalent in other furs or goods. The M-B (as it was known) took the place of money in barter with Indians. HBC men were mostly lowland Scots and Orkneymen willing to accept low wages and living standards which, nevertheless, were considerably better than they could expect at home. Being literate and better educated than their English counterparts, they became company clerks who could be relied on to handle accounts and keep accurate records. Generally speaking, HBC men were servants of the company for life. If they showed promise they might become factors of small trading posts, and wintering partners with a stake in company ownership and profits. In the heart of the country where Indians brought furs to trade, company men built outposts along the main rivers. Those who wintered over (*hivernants*) acquired useful local knowledge and often took Indian bedmates who produced families of métis children.

Later, in the 1820s, HBC Governor George Simpson imported young women from Britain as potential brides. He had already fathered at least five children by four different Indian women before marrying his eighteen-year-old cousin, Frances. An illustration of his callousness is a note he wrote to the factor at York Factory concerning a former doxy: 'if you can dispose of the Lady it will be satisfactory as she is an unnecessary & expensive appendage. etc.'

Eventually the HBC abandoned its monastic demands for celibacy and chastity among employees and allowed them to marry Indians. These 'blanket marriages' suited the company because it was not responsible for Indian wives, who usually stayed behind in Canada once the employee returned home. An Indian wife also afforded her white partner entry into the safety of her tribal society, and thereby cheap insurance against being scalped. She taught him bush survival skills – how to snare rabbits, trap and skin animals, and catch fish. She also made his moccasins and prepared furs for market.

In the mid-eighteenth century some French Canadians were the first to establish forts inland, and became the North West Company (NWC). The two widely separated points of entry into the remote and inclement land of Canada, York Factory and Montreal, became the headquarters of the HBC and NWC respectively. NWC supply ships travelled up the St Lawrence River to Montreal, longitude 74°W, where they established business houses. The HBC fleet sailed through Hudson Bay to York Factory, longitude 92°W, at the mouth of the Hayes River. Being 20° farther west, and 1,500 miles nearer the hub of the Athabasca fur country, the HBC had considerable advantage over the NWC because of shorter access to the interior. Nevertheless HBC fur trading never matched that of the NWC.

The NWC had no corporate charter, and its loose organization depended on strong ties between Roman Catholic French Canadian voyageurs and their Presbyterian Highland Scots employers. At first, small groups of itinerant traders peddled with Indians on their own turf, often taking Indian women as partners. The libertine behaviour of feral Frenchmen, however, rarely allowed them to winter over in the same place twice. They frequently carried off women against their will – virtually bonding them as slaves – or bought and sold them between each other. These traders often sought favours from post officers with gifts, and offers of services in exchange for transient liaisons with their own wives. This conduct, although socially acceptable by Indians, reflected the NWC's informal and flexible trade dealings.

Nor'Westers worked on short contracts lasting one to three years, and then renegotiated their terms. The paddling skill of the

NWC's inland navy brigades of 2,000 canoemen voyageurs (*engagés*) was unmatched on the vast network of rivers that led into the heart of prime fur country.

Nearly half the major rivers flowing east from the Rocky Mountains emptied into Hudson Bay, whereas only one tenth of them drained into the St Lawrence. By spring the NWC needed to have its cargoes ready at Grand Portage (their wilderness head-quarters on Lake Superior) for instant dispatch as soon as ice went out from the northern rivers. These seldom opened before mid-May and were frozen again by late September. With less distance to travel, the HBC could more easily deliver supplies and trade goods into the very heart of the continent. However, in contrast with the NWC's five-month open season, the HBC's sea route was only ice-free for two months, when shipping was open to and from Europe.

The HBC controlled Hudson Bay itself. Most factors stayed at York Factory waiting for Indian middlemen to bring furs there, rather than going inland to fetch them, as did the NWC. HBC officers had to refer all major questions to ten board members sitting at Fenchurch Street in the City of London, none of whom had ever seen a portage and whose information about the country was usually out of date. Replies to factors' letters could take several months – or even years – so they could expect no quick deci-sions.

Franklin could not have chosen a worse time to mount an expedition that depended so heavily on company goodwill. It presages how he and his men got themselves deeper and deeper into trouble on their first land expedition into Arctic Canada. Meeting the four NWC partners detained by the HBC at York Factory should have raised his suspicions. In fact, before Franklin arrived in the winter of 1816–17, the NWC had taken prisoner HBC's John Clarke at Fort Wedderburn, seized the fort, and forced the occu-pants to surrender a large quantity of trade goods. A year later Colin Robertson of the HBC was arrested by the NWC at Fort Chipewyan and kept prisoner until he escaped from Cumberland House the next summer. The HBC had imprisoned Simon McGillivray of the NWC; and an HBC constable, George Spence, 'took members of the NWC prisoner for shorter periods'. So there was plenty of give and take – mostly take.

To be in the middle of a tit-for-tat war between those on whom he depended was dire for Franklin, despite his carrying a circular letter to all HBC factors from William Williams, then governor of the HBC at York Factory:

> I most particularly enjoin you individually and collectively to render every possible assistance he ['Lieutenant Franklin, Commander of an Expedition fitted out by our Government in England to explore the North East Continent of America'] may require in Supplies, provisions, men, dogs and sledges, interpreters and hunters, in fact everything conducive to make so arduous and interesting an undertaking as facile as possible.

An understanding of the geography – especially of the Canadian Shield – makes it easier to comprehend Back's twenty-year association with the northland and the peoples who travelled throughout it. The Precambrian Shield is a vast dome of crystalline rock – mostly granite, gneiss, and schist – exposed to the surface in an area occupying half the size of present day Canada. Glacial ice sheets once eroded and smoothed the ancient rolling bedrock, gouging out hollows that formed a myriad of small lakes. From the explorers' point of view this barren land was utterly savage – a vast wilderness interlaced with lakes and wild rivers that ran at random in unpredictable directions. It was an endlessly rugged, scabrous landscape of jagged rock and sparse forests of skimpy trees.

The Shield encircles Hudson Bay like a giant horseshoe whose horns almost meet at the northern tip of Baffin Island. The large inland waterways follow the western edge of the Shield; the St Lawrence River and the line of huge lakes – Superior, Winnipeg, Athabasca, Great Slave and Great Bear – are virtually inland seas that extend west and northwards. To the east lies the dog's head that is Labrador.

Draining the western Shield into Hudson Bay is a sprawling system of rivers – Thelon, Churchill, Nelson, and Hayes; and into James Bay – the Albany and Moose. The wilderness they cross is still known as the Barrens. Inland, a chain of interconnecting lakes and rivers, with relatively short portages between them, leads as far as the Rocky Mountains in the west and north to the Arctic Ocean. The present treeline is a transition zone with, to the north, Arctic Barrens and tundra – the treeless, rocky, marshy land of permafrost. Black spruce forest stands to the south. The most productive fur-bearing country lay around the edge of the Shield. Following the NWC's river route to the Arctic from its headquarters on the St Lawrence River is like running a finger clockwise round the rim of an upturned dinner plate.

Beavers made many waterways navigable by building dams which in turn formed a stairway of small lakes. Canoes could be hauled over one dam after another, from one lake to the next. Hunters and traders steadily intruded into this country, forcing the beaver to withdraw northwards. Consequently pelts became increasingly scarce and as a result the fur trade came to a close.

On 30 August 1819 the *Prince of Wales* anchored at York Flats about five miles from the shoaly mouth of Hayes River. York Factory comprised a stockaded compound inside which were several fur warehouses and dwellings for company employees. Back sketched

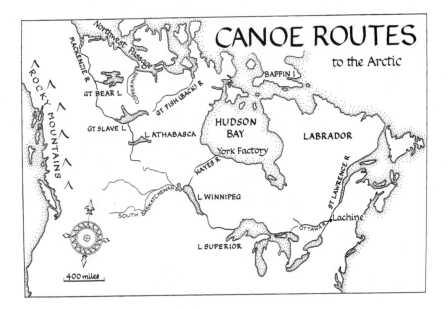

the fort and explored the flat surrounding country which was inhabited by Swampy Cree Indians. He found them malnourished and miserable from whooping cough and measles contracted from Europeans. He notes how nearly all the men suffered from sore, red eyes that often led to blindness, in some cases the result of measles in childhood. Hood describes how Franklin himself caught whooping cough so severely that it 'threatened strangulation'. Hood continues: 'But his [Franklin's] mind was too eagerly bent on the service which he had undertaken to be relaxed by the attacks' – a Royal Navy stoic indeed.

Governor Williams ordered his carpenters to refit a York boat for the expedition – a heavy old clunker, but the only one he could spare. The British crew comprised four officers – Franklin, Richardson, Hood and Back plus sailors John Hepburn and Samuel Wilks, and four boatmen brought from the Orkneys. Only one HBC man, a steersman, was available, all the rest being on the river already. The boat could carry only three tons of gear, so the expedition had to leave half its supplies – thirty-five loads including bacon, some tobacco, gunpowder and ammunition – at York Factory with instructions to the factor to forward them as soon as possible.

Expedition gear comprised personal clothing and bedding; each officer carried a compass, spyglass, and chronometer. Among many scientific instruments were magnets, sextants and artificial horizons, and a barometer, dipping needle and electrometer. The cargo was made heavier by all the guns, ammunition, and cast iron cooking utensils, together with knives, chisels, axes, nails, and fish nets to be used as gifts to the natives. Books were plentiful: bibles, prayer books, commentaries on scripture, leather-bound notebooks for recording scientific observations, and manuals of navigation and astronomy. There were several volumes of previous travellers' accounts of their journeys, natural history and geology tomes, and medical and surgical texts. And then there was enough basic food for three years. Although unnoticeable in a Royal Navy three-masted ship, all of these weighed heavily in a York boat.

HBC York boats, patterned on Orkney fishing smacks, were originally built at Albany House at the mouth of the Albany River, which flows into James Bay, the southernmost part of Hudson Bay.

Angled bow and sternposts gave the craft exceptional strength and provided a pivot for hauling it over portages. An almost flat bottom allowed it to navigate shallow rivers because the twenty-four-foot keel only drew two feet of water when loaded. The standard three-ton cargo comprised seventy *pièces* weighing up to ninety pounds each. When under sail on big lakes, however, the craft drifted strongly to leeward. Being built of soft pine and spruce – the only wood available – York boats were very heavy. Usually they lasted just three seasons because of repeated damage from running rapids and being dragged over portages. Their annual journeys to and from Hudson Bay originated at Methye Portage near Isle à la Crosse, at the junction of the Athabasca and Saskatchewan river systems.

A York boat crew usually comprised eight oarsmen. Navigating rapids required great skill by the steersman who stood in the stern with a long sweep oar, and by the bowman who fended off rocks. Carrying heavy boats across the many portages en route was hard labour; half the crew at a time changed places with the other half for a rest every thirty minutes. William Auld, an HBC officer for twenty-one years, wrote (sparely on grammar and spelling) to the London committee about the training boatmen needed:

> Your rivers never freeze ours are only a short time open were our people perpetually during *three* full years constantly working among the Rapids no question but they would in that time become expert and able *Voyageurs* . . . I intreat you to dismiss from your mind the spancaly-dressed wherry-man with his plush breeches and his silver badge nor conceive the *descent* of the solitary bargeman at London Bridge with that through the shallow horrors of rocky chasms as at all *synonimous*. Here the slightest mistake is big with fate allow a wrong impulse and the vessel is overwhelmed in an instant.

On 9 September 1819, the expedition left York Factory to a send-off of three rousing cheers from the HBC governor and his officers gathered on the bank, and a 9-gun salute. Beyond tidal water the current became so strong that the boat had to be tracked upriver on a long rope.

On the sixth day out, two HBC crews following the expedition advised Franklin to lighten his boat in order to make tracking upriver easier and quicker. Also the men were sinking deep into the soft mud and cutting their mooseskin 'country shoes' on sharp stones. At Rock Depot Franklin cached another sixteen *pièces* of cargo – this time the turn of sugar, biscuit, tea, rice, and portable soup – with orders for them to be forwarded later.

When a rapid became too steep to allow tracking laden boats upstream, Back and his colleagues had their first of many tedious and tiring experiences of portaging. Each time they had to unload cargo and carry it – and often the boats too – sometimes across portages several kilometres long, which quickly impressed the Royal Navy men with the weight of their sturdy craft. Back's account in his journal of the first large rapid gives a foretaste of the lucid prose he could write, and makes clear the very real difficulty and dangers they had to face:

> . . . entirely surrounding the boat were innumerable quantities of large stones, and the water rushed against them with an impetuosity almost irresistable. We grounded near the centre of the rapid, the men (but four) leaped out and tried to force her ahead, whilst the officers aided them with poles . . . the line to which we were secured broke, and she was immediately hove broadside on to the stream (for our strength was altogether inefectual) and thus situated drove with such velocity against a stone, as made us imagine she was certainly stove, at the shock we were mostly thrown down and narrowly escaped falling into the stream. Indeed one of the crew, who was hanging by the gunwhale, was so exhausted, that had it not been for immediate succour, he would in all probability have been bruised to death.

At Rock House they moved from a treescape of trembling aspen, poplar, and tamarack into spindly spruce, pine, and fir forest that covers much of Canada. Autumn leaves of deciduous trees were turning golden, but absent were the deep red and rich orange of more southerly maples. Before Oxford House a succession of rapids required portaging. Over the years a path a dozen feet wide had been cut through the bush for manhauling clumsy York boats and canoes. On the cleared trail boatmen laid rollers, set three feet apart, of freshly cut poplar whose smooth slippery bark made hauling easier, especially when wet. On steep ground occasionally they winched the boat with block and tackle.

Nonetheless, York boats had some advantages over birchbark canoes: on large open lakes they were more seaworthy and sailed better, and in rivers they withstood battering by chunks of floating spring ice. They were only a little slower than large freighter *canots du maitre*, and carried about the same weight of cargo. However, they could not match the speed of the smaller *canots du nord* and the light express *canots légers*.

In his journal Back describes the many portages and difficulties along the way like an enthusiastic Boy Scout relishing the challenge of his first camping trip. He does not mention how much, or little, help the other British officers gave the crew. York boatmen frequently had to jump into the river to lift their craft over rocks. Then they had to carry immense loads across portages. They spent all day in wet clothes at temperatures near freezing, so they were often in danger of hypothermia and immersion cold injury. On lakes with the wind abaft, York boatmen would raise a square sail that hung from a yard on a short mast stepped amidships, and secured by shrouds rigged like a Viking longboat. It was often garishly painted. The steersman stood in the stern to control the loose-footed sail which he could haul close to the wind with sheets. On lakes he used a tiller and rudder made of hardwood, instead of a long sweep oar, that gave leverage for changing direction quickly in rapids.

Back recounts the near demise of his leader, who was walking on some moss on a rocky bluff beside the rapids close to a waterfall: 'by some accident, he slipped and notwithstanding his attempts to stop himself, went into the stream, it happened to be deep and after many fruitless trials to get a landing, he was fortunately saved by one of the boats, which by dint of chance was near the spot.' The only misfortune for Franklin was breaking his chronometer's second hand, which was later replaced without disturbing the clockwork.

On 6 October 1819 the expedition met some Cree Indians on the northeast shore of Lake Winnipeg just before reaching Norway House. This HBC post got its name from a Norwegian labour gang imported to build a winter snow and ice road to York Factory in order to bypass the Hayes River rapids. The project was doomed, however, because by then the focus of the fur industry had moved far inland. This was partly because beavers were being annihilated by hunters using newfangled steel traps baited with castoreum – a bitter, orange-brown alkaloid produced by beavers' perineal scent glands; partly because natives were killing cub beavers for food, the tail being a special delicacy.

With a good breeze behind them the expedition's York boat left Norway House and coasted along the north shore of Lake Winnipeg, sailing through the night. Back describes northern lights, the aurora borealis, dancing across the sky and falling in coloured curtains, which reflected 'the red, violet and orange tinges as clear as when seen in a rainbow. It seemed as if lustre were added to the stars through them, for they shone with redoubled brightness.'

The large northern lakes – Winnipeg, Great Slave, and Great Bear – were like shallow inland seas whose shore could not be seen from the middle. Squalls and high waves make boating on them, even under reefed sails, as dangerous as any sea voyage. Certainly the navy men felt more at home on open water than on rivers, despite the flat-bottomed York boat's leeward drift. For the present the sailors were happy with their craft, since pounding waves could easily break the backs of birchbark canoes which, having no keel, also drifted badly.

Grand Rapids on Lake Winnipeg lay 160 miles from the expedition's projected winter quarters at Cumberland House. Situated at the mouth of the Saskatchewan River, that fort became a hub of fur trade routes where boats from Hudson Bay met those from Montreal. Near Grand Rapids, Back met a Canadian voyageur canoe whose cargo from Europe had arrived at Montreal the previous November, before the St Lawrence froze.

Canoe brigades of both trading companies passed round the portage at the foot of Grand Rapids, where carts used to ferry baggage had been destroyed in rival skirmishes. The HBC men with the expedition nervously expected retaliation because that was where Governor Williams had seized the Nor'Westers, McTavish and company (now detained at York Factory).

By contrast with the comparatively short HBC route, crews of NWC *canots du maitre* set out from Lachine, upriver of the St

Lawrence rapids, near Montreal. The 3,000-mile journey from Lachine to Athabasca crossed more than fifty sizeable lakes and involved 120 portages round impassable rapids. Because it took two years for supplies to reach their destination, NWC traders accumulated big overheads before they reaped any profit.

Wealthy NWC French and British family businessmen dominated the Montreal fur trade. Many of them had served their apprenticeship in the interior – *hommes du nord*. If they had spent a full season and wintered over in Indian fur country – *le pays d'en haut* – they thereby accrued merit and qualified for the exclusive Montreal Beaver Club. Every fortnight members, each wearing a gold medal engraved with the motto 'Fortitude in Distress', held bibulous banquets when they sat on the floor pretending to paddle a *canot du nord* to the drunken refrain of voyageur songs. This bacchanalia, reliving *le grand voyage*, helped traders, who had developed cabin fever from living too many winters in the bush, to ease themselves back into society.

In order to reach Lake Superior, NWC voyageurs paddled the Ottawa, Mattawa, and French Rivers, which involved crossing a total of thirty-five portages. After forty outbound days they reached their halfway rendezvous, Grand Portage at the west end of Lake Superior. There they turned round and returned to Lachine, where they were known pejoratively as *mangeurs de lard* – pork-eaters.

Franklin's expedition and their cargo transferred to lighter *canots du nord* of the Athabasca brigade at Grand Rapids, the central warehouse for collecting and distributing furs. These canoes were only twenty-four feet long, carried one and a half tons of freight and a crew of six, and so were suited to work on the turbulent northern rivers that led to their wintering quarters over a thousand miles into the backcountry. The expedition crew must have been glad to leave behind their cumbersome York boat.

The birchbark canoe – an aboriginal invention modified over centuries – was the key to opening the interior landmass of Canada lying between three oceans. Early fur trappers and explorers used this basic tool to paddle across a vast inclement land by a labyrinth of rivers and lakes which comprise one sixth of the world's total fresh water. Canoe highways run around the western perimeter of the Canadian Shield through taiga – boreal forest of stunted spruce and swampy bogs. Then the highways cross Barren Lands of permafrost Arctic tundra covered with mosses and lichens. Indian men and women (mainly Algonquin and Iroquois), who had travelled for centuries throughout the north by canoe, held the secrets of building them and gradually taught Europeans their art.

Louis Franquet, an engineer and inspector of fortifications, penned a report around 1750 noting that Indians made excellent birchbark canoes. Traditional division of labour dictated that men did the woodwork and assembled the boats, while women and girls sewed the bark with spruce roots, and gummed the seams. Large canoes were built mostly on the St Lawrence River in factories managed by Quebecers, and were paddled by French voyageurs. As a result, French terms predominate in canoeing folklore.

The Le Maitre family originally had a birchbark canoe factory at Trois Rivières. They built thirty-six-foot freighters, which carried a crew of twelve and a cargo of seventy *pièces* weighing three tons in total. Peter Labor writes of the versatile *canots du maitre*, Master of the Inland Seas: 'The canoe was developed by Aboriginal builders to meet the needs of geography, adapted by the French, Scottish and British entrepreneurs to meet the demands of the economy, and animated by mostly French-Canadian and métis voyageurs who made a shell of bark, roots and sinew dance and fly like a living creature.'

The best forests for garnering bark of white canoe birch (*Betula papyrifera*, also known as paper birch) grew north of the St Lawrence and the Great Lakes – Huron and Superior – bordering the Canadian Shield. Canoe-builders favoured birchbark because, being more resinous, it did not stretch and shrink, rarely rotted, and tolerated freezing and heat. By contrast, elm was stiff and heavy, and spruce never dried completely so was difficult to sew. Because birch grain ran round the tree, sheets the full length of a canoe could be laced together and rejoined smoothly edge to edge, without folding or crimping odd-shaped pieces. Women sewed with awls instead of needles to lace patches and wedge-shaped gores using thongs, known as watape, cut from roots of black spruce (*Picea mariana*). Roots, split lengthwise in two half-round strands

up to twenty feet long, were tough and durable, yet flexible when
wet.

Indian warriors who settled along the St Lawrence River soon
realized on which side their bread was buttered. So they protected
French colonizers from hostile tribes, and built canoes for their
military campaigns – until the French themselves learned how.
Natives – especially men from Trois Rivières, Kahnawake and Oka
– provided voyageurs to paddle the canoes.

HBC factor, Colin Robertson, who moved to Montreal and
opened an office for agents working in direct competition with the
NWC, wrote in 1819: 'I have frequently heard the Canadian and
Iroquois voyagers disputed as regards their merits, perhaps the
former may be more hardy or undergo more fatigue, but in either a
rapid or a traverse, give me the latter, from their calmness and
presence of mind which never forsakes them in the greatest danger.'
Even Governor George Simpson picked for his express canoe a crew
from Kahnawake, 'than whom there are no better in the world'.
Praise indeed from one not lavish with it.

Voyageurs who penetrated farthest north became the stuff of
their own legends. At Norway House, NWC trader Alexander Ross
once met an old voyageur, who confided to him:

> For twenty four [years] I was a light canoe-man. I required
> little sleep, but sometimes got less than I required. No
> portage was too long for me; all portages were alike. My end
> of the canoe never touched the ground till I saw the end of it.
> Fifty songs a day were nothing to me. I could carry, paddle,
> walk, and sing with any man I ever saw. During that period,
> I saved the lives of ten *Bourgeois*, and was always the favourite,
> because when others stopped to carry at a bad step and lost
> time, I pushed on – over rapids, over cascades, over chutes; all
> were the same to me. No water, no weather, ever stopped the
> paddle or the song. I had twelve wives in the country; and was
> once possessed of fifty horses, and six running dogs trimmed
> in the first style. I was then like a *Bourgeois*, rich and happy: no
> *Bourgeois* had better-dressed wives than I; no Indian chief finer
> horses; no white man better-harnessed or swifter dogs. I beat
> all Indians at the race, and I spent all my earnings in the

enjoyment of pleasure. Five hundred pounds twice told, have passed through my hands; although now I have not a spare shirt to my back, nor a penny to buy one. Yet were I young again, I should glory in commencing the same career again, I would willingly spend another half-century in the same fields of enjoyment. There is no life so happy as a voyageur's life; none so independent; no place where a man enjoys so much variety and freedom as in the Indian country. *Huzza! Huzza! Pour le pays sauvage!*

At the head of the Pigeon River, near Grand Portage – the height of land where water flowed either to the Arctic Ocean or Hudson Bay – by tradition a senior guide would cut a scrub cedar bough, dip it in water, and order each novice to kneel and swear allegiance to the northmen's code of honour – *Je suis un homme du nord* – I am a man of the north. This also implied the promise always to perform this ceremony when passing the height of land, and never to kiss another voyageur's wife without his permission.

Rapids were the main river obstacle to Franklin's voyageurs, but they also provided their greatest excitement. If a rapid was too wild to run they would try to line the canoe downstream, or, if that were impossible, to portage it. Travelling upriver they paddled until the water became too heavy. Then they would unload half the cargo (*demi-chargé*) and pole and track the canoe upstream; if totally unnavigable they unloaded fully (*déchargé*) and portaged it. Unloading entailed a return journey to pick up stashed cargo, thereby doubling the labour. Two men could carry a *canot du nord* upside down on their shoulders. With a larger canoe four men, using carrying sticks lashed across the gunwales, rested it on their shoulders, holding it steady with cords.

Many portages were built by Indians aeons ago, and the paths remain well trodden today. Some were even flagged with stone steps. Each voyageur usually trotted with two ninety-pound *pièces*, one on his back like a packsack supported with a leather tumpline across his forehead, the other on top nestled into the nape of his neck. He would set down his load for a rest at a halfway *posé*, and return for another load. To carry all the cargo across a portage often required three trips. Bonuses were paid for bigger loads, and one man is even recorded carrying 470 pounds.

On big lakes, to avoid buckling in sudden squalls and steep waves, a guide might unload half his canoe and spread the remaining cargo low on the bottom, keeping the bow and stern empty. High canoe ends were liable to catch strong crosswinds. However, together with greater freeboard, they protected the *avant* (bowman) and *gouvernail* (steersman) from being doused with water shipped in deep swells.

In rough weather canoes traversed from headland to headland across bays and inlets, or hugged the shore inside offshore islands. Landing was impossible on many rocky shores of Canadian Shield granite. If waves were too big, voyageurs would lay up to rest until the wind – *la vieille*, the old lady – died down. With a favourable wind they lashed canoes together, hoisted sails, and made good speed.

On 23 October 1819 Franklin's Arctic Land Expedition arrived at Cumberland House. As calculated by the immaculate survey measurements of Hood and Back they had travelled $685\frac{1}{2}$ miles from York Factory. Winter was approaching, which confirmed Alexander Mackenzie's opinion that this season they would get no further inland than Isle à la Crosse.

Franklin made their winter quarters at Cumberland House. Five buildings stood within the stockaded HBC fort, built forty-five years before by Samuel Hearne on his return from the Coppermine River. The surrounding country was thickly wooded, riverbanks bare and swampy, and lake edges recently frozen. Back went for a walk, got lost, and stepped on an iron-spring fox trap, luckily without injury. He found he had completed a circle – a common mistake when lost in the bush – and vowed from that day never to go into the forest without a compass.

In the coming sedentary six winter months the officers kept themselves busy by making daily scientific and meteorological observations. They soon discovered the hazards of holding cold metal instruments in bare hands, and Back found that 'you lose every sensation in the fingers, and if suffered to remain in contact with any metallic substance, becomes almost frozen to it, the certainty is that the skin remains behind.' Anyone whose lips have touched metal in winter knows this to be painfully true.

Since no one at Cumberland House seemed to know about conditions in the country to the north, Franklin decided that, as soon as snow and ice allowed, he and Back would travel overland to Fort Chipewyan on Lake Athabasca to recruit hunters and guides for their onward journey the following spring. Franklin did manage to enlist some men, although local Indians and traders appeared wary of the foreigners and suspected that expedition members were competing traders. Seaman Samuel Wilks was discharged, having been 'unequal to the fatigue of the journey'. Franklin and Back remained at Cumberland House only until 18 January 1820 before setting off north; meanwhile Richardson and Hood continued their studies and arranged for stores cached along the way to catch up with them during the winter.

CHAPTER 6

To Fort Chipewyan

1820

Fort Chipewyan May 27, 1820, by Back.

On 18 January 1820 John Franklin, George Back, and John Hepburn set out from Cumberland House on snowshoes, together with Indian guides, heading for Fort Chipewyan in order to lay preparations for next year's movement north, and to reconnoitre the rivers. Their westerly route took them to Carlton House by way of the frozen Saskatchewan River, then north to Isle à la Crosse.

One guide went ahead on snowshoes to stamp a trail in the soft snow so the loaded dog sledges might follow more easily. Their snowshoes allowed them to walk on the snow surface without breaking through. They are, however, diabolical footwear for a beginner, like being strapped to tennis rackets (voyageurs called them *racquettes*). They upset and overbalance the wearer, catch on undergrowth in bush, blister feet at tie points, and chafe ankles with every swinging step. Franklin recalls 'a species of suffering and fatigue which greatly exercises the temper and patience of the Novice'.

Snowshoes are made of ash frames laced with thongs of moose or caribou hide (babiche). Each Indian tribe has its own distinctive style, dictated partly by the texture of local snow and partly by the type of country. Some are pear-shaped with rounded ends, others have turned-up tips and long tails. Two crossbars spread the frame like thwarts of a canoe and anchor the babiche. A space in front of the forward bar allows a moccasin to pivot forwards when walking, but the bars can cause hideous blisters to unpractised feet. The heel rises free with each step, dragging the tail on the snow. 'In a long journey the feet, though well covered with socks are much galled by the bars and straps,' wrote Hood. 'All the superiority of European art has been unable to improve the native contrivance of this useful machine.' Back's three-feet-long snowshoes confirm that he was probably only about five feet tall.

Soon after arriving in camp, drivers unharnessed their dogs and untied their booties, a ritual that dog mushers still perform today. The officers' own moccasins, made of scraped moose or caribou hide, were tied with thongs above the ankles. Although not waterproof, they were supple for wearing with snowshoes.

Each night the party bivouacked, often at −40°F (−40°C), under the 'sublime canopy of the heavens'. Some men felled trees for firewood, others cleared the ground and laid a bed of pine branches. Back notes 'if you wish to avoid being frost bit it is absolutely necessary when once laid down under your blanket and buffalo skin that you do not move one jot, though you may ache in every joint.' Everyone slept in a circle with feet pointing towards the fire. On one occasion, Back's buffalo robe and left moccasin got too close to the embers and caught alight, so he jumped into the snow to quench it and to ease his pain.

New fallen snow and steady low temperatures slowed the party's progress through hilly country beside the Saskatchewan River. The voyageurs' provisions, especially pemmican, were scanty because from the start of the journey they refused to ration themselves. Also by passing up moose and caribou carcasses left behind by ubiquitous wolves, men and dogs went hungry. They were able, however, to resupply at Carlton House, which post provided pemmican for the canoe brigades.

Pemmican – from the Cree word *pimikan* – provided a concentrated subsistence food for long journeys. It was crucial to opening the Canadian northland and exploring the Arctic. Plains Indians originally made pemmican from pulverized dried lean buffalo (bison) meat mixed with melted fat. Women cut meat of one or two bison into thin strips which they hung to dry either in the sun or over a smouldering fire of poplar or willow. Smoke kept flies off the drying racks, and added flavour to the meat. After pounding it with stones or wooden mallets (beat meat) the women put the pulverized powder in a rawhide sack with the hair outside and seams greased for leak-proofing. They added melted marrow – soft fat from crushed bones mixed equally with hard tallow extracted by rendering bone fat in huge kettles. Finally they sewed the sack tight and mixed the contents by frequent turning. For flavouring they sometimes added wild berries – saskatoon or chokeberry.

Each bag of pemmican – the standard ninety-pound *pièce* – was rectangular, and could be squashed flat for stowage. A voyageur's daily ration of pemmican was one and a half pounds, equivalent to eight pounds of fresh meat. He usually ate it as soup or stew (*rubbaboo*) made by adding flour, wild onions, sugar or scraps of vegetable or meat, commonly pork; sometimes he fried it in its own fat (*rousseau*). It dried hard, so it was tough to chew if eaten raw. Back says that his less-than-top-quality pemmican 'so hardened our jaws that I verily believe it would have been of little consequence whether our next meat had been granite or limestone'.

On 31 January Franklin, Back, and Hepburn, with their guides, reached Carlton House, having travelled 240 miles in fourteen days – good going for the time of year which gave the lie to George Simpson's opinion of Franklin's fitness. Back enjoyed his first wash and shave – 'cutting off the muzzle lashing' in his navy slang. The HBC fort consisted of several buildings enclosed by a high square stockade with towers at each corner. Buffalo roamed the riverbank near the fort where the soil was fertile enough to produce wheat, barley, oats, and potatoes.

Franklin and Back went by horse sledge cariole to visit the

neighbouring NWC fort three miles away where they were welcomed with a volley of gunfire. The two companies used to share the same compound but their current enmity had caused the present separation. Voyageurs spent the day 'in gaiety', dancing with 'the dusky damsels [who] would never cease coming in'. The Englishmen, however, couldn't join in because their joints were stiff after long days of snowshoeing. Missing out on a dance must have irked a confirmed ladies' man like Back and contradicts his claims of fitness. Like voyageur paddling songs that featured round campfires at any season, this jolly scene was in character with easygoing NWC Frenchmen. It contrasted with the lugubrious atmosphere of the HBC fort where the men sat around eating, drinking, smoking, and talking about buffalo and the price of fur, followed, as Back tells, by 'a vast vacancy in conversation, which is by this means filled up – viz with a pipe'.

Back usually refers to his voyageur guides as 'Canadians', and often makes observations about them in French, particularly on the subject of dogs and how they were treated. He once upbraided Paul, his one-eyed cariole driver, for cracking his whip at the dogs, and remarked that he was a poor image of his biblical namesake.

'"True, sir," Paul replied, emboldened by a dram of grog (liver courage) before a portage, "*il eut deux yeux, moi, j'en'ai q'un, mais j'en doubte beaucoup si cet Monsieur dont vouz parlez eut l'usage de raquette* – he had two eyes, I have only one, but I doubt very much if this gentleman of whom you speak knew how to snowshoe."'

On another occasion, Back chided Paul for trying to pass another team to be first into the fort. Paul explained he did it, '*pour l'honneur de mes chiens, pour vous montrer seulement que c'est dans le pouvoir de ces beaux animaux* – for the honour of my dogs, to show you that these beautiful animals can do it.'

Franklin also was upset by what he describes as 'the wanton and unnecessary cruelty of the men to their dogs, especially the Canadians who beat them unmercifully and habitually vent on them the most dreadful and disgusting imprecations'.

Back and Franklin took two weeks on the leg of the journey from Fort Carlton to Isle à la Crosse. They traversed rolling country forested with willow and poplar, pine and spruce, often with buffalo and wolves for company. Franklin writes that they had 'completely surmounted the pain which the walking in snow-shoes had occasioned'. Back confidently notes: 'So little did I feel any languor from the journey that I was in every measure more capable of undergoing fatigue than at the commencement.'

A volley of muskets welcomed the party to the HBC fort at Isle à la Crosse where Indians used to congregate annually to play their traditional game. This was eponymously named lacrosse (the sticks being shaped like a bishop's crosier) in 1638 by a French missionary, Jean de Bréboeuf. Originally it was a violent free-for-all but, after acquiring rules in 1867, it became the popular national sport of Canada.

A memorable feature of the journey towards Fort Chipewyan was Portage La Loche, later known as Methye Portage. In a passage in his journal Back waxes lyrical about the view; written in the style of Victorian landscape artists, especially Ruskin, it shows his equal skill with either pen or pencil:

> Breaking through the thick foliage of the pine and cypress, he stands at once on the summit of an immense precipice, and like one bewildered in some vast labyrinth, knows not how or where to fix his eye. The view is that of a valley some thousand feet beneath you, in length upwards of 30 miles, in breadth three or four, and in the centre a meandering river holds its course near, covered with snow, farther distant, less light, decreasing in brightness, till it becomes insensibly lost in the deep blue mist of the distant perspective, it is bounded on each side by immense hills, the fragments of gigantic mountains, irregularly broken, like to the confusion of an earthquake, undiscribably grand, the one side is burnished over with the luxuriant foliage of the pine and cypress, the other with the cold and sterile poplar, half lost in snow, while here and there on the summit, scattered promiscuously, dark towering forests hang half suspended, the valley is filled with trees of various kinds and adds a finish to the scene, the path on which you descend is so narrow, that without great care, you may be precipitated by one false step to certain destruction. I do not pretend to describe the beauties of this view, the

pencil being a more powerful vehicle than the pen for that purpose, for the whole is apt to vanish before the minute parts can be described.

On the farther side of Methye Portage the drivers unharnessed their dogs to better control the sledges when sliding steeply to the valley floor. For one day, foul weather confined the party to sleeping under blankets, not in the open air – as was their custom – but underneath trees, which showered them with new-fallen snow – the mistake of a *cheechako*, a newcomer to the north. This was the first day since leaving York Factory that Franklin's crew had been stormbound, ample witness to their tenacity considering the often terrible weather.

On 26 March, after a journey of sixty-nine days, they reached Fort Chipewyan on Lake Athabasca, and were met by the NWC partners. Franklin writes in his *Narrative*: 'Thus has terminated a winter's journey of 857 miles . . . a great intermixture of agreeable and disagreeable circumstances . . . [on] balance, the latter would much preponderate.' He is referring to marching in snowshoes 'with a weight of between two and three pounds constantly attached to galled feet and swelled ancles'. Soon afterwards he seems to have recovered, and continues: 'Mr Back and I did not need this rest having completely surmounted the pain which the walking on snowshoes had occasioned.'

This winter journey covered an average of about sixteen miles per day, excluding rest days. It confounds the disparaging view of George Simpson, then Governor of the HBC, who wrote in his *Athabasca Journal* on 8 February 1821, even before the expedition had run into serious trouble: 'Moreover Lieut. Franklin, the Officer who commands the party had not the physical powers required for the labor of moderate Voyaging in this country; he must have three meals p diem, Tea is indispensible, and with the utmost exertion he cannot walk above Eight miles in one day.' Many subsequent detractors used this statement to dog Franklin who, while he may not have been a master of forethought and planning, was unquestionably tough.

Back – younger and even tougher – was in his element with the physical challenge, as he showed repeatedly in later journeys. On 25

May 1820 Back wrote a long cross-written letter to his brother Charles from 'Fort Chipewyan Interior of America'. In cross-writing a finished page is turned sideways and written over at right angles in order to get more words on each page thus saving on scarce paper. It is also a work of art. Back's letter to his brother is written in an unusually intimate manner, without the restraints of a journal that his superiors would read. (More is the pity that we have so few of his personal letters to illustrate his character.) He writes: 'There was a wide difference between Franklin and me, and he suffered every evil I have mentioned whilst mine was a slight chafing in the toes occasioned by the Snow Shoes, he had never been accustomed to any vigorous exertion; besides his frame is bulky without activity. In fatigue I found my constitution could surpass even the old travellers and as for the climate it has no effect on me but to spur me on in my undertaking.' He added a postscript: 'I was not frost bit the whole winter – the whole party except myself was.'

Back's conceit was the trait that probably began to alienate him from his boss. It recurs occasionally (usually only by hint) in the months and years ahead by veiled critical journal entries. The gilt of his Spitzbergen certificate from Franklin was beginning to tarnish. The NWC fort impressed Back as the best built of any they had so far seen, and capable of housing several hundred people. He also notes that McVicar, chief trader at Fort Chipewyan, had prepared a house where 'a pleasant-looking girl' was busy roasting a joint for them. The less imposing HBC fort stood on an island a mile away. Franklin realized that his expedition could not go beyond Great Slave Lake without the help of the NWC. This impressed on him the importance of their recent journey in making arrangements for the following spring in preparation for the summer season of exploration. The companies were still barely speaking to each other and consequently all their trading posts were short of supplies. Franklin was frustrated at not gaining guarantees of help, both with manpower for canoes and provisions for the next stage of his journey. Goodwill was abundant, but hard results scanty.

In May the NWC partners at Fort Chipewyan wrote to Franklin saying they would do their best to help him in their present difficult circumstances, and that they were 'extremely sorry to find that the existing troubles in the country and more particularly the recent extraordinary transactions taken place in this quarter, has already deprived us and may deprive us still more, of the means of contributing towards the successful issue of the expedition to the extent we most ardently desire'.

The NWC canoe brigades were ready, waiting for the ice to go out so they could transport the winter's fur harvest in the opposite direction to where Franklin wanted to go. His request for boatmen, however, brought an unexpectedly terse response: 'For whether the seizure of our people is by legal authority [the letter of assurance from the Company] or not, does not the less deprive us of their services, and those who are most useful to us would be of most service to you.'

Franklin arranged a meeting between rival officers in a tent on neutral ground between the forts. A NWC officer, familiar with both French and Indian languages, would manage Canadian voyageurs, and engage Indians to hunt and build a post for wintering somewhere on the Coppermine River. The HBC men advised him that for his projected journey a party of twenty was the minimum necessary, travelling with a month's provisions in light *canots du nord*.

Boileau, a métis, used charcoal to draw a map on the floor to show the country north of Great Slave Lake as far as the Coppermine, where he said indigenous Indians would give them more information. An old Indian named Blackmeat then took the charcoal and drew a triangle from Kathawachaga Lake to the mouth of the Coppermine, east along the coast to Bathurst Inlet, and back following what he called the Anatessy (Burnside) River, where he claimed he had killed several Eskimos on skirmishes. He described a river that also drained into the Arctic Ocean and was so shallow as to be suitable only for small Indian canoes – the Thlew-ee-choh, or Great Fish River (which will feature large in Back's later story).

Nothing particular occurred until May when the lake began to unfreeze and pulsatilla, the pasque flower (known locally, and incorrectly, as the spring crocus) appeared, heralding spring. The lake opened by 1 June, when deciduous trees were dressed in tender green leaf buds. Along with migrating swans and geese on their way north to their breeding grounds were those dreaded harbingers of summer – mosquitoes.

Back deplored how the Chipewyan Indians, once zealous hunters and brave and determined warriors, had plunged into a 'vortex of indolence' which he attributed largely to vice and debauchery, encouraged by European traders plying them with alcohol – 'all for the poor fur of the harmless beaver'. He was particularly sympathetic to Indian women, unmercifully beaten by their men, yet who did most of the labour – dressing skins, preparing food, pitching camp, dragging sledges and paddling canoes. Meanwhile Indian men hunted, sat around camp, smoked pipes and talked among themselves. Also they indulged their sons and neglected their daughters and, whenever they felt like it, swapped or borrowed wives.

Franklin was still having difficulty recruiting boatmen: 'Most experienced voyagers still declined engaging without very exorbitant wages . . . bow-men & steersmen to receive 1600 livres Halifax per annum, middle men 1200 exclusive of their necessary equipments.' Stores left behind at York Factory for forwarding, as promised by Governor Williams, still had not caught up with them. Also, supplies at the posts were so scarce that Franklin sent his Indian guides and their families to subsist on fishing at a nearby lake.

On 13 July Richardson and Hood arrived by canoe bringing ten men and all the stores they could procure from Cumberland House. They had taken a more direct, northerly, route than Franklin and Back, by way of Frog Portage and Churchill River. At several portages round serious rapids and waterfalls they found wooden crosses – 'the mournful records of former failures'. Then at Otter Falls tragedy struck when a canoe, being tracked upstream along the edge of the rapid, capsized with two men aboard and was swept downstream by the current. Hood and some other voyageurs jumped into a canoe and shot the rapids in an unsuccessful attempt to rescue their companions. The steersman reached the bank, but the foreman, Louis St Jean, drowned – a sad event that put a damper on the party.

CHAPTER 7

Fort Enterprise

1820

Winter view of Fort Enterprise: snow melting May 13, 1821. Drawn
by Back, engraved by Finden.

On 18 July 1820, after four months waiting for summer to arrive,
the expedition left Fort Chipewyan and paddled off down the Slave
River in three canoes. Stores of food, along with ammunition,
spirits, and tobacco, were scarce at the fort. The men had to ditch
ten bags of mouldy pemmican acquired from the NWC, so they set
out north with only one day's food remaining. They tried setting
nets but caught only a few small fish, not enough for a satisfying
meal. This was an inauspicious start to a journey destined for some
of the most desolate country on earth – unless, that is, you know
how to live off the land.

George Back was tormented at every turn by mosquitoes, and he
tried smoking out of his tent what he called those 'creatures [that]

have no regard for decency'. Throughout his journeys mosquitoes were one of the few discomforts that got under his skin. He complains constantly about them – as do the diaries of many northern travellers. Ubiquitous standing water in the North West Territories makes ideal breeding for mosquitoes, and swarms are sometimes so thick that clenching one's teeth is the only way to avoid inhaling them. They can drive man and beast crazy.

The expedition encountered a series of portages that passed round waterfalls in the middle of the Slave River. They had some accidents with the canoes. One was rammed amidships and nearly cut in half, and the back of another broke when the man carrying it slipped and fell. Voyageurs, nevertheless, quickly and skillfully repaired the boats with spruce resin – a frequent maintenance ritual, called gumming, that had to be performed at the bottom of most rapids.

After a week the canoes entered Great Slave Lake and crossed to Moose Deer Island opposite the mouth of the Slave River. Two trading posts stood there (both later moved to the mainland) – the NWC's Slave Fort comprised some houses and a canoe shed, and Fort Resolution of the HBC. The latter, Back tells, was 'a house with a few miserable stockades in front to prevent the NW men from beholding what is going on'. Both companies were desperately short of supplies and had little to spare for the expedition. However HBC factor McVicar gave all he could, and more, literally parting with the shirt off his back. His generosity earned him the lasting enmity of Governor Simpson, and thereby jeopardized his job. Fortunately, next day some returning Chipewyan hunters brought a good stock of meat, which they were glad to sell.

Hugging the shore, Franklin's party paddled to Stony Island, from where they cut due north across Great Slave Lake. Although exposed to the winds of this huge body of water, they were able to shelter among a myriad of small islands that lay towards the lake's east arm. Once past Gros Cap they followed the shore to Fort Providence, where William Ferdinand Wentzel greeted them. A twenty-year Norwegian employee of the NWC, who spoke the Copper Indian language, he had agreed to accompany the expedition northwards.

Wentzel had engaged some Copper Indian (synonymous with

Yellow Knife) hunters, who came to meet Franklin along with their chief, Akaitcho, and his escort. In order to make an impression on the natives, the British officers hoisted a silk Union Jack over their tent and decked themselves out in full uniform with medals. Akaitcho entered the fort wearing a white cloak covered with a blanket. He sat down ponderously, smoked a peace pipe, drank some spirits with his companions, and then launched into a harangue. He told Franklin that it was too late in the year to go much farther, but that this season he would escort them some way north to 'a land where animals abounded.'

Franklin replied that he had been sent by command of 'the Greatest Chief in the world, who was sovereign also of all the trading companies in the country.' His orders were to find a sea passage whereby large ships could bring quantities of goods which would benefit the Indians. He assured Akaitcho that he wanted to make peace between Indians and Eskimos. Nevertheless Akaitcho warned the British officers to be cautious of Eskimo treachery. Franklin promised that if the Indians would accompany the expedition as hunters and guides they would receive rewards of cloth, ammunition, tobacco, and iron tools; also he pledged to settle the Indians' debts to the NWC. To all of this Akaitcho agreed.

Keskarrah, an old Yellow Knife guide, drew a map on the floor with charcoal showing the course of the Coppermine River leading to the Arctic Ocean. His fellow guide, Akaitcho's elder brother White Capot (who had been with Samuel Hearne), disagreed and suggested a route that went north west to Great Bear Lake and then cut across to the Coppermine.

The gravitas of this meeting suffered a setback when Franklin's tent suddenly burned down. Hepburn had fallen asleep while watching the glowing embers and trying to smoke out mosquitoes. Some dry grass caught fire, the tent went up in flames, and Hepburn only awoke when a burning tent pole fell on him. He escaped carrying several powder horns and some valuables just in time before there would have been a volcanic explosion.

In spite of this episode the expedition set off in high spirits from Fort Providence. It now comprised four officers and Hepburn, together with Wentzel, the Indian hunters, three interpreters, and

sundry wives and children brought to make moccasins and clothing. Hepburn, being other ranks, lived and messed with the
francophone voyageurs. His companionship with them was limited
since he spoke no French. The Yellowknife River develops from a
maze of small interconnecting lakes set amid scrawny forest which
gradually peters out towards the treeline. Indeed, a large scale
modern map shows a tapestry of equal parts blue and green.
Travelling upstream involved constant poling and tracking, and
cutting a path through the bush round overgrown portages.

Back enthused over the views, again as apt and vivid with pen as
with brush or pencil:

> The scenery was truly romantic. Every winding displayed
> some picturesque view of craggy rock, wood, lake or river; at
> other times the roaring of the rapid breaking over huge
> fragments of fallen rocks and rushing between confused heaps
> of trees laying in all directions. And the solitary Fishing Eagle
> high perched on some tall pine gave an indescribable wildness
> to the scene. The rocks of which the country seemed formed
> were high and broken, primitive.

Where the Yellowknife River flows into Great Slave Lake they
again met Akaitcho with his hunters and their families, and also a
young slave whom he had seized previously in a spat with rival
Dogribs. Hood's drawing of nearby Lake Prosperous shows the
expedition setting off north in a brigade of seventeen canoes of all
styles, shapes and sizes, some with sails hanging limp on the
windless day.

Back, an inveterate fisherman, cast a fly line, for which Akaitcho
chided him saying, 'The fish are not such fools as to catch at
feathers, nor will those small hooks bear the weight of our fish.' He
was confounded when Back skillfully landed a dozen grayling,
which persuaded him that perhaps white men could survive in
Indian country after all. Known by Indians as 'blue fish', Richardson named the species Back's grayling.

Caribou had not appeared as the Indians expected, and fishing
nets were constantly empty. The voyageurs complained vociferously
about labouring over countless portages on a diet of dried rotten
meat, a little arrowroot and some portable soups. Franklin sent the

hunters forward with extra ammunition and ordered them to make smoke signals if successful. This would have been an ideal occasion for the officers themselves – and particularly Hepburn, a marksman by repute – to accompany the hunters to learn and practise some of their skills. Naval hierarchy, however, discouraged such mixing of rank – to everyone's eventual and eternal loss.

A night watchman posted at one camp noticed that some tinder dry caribou moss, previously smouldering underground, had caught fire. Fanned by wind, flames spread quickly around camp, threatening to destroy canoes and precious cargo. Nevertheless, with much hard work the men doused the fire.

At Reindeer Lake word arrived that the Indian hunters had killed eighteen caribou, but they were too far ahead to carry the meat back to camp. The men left behind caught just enough fish – trout, grayling and suckers – for one meal only. Such hand-to-mouthing boded badly for an expedition planning to travel for more than a year across Barren Lands. Disgruntled mutinous voyageurs refused to go farther. Back tells how his unwontedly assertive boss threatened to blow out their brains unless they picked up their loads. At this they meekly complied.

'I must admit, however,' Franklin concedes in his *Narrative*, 'that the present hardships of our companions were of a kind which few could support without murmuring, and no one could witness without feeling a sincere pity for their sufferings.' This suggests that the British officers did little or nothing to help carry loads over the many long portages before reaching Winter Lake where they intended to hibernate. Indeed, Finden, the engraver, occasionally put them in uniforms not present in Hood's original drawings, as if to emphasize their superiority. Hunters brought in two caribou, which temporarily filled the bellies of the hungry voyageurs who, when paddling, needed at least 4,500 calories, equivalent to eight pounds of meat a day.

Fort Enterprise, site of the expedition's winter camp, stood on a sandy terrace above the north side of the short Snare River. It overlooked rapids that drain Winter Lake into Roundrock Lake, a centuries-old caribou migration crossing between tundra and boreal forest. The actual height of the fort above the river was considerably less than Back's drawing suggests. A stand of large spruce, thirty to forty feet high and two feet in diameter, surrounded the fort. Berry bushes grew abundantly roundabout, and pale green caribou moss covered the ground like a thick pile carpet.

An apparently endless horizon of treeless tundra, bare rocky plates surrounded by millions of small lakes and swampy muskeg bog, stretched to the Arctic Ocean. Looking south across the river, Back notes that 'the characteristic feature of the whole consists in its sterility and whichever way you turn the sight is arrested by hills.' The site was certainly daunting for sailors from pastoral Britain preparing to spend a winter there with the prospect, next spring, of launching into an unknown ocean to the north. They were now 553 miles from Fort Chipewyan and the voyageurs, each carrying 180-pound loads, had portaged to-and-fro ferries of about 150 miles in total.

Across the river some hunters built a fire so that smoke would signal their position to Akaitcho, but the wind rose blowing it into a forest fire that burned for three days. Luckily, flames did not jump the river, and rain eventually damped it leaving their former 'fine prospect' a hideous charred wasteland.

The officers immediately set men to cut timbers for building houses, others to hunt for meat. Hepburn went off chasing caribou, but failed to return. Just three hunters and a boy volunteered to search for him, the rest having changed their minds about accompanying the expedition since the discussions with Akaitcho. Hepburn eventually turned up, tired but fit, after three days of anxiety for his companions, having, Back reports, 'got bewildered in the foggy weather and had been wandering about ever since, [having] eaten only one partridge and some berries and a deer's tongue'. He was found strolling about carrying on his back a large deer, which he refused to hand over until he reached camp, exhausted though he was.

Towards the end of September 1820 flocks of geese flew south. At night ice formed on shallow pools – signs of departing summer and a long winter ahead. Hood describes 'long flights of snow geese, stretching like white clouds from the northern to the southern horizon, and mingling their ceaseless screams with the uproar of the wind among the hills'.

Caribou began moving from tundra to forest, so the hunters got their guns prepared. Dogrib Indians hunted in pairs; the man in front would imitate an animal by carrying in one hand a small bundle of twigs which he rubbed against a rack of caribou horns still attached to part of the animal's head in the other. Under his arms he held the muzzles of both their guns horizontally, while his companion trod in his footsteps with fingers ready at the triggers.

Hunters imitated their quarry's high stepping gait by raising their legs together and then stamping them, meanwhile nodding their heads. Caribou, being intensely curious, will halt and take notice if a person stands still with arms held high imitating horns. By these ruses the hunters could get into the middle of the herd and pick out the fattest animals. The rear man then pushed his comrade's guns forwards and fired both simultaneously. Copper Indians, by contrast, dressed in white, and waved their guns, imitating a caribou rubbing its horns against a stone.

Akaitcho appeared at the fort mourning his brother-in-law (since he had thirty younger wives this could become a time-consuming prospect). He again warned the officers against descending the Coppermine River this season because they would be leaving the forest behind and entering the Barren Lands.

'I will go in spring,' Akaitcho told Franklin, 'but not now, for it is certain destruction. But if you are determined to go and die, some of my young men shall also go because it shall not be said that you were abandoned by your hunters.' He advised against ever trying to make a voyage along the seacoast, since he was sure they would inevitably perish. Franklin was sceptical, since he believed that the métis interpreter, Pierre St Germain, had sowed doubt among the Indians. After endless debates with Akaitcho and his brothers, Longlegs and The Hook, finally they all agreed to form a small party to scout the upper Coppermine in a light canoe. Franklin ordered Back and Hood to get ready for this foray.

On 28 August the party, under Back's command, set off north towards Point Lake, part of the Coppermine headwaters, a mix of narrow rapids and wide meandering lakes. They had food for only eight days and, as they were in the Barrens, there would be no wood for fuel. Back summarized their quandary: 'after all we could but gain ten months earlier information with the great risk of not only losing the canoes by being obliged to leave them where there was no wood, but of losing the lives of some of the party.' He realized that ultimately they depended entirely on the Indians.

At the top of Little Marten Lake they had run out of paddleable water, so they cached some food and the canoe. On its bottom St Germain drew with charcoal a man and a house so any Indians finding it would recognize that it belonged to white people. Then they walked over some hills to Big Lake. Back says that he and Hood were 'so embarrassed by lakes of one kind and another that our direct distance was trivial in comparison to that actually walked'.

Men complained of pains and exhaustion. Back observed: 'no one had yet slackened his pace, nor was it necessary, for the delay occasioned by travelling with an Indian is sufficient for the repose of any person, however incapable he may be of sustaining fatigue.' In his next breath, however, referring to a dispute with the guide about the return route, Back concedes: 'in passing through strange country it is saving of time to trust to the local knowledge of your guide in preference to your own.' A humbling admission by a man so cocksure and opinionated. Their compasses were fickle from being so near the north magnetic pole which wanders slowly but constantly in what modern aeronautical charts designate as an 'area of compass unreliability'.

Their reconnaisance over, they turned around and Back and Hood collected the stashed canoe. On returning to Fort Enterprise they discovered that Franklin, Richardson, and Hepburn, with Keskarrah to guide them, had set off the previous day on a week-long 'pedestrian excursion', slightly farther to the west. That party also reached Point Lake and then turned round. At one camp Keskarrah chastised Franklin about cutting down one of four stunted trees for firewood because 'they had been long serviceable to his nation and that [they] ought to be content with a few of the smaller branches'. With the temperature just below freezing, Keskarrah then stripped naked, toasted himself over the embers, curled up under his deerskin, and instantly fell asleep.

While the officers had been away on their various jaunts, Wentzel had roofed the three winter log houses, built with axes alone. Rather grandly called a fort, the houses now formed three sides of a square. The officers got the middle house, measuring fifty feet by twenty-four feet, which comprised a hall, three bedrooms and a kitchen; floors were made of planks and windows were covered with caribou skin parchment. Walls and roof were plastered with clay brought from two mud pinnacles (hoodoos) that stood on a nearby esker; in severe cold weather, however, the clay cracked and let in wind. Nevertheless, with fires blazing in rock fireplaces the house was cozy. The men learned to use crooked knives to build furniture and became skilled carpenters, so everyone became more comfortable. Men's quarters stood adjacent to the officers'. A storehouse was already stocked with a hundred caribou carcasses, some dried meat, and a thousand pounds of suet for making pemmican.

In the morning a thermometer inside the house frequently recorded $-40°$F. The sun appeared only briefly each day and shone at such an oblique angle that it provided little heat, and woodcutters broke several axes felling frozen trees. With bare hands, at $-46°$F, Hood plotted the latitude of Fort Enterprise to the nearest minute. At night the aurora gave a brilliant coloured display, like fireworks, and prismatic parhelia surrounded the moon.

The officers passed the dark winter days writing up their journals, recalculating scientific observations, and drawing specimens they had collected. They read and reread letters, outdated magazines and newspapers that had arrived in November. One announced the death of King George III on 29 January of the previous year – 1819 – from dementia (probably due, as we now believe, to porphyria). Occasionally they walked on the river. To distract the Indians from hunger, Back taught them to toboggan down the snowy bank in front of the fort. Capsizes caused much mirth, but in one upset a fat Indian woman ran over Franklin, severely spraining his knee, which caused him pain for weeks afterwards.

In the evenings everyone played games in the hall, one appropriately called 'prison bars'. Boredom, however, was seemingly no problem. On Sundays the voyageurs dressed in clean clothes to attend divine service read by Franklin in English; for most of them, being French-speaking Roman Catholics, not much can have sunk in.

Early that winter at the fort they were 'in the midst of plenty, surrounded by numberless herds of deer' – the migration of the several-thousand-strong Bathurst Inlet caribou herd. The expedition's diet almost exclusively comprised caribou meat, varied occasionally with fish. The men killed about fifty caribou each day to lay down for next spring's excursion down the Coppermine River. They had also put away 3,000 pounds of whitefish. Hepburn made candles from strips of cloth dipped in caribou fat, and soap by mixing fat with wood ash and salt.

Now entering winter, the party was short of clothing and entirely out of ammunition, which they expected should have caught up with them at Great Slave Lake. Franklin even ordered men to melt pewter mugs to make musket shot. While other Indians went hunting, Keskarrah stayed at Fort Enterprise hoping Dr Richardson would treat his wife, who had a huge skin cancer eroding the front of her face and nearly destroying her nose. Keskarrah said prayers to the water spirits and made offerings by throwing into the rapid below the fort a bundle containing a knife, some tobacco and other odds and ends.

Back volunteered to return to Fort Chipewyan in search of the missing supplies – or perhaps Franklin nudged him. The boss's frayed nerves needed a break from the irritations of his boisterous, cocky and critical junior officer. Or might there have been another reason?

The charms of Keskarrah's fifteen-year-old daughter impressed Back and Hood, both in their lusty twenties, stuck in a strange land far from home and girls. As winter approached, rivalry heated up between the two over Greenstockings, as the officers called her, according to Franklin, 'from her dress'. Her beauty is evident in Hood's painting, showing her seated beside her father threading snowshoes. Nor were her charms lost on men of her tribe. She had already been married twice, 'and would probably have been the wife of many more if her mother had not required her services as a nurse'. Her mother was also concerned that the Great Chief in England might send for her daughter, renowned as she was.

The antagonism between Back and Hood became so acute that they allegedly challenged each other to a duel. Perhaps it was half in jest between two young men who would hardly have jeopardized their careers – let alone their lives – in such a barmy affray. But the story was taken at face value many years later in the memoirs of Lieutenant Joseph René Bellot who was on an expedition to the Arctic along with seaman John Hepburn. In 1855 Bellot records their gossipy conversation: 'Mr Hepburn tells me that [Back] and [Hood] had a quarrel one day about an Indian woman and were to fight a duel; but he overheard them and drew the charges of their pistols at night. Poor [Hood] had by the same woman a daughter whom the family have recently sent for.'

This latter development resulted during Back's absence – voluntary or engineered – many miles to the south during the winter. While Back was locking horns with George Simpson over the expedition's laggard stores, Hood was at Fort Enterprise cozily tucked up under his buffalo robe with Greenstockings.

CHAPTER 8

Back's Winter Journey

1820–21

Manner of making a resting place on a winter's night, March 15,
1820. Drawn by Back, engraved by Finden.

George Back set out on 18 October 1820 from Fort Enterprise, on
Franklin's orders, in search of the expedition's mislaid cargoes. The
advancing expedition had outrun its supply lines and broken the
golden Royal Marine rule (perhaps less obvious to sailors) – 'Never
get separated from your gear.' The stage had been set way back at
Rock House on the Hayes River when, finding their York boats low
on freeboard, Franklin ordered sixteen packages of cargo, each
weighing ninety pounds (over half a ton), comprising sugar,
biscuit, tea, rice, and portable soups, to be unloaded and forwarded
next season by canoe with the HBC Athabasca brigade.

Back's southbound party comprised his servant Gabriel Beauparlant, Wentzel of the NWC, voyageur Solomon Belanger, and
two Indian hunters with their wives and one child. The first night

they camped in a clump of trees beside a lake with plenty of caribou still around, despite the main migration having already passed. Back notes the quickness with which an Indian 'discerns or hears an animal, always on the wing of anxiety', and that they 'cannot avoid pursuing an animal when they see it and you cannot displease them more than by forbidding them to do so'.

To avoid running short on their return, the party cached meat along the way, placing carcasses in a tree or on a frame, well out of reach of wolves that howled around their camps. The curiosity of caribou impressed Back, especially when a hunter 'made faint halloo, they sprang some height from the ground and trotted about 200 yards . . . they then turned round with their heads and ears erect, seemed as if listening.' He continues: 'Nothing can be more rugged than the country around here, deep vallies covered with huge stones, yet the deer fly as it were over these difficulties with apparent ease seldom making a false step and springing from rock to rock with all the safety of a mountain goat.'

October was the worst possible month for traversing this country because lakes were only partly frozen and still unsafe to walk on. Although two inches of ice will support a man it is impossible to tell where the under surface has been eroded and thinned by water currents. Even the thickness of ice forming at the edges of lakes was unpredictable, and therefore hazardous. Back's party could not yet use snowshoes because the snow was not deep enough to fill spaces between rocks and to smooth out rough terrain. The men's deerskin moccasins became slippery when wet and caused them to tumble, so they could easily sprain or break an ankle – a potential calamity.

Then they began to run out of food when they saw no caribou for ten days. One woman caught a jackfish by jigging through a hole in the ice, using lichen as bait. She gave the fish to Back, saying, 'We are accustomed to starvation, but you are not.' Soon the party's only food was some ersatz pemmican made from the remains of an old caribou skin food bag. Yet this was a luxury after starving for three days.

Near the mouth of the Yellowknife River they lashed tree trunks together to make a raft which carried three persons across at a time. They arrived at Fort Providence hungry and exhausted after frequently breaking through the ice. The Indians complained of feeling ill but, after a flagon of mixed spirits, Back noted that 'their griefs were buried in oblivion and in a quarter of an hour they pronounced themselves excellent hunters and capable of going anywhere. They had not only conducted themselves in the most exemplary and active manner towards the party with a generosity and sympathy of feeling, but the attention and affection which they manifested for their wives evinced a benevolency and kindness of disposition.' This was praise indeed from a brash young naval officer who one might not expect to show such sensitivity.

At Fort Providence Back had the first of a series of confrontations with the NWC. Nicholas Weeks, an apprentice clerk in charge of the post, announced that only five of the original sixteen *pièces* had arrived. They were still at the HBC fort on Moose Deer Island, across Great Slave Lake at the mouth of Slave River. Moreover, they consisted mostly of useless articles – three kegs of watered-down rum, a keg of flour, half of the sugar, a roll of tobacco and forty pounds of ammunition. Weeks claimed that a NWC partner, Edward Smith, had ordered him not to give any supplies to the expedition. Nevertheless Back knew that Smith was reliable and he did not believe Weeks, whom he considered 'a slanderous and malignant vagabond, replete with hypocrisy and a discredit to all society'. Finally Back confronted Weeks and accused him of ordering Indians not to supply the expedition with meat, and of spreading dissension among the voyageurs.

Back decided to go to Moose Deer Island to sort things out for himself and, if necessary, to go farther south to Athabasca 'to inform myself particularly of the cool and negligent manner in which the Expedition had been treated'. He continues: 'I was aware of the difficulty of extracting the truth precisely from two jealous rivals who were each implicated in the cause and had each a motive for swerving from direct veracity.'

Before setting off, Back sent Solomon Belanger and his wife north to Fort Enterprise with mail and a hundred musket balls, reluctantly loaned to him by the stingy Weeks. Back had received a letter from a senior Athabasca NWC partner, reporting that the HBC had forwarded a number of packages as far as Grand Rapids on Lake Winnipeg, but that the NWC canoes were too heavily laden to take them farther. Also a NWC canoe, specially detailed to carry the expedition's goods, had called at Cumberland House, but was told by the HBC factor in charge that he had nothing for the expedition: 'for our situation this season is such that he [Franklin] cannot expect supplies from us.'

Governor Williams wrote to Franklin from Rock Depot on 23 July 1820: 'The most useful part of your packages at York Factory and the Rock are forwarded by the [HBC] Athabasca Brigade.' Back noted a letter from George Simpson (whom he scathingly refers to as a senior clerk – in fact he was boss of Fort Wedderburn and the entire HBC Athabasca district and would later become Governor): 'I shall be happy to render the Expedition any assistance in my power connected with the department and trust you will command my best services on all occasions.' This prefaced a squabble about to erupt between these two men, both short in stature but strong in opinion.

A band of Slave Indians, terrified of being pillaged by their Copper neighbours, had taken refuge at Fort Providence. The young men put on a dance, each dancer holding four feathers and moving round in a circle, occasionally jumping sideways, some, according to Back, 'in a state of nudity, singing an unmusical wild air with an appropriate story, the distinctive marks of which were ha! ha! ha! uttered vociferously and with great distortion of the body, the feathers being kept constantly trembling'.

The chief could not give Back any new information about country to the north, but Back presented him with a medal, saying it bore the stamp of 'the Great Chief across the Oceans' who would decide whether to have goods for them sent out to the trading posts by the nearer (north west) passage, or by the longer journey from the south. This oration clumsily hinted that Indians should cooperate with the expedition.

At Fort Providence Back saw a parhelion sun dog, formed by rainbow-coloured crystals, which he describes in terms only an artist would use: 'an inner circle – light carmine and red lake which, mixed with a rich yellow forming a purplish orange, outer edge pale gamboge'. When he saw the aurora borealis he recounts how NWC voyageurs, on seeing unusually vivid sparkling flashes of light, 'fell on their faces, fearing they should be killed . . . [by]

the fluid which was there within two feet of the earth flitting with incredible swiftness and running in parallel line to its surface. It continued for upwards of five minutes, and made a loud rustling noise like the waving of a flag in a strong breeze.'

Unable to resolve the situation with Weeks, a frustrated and angry Back set off south for Fort Chipewyan on 7 December 1820, accompanied by his servant Beauparlant, Wentzel, and two voyageurs, each hauling a sledge across Great Slave Lake. Because the weather was so foul and cold the men suggested Back should ride on a sledge. He reluctantly agreed and, seated on a caribou skin covered with a blanket, he mused: 'The recollection of having been five years a prisoner in France made me something averse to being tied (even by friends) . . . so forcible is the idea of Liberty in the mind of an Englishman that even a cobweb becomes a chain when thrust on him contrary to inclination.' Back rarely mentions his teenage imprisonment, but the benefits he derived from it are evident – his sheer physical toughness, his ability to converse with his voyageur companions in their own language (he often slips into French in his journal), and his developing skill as an artist.

Four days later the party reached Moose Deer Island. Edward Smith and Robert McVicar respectively were in charge of the NWC and HBC forts, and both confirmed the tardy arrival of a paltry five *pièces*. Back demanded supplies from them because: 'It was not an appropriate time to jaw but I found myself obliged to take up the cudgels directly.' He got less than half he asked for, but immediately he sent the stores off to Fort Enterprise in the care of Wentzel and the two Eskimo interpreters, Augustus and Junius. Both the latter came from north of Fort Churchill on Hudson Bay and spoke the common Eskimo (Inuktitut) language. The ebullient Augustus (Tattanoeuck) spoke some English so he lorded it over his more placid friend Junius.

Back notes of his earlier dispute with Weeks that: 'This affair was not so trivial as may at first appear for the contagion had expanded itself to such a degree amongst the loquacious and fickle-minded Indians that our vital interest was connected with it, and had I not fortunately succeeded in procuring a few goods, the Expedition could not have proceeded beyond its present situation.'

Still short of stores that the expedition needed, Back decided to go farther south to Fort Chipewyan on Lake Athabasca. This despite Smith's warnings that it would take sixteen days by snowshoes, probably no spare supplies could be had anyway, the dogs would be unfit to return, and his food would turn mouldy.

Back, together with Beauparlant and one voyageur, set off on 23 December in fine but extremely cold weather. Each man hauled a sledge loaded with pemmican, because the dogs became 'quite fagged' pulling through deep snow, and their feet were raw despite booties which had to be retied repeatedly.

Generally they followed the Slave River through forests of spruce, willow and poplar, but they had to portage frequently round open rapids. At one point the dogs, fearing Back was about to beat them, ran the sledge over their master's snowshoes and upended him. Added to this insult Back's snowshoe thongs had rubbed his toes raw, and his knees and ankles were swollen from a sprain. Furthermore, the dogs had trotted off and needed to be caught and re-harnessed.

Passing through Portage of the Drowned, Beauparlant's face became frostnipped. '*Mais c'est terrible*,' he remarked when the sun shone, 'to be frozen and sunburnt in the same day.'

They pushed on in the teeth of freezing wind along the river, rough with heaped-up ice. On 2 January 1821 the party reached Fort Chipewyan, ten days and four hours after leaving Moose Deer Island. Back noted factually of this remarkable record that it was 'the shortest time the distance has been performed in the same season of the year'.

Since it was New Year party-time, when voyageurs were generally blind drunk for about four days, Back put off making any demands until everyone had sobered up and the 'scene of debauchery was over'. Next day, however, he asked both companies for supplies of ammunition, tobacco and spirits, guns and flints, axes and files, and clothing, without which the expedition was unable to proceed.

The NWC replied: 'our inclinations to render assistance to the Expedition remain unshaken.' George Simpson, Governor of the HBC, who was staying at nearby Fort Wedderburn, was less solicitous. Over the next two months he and Back carried on

Admiral Sir George Back, 1867

EXPEDITION BESET

A scene from Back's first Arctic Voyage under Franklin: *Dorothea* and *Trent* stuck in ice in a bay in Spitzbergen

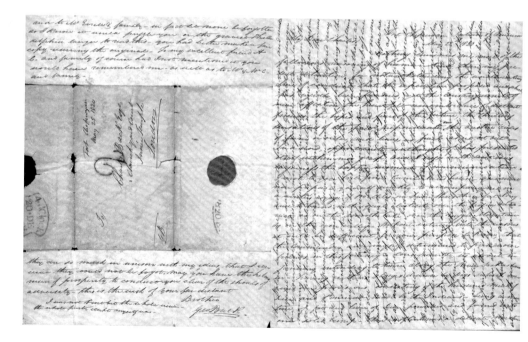

ICE OFF RED HILL.

Cross-written letter, George Back to his brother Charles, Fort
Chipewyan, 25 May 1820

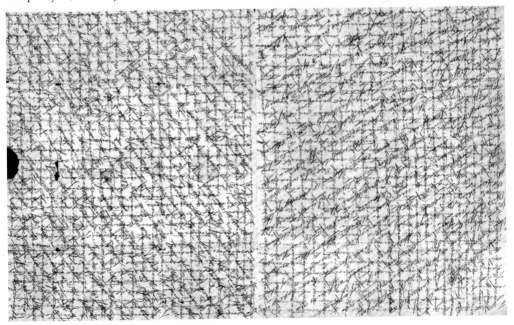

Marten Lake, visited by Back on Franklin's first expedition, as painted in 1820 by Hood

Setting out on Point Lake, June 25, 1821, by Back

Setting out on Point Lake

Rocky defile Rapids and a distant view of the
Copper Mountains.

Rugged landscape north of the Arctic circle: *Rocky defile Rapids and a distant view of the Copper Mountains*, by Back, July 1821

Back's *Portrait of a Stone Indian*:
The Stoney or Rocky Mountain
Sioux are linked to the Dakota
and Assiniboine nations

In the Arctic Ocean: *Canoes off Cape Barrow*, painted by Back, July 25, 1821

'Broaching to' Canoes crossing 'Melville Sound' -

Royal Navy sailors show their mettle: *Broaching to — Canoes crossing Melville Sound*, by Back

Landing near Point Evritt, by Back

Expedition camped at Point Turnagain, painted by Back on the day
Franklin decided to head home, 21 August, 1821

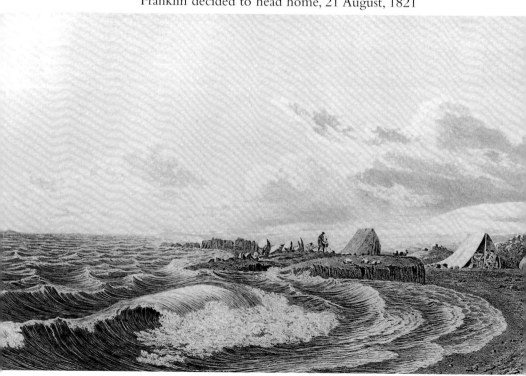

petulant and acerbic exchanges by letter. The following extracts from Simpson's *Athabasca Journal* give an unusually intimate portrait of these two feisty and sparky men in an era when expressing personal feelings, especially on paper, was not commonplace.

Simpson to Back – 4 January:

> I regret that at present I am unable to comply with your demand . . . I am anxious to render every assistance . . . in conveying the five Pieces delivered to you at Gt. Slave Lake and the eight pieces delivered to the North West Coy . . . Any further assistance I may be enabled to render this season entirely depends on the arrival of supplies expected in a few weeks hence from a distant establishment.

a note added to the copy of the above letter:

> Mr Back afterwards came over to dinner and remained all night: he seems much dissatisfied with the N.W.Coy. who have not rendered that assistance which the Expedition had reason to expect . . . I explained to Mr Back that this excuse was merely trumped up for the purpose of deceiving them.

Back to Simpson – 5 January:

> I regret deeply that you cannot supply the Expedition with the articles specified in the demand, without which I apprehend its interests will be severely injured, insomuch that it may be a subject of consideration whether it can proceed farther than its present situation under the gloomy and unexpected circumstances which appear to surround it.

Back to Simpson – 15 January:

> The time is now approaching when I must return [to Fort Enterprise] . . . you can remedy any defect hereafter arising from our demands, especially as your expected pieces must arrive sooner or later, whereas this is our last resource, and failing in this we lose all. . . . I trust you will comply with my desire were it only for the reputation of the Honble. H.B.Coy.

Simpson to Back – 16 January:

> I am not at present enabled in any shape to administer to your wants . . . The District of Gt. Slave Lake must labour under serious difficulties from the liberal supply furnished by Mr McVicar . . . I do not see that the 'reputation of the Honble. Hudson's Bay Coy' stands in any danger of being tarnished, nor can the imputation lay against them of not evincing the most lively interest in the objects of the Expedition.

Simpson writes a chiding letter on 26 January to McVicar at Great Slave Lake:

> I therefore regret exceedingly that you have given Mr Back such a liberal supply as I fear it will expose you to very serious difficulties; that Gentleman seems to think that every thing must give way to his demands . . . their necessities are a very secondary consideration to our own difficulties; we have already done more for them than was either required or expected by Lieut. Franklin, and if the fate of their mission depended on it we must not loose sight of our own Interests to promote their views.

Back saw several sledges arriving at the HBC fort loaded with supplies, so he writes with pique to Simpson on 5 February accusing him of equivocation.

Simpson to Back – 5 February:

> . . . if you will take the trouble of referring to my correspondence I think you will find that any promise made of further assistance is qualified with the proviso of my receiving the expected supplies from Isle alà Crosse . . . I have not in any instance amused you with 'equivocation'.

Back to Simpson – 5 February:

> I need no prompting as to references or any former correspondence. This I know – that you have had several arrivals during my residence here and I imagine they were not all empty.

Simpson to Back – 5 February:

> The object of my referring you to former correspondence was
> to correct an error into which you appear to have fallen in
> regard to my promises of additional supplies . . . The arrivals
> you allude to have no connection with the Goods expected
> from Isle alà Crosse and your conjecture that 'they were not
> empty' is perfectly just, but I presume you will give me leave
> to know the purposes for which they are intended.

Simpson adds a note to his own journal dated 8 February:

> Mr Back paid me a visit preparatory to his departure; from his
> remarks I infer there is little probability of the objects of the
> expedition being accomplished, not so much on account of
> any serious difficulties to be apprehended, but from a want of
> unanimity amongst themselves; indeed it appears to me that
> the mission was projected and entered into without mature
> consideration and the necessary previous arrangements totally
> neglected . . . they evince a strong party feeling and consider
> themselves no where at home except in a N.W. Fort where
> they harangue the Indians . . . to our prejudice; Mr Back's
> servant I understand has been employed as a spy on our
> proceedings when sent with notes or messages from Fort
> Chipewyan.

To add to Back's discontent at Fort Chipewyan, he received a
letter from Franklin at Fort Enterprise dated November 1820: 'We
get on very well en famille, not a single dispute or unpleasant word.
You will hear of the change that has taken place in family affairs.
Perhaps you were prepared to expect the pleasure of having a
female companion in your room. Hood says he shall inform you of
the circumstance, I need not therefore enlarge upon the subject.'

That Franklin would condone one of his midshipmen cohabiting
with a native girl in the officer's mess seems strangely out of
character. But one can only imagine Back's chagrin on receiving
this news. It is understandable that later he should indulge in sour
grapes when describing Yellow Knife Indians:

> Polygamy is common among them and depends entirely on
> the disposition of the man, who, if he is a good hunter, may

have as many wives as he pleases. The women are . . . sure of being married in their 12th year and chastity not being considered a virtue they give disgusting loose to their passions, which very frequently carries them beyond the limits of decency or moderation, even in the gros opinion of an Indian. It cannot be denied, however, that they receive kind treatment from the men.

In the Fort Resolution census of 1823 (since lost) Greenstockings's child was registered as the 'orphaned daughter of Lieutenant Hood'. She was conceived therefore some time in February, while Back was struggling northwards on his return to Fort Enterprise. Hood died on 20 October 1821 during the expedition's catastrophic retreat from the Arctic Ocean to Fort Enterprise, so he never got to see his child.

Back was to meet Greenstockings again on his Great Fish River Expedition a dozen years later, when her bloom had faded. We shall see, however, that the sight of her still raised his pulse rate.

Back left Fort Chipewyan on 9 February, after a hearty breakfast washed down with firewater – a *coup de l'eau de vie* – *façon de NW*. He was touched, literally and metaphorically, by the host of Indian women who turned out to hug and kiss him farewell. In the stampede he mistakenly trod on the foot of an old Indian lady, who upbraided him severely. As a sign of sorrow at parting, someone had raised the Union Jack upside down.

The dogs soon became exhausted from hauling three heavily laden travois (V-shaped frames of two poles apiece), and their feet were raw from ploughing through deep new snow. Back's 'tedious snowshoes' chafed and caused him acute pain and swelling in his 'genu' (meaning *genou*). Franklin's letter about the changes in 'family affairs', can only have worsened his discomfort.

The party reached Moose Deer Island on 20 February, a record passage of eleven days from Athabasca. Back spent time settling the expedition's accounts, and arranging for goods he had acquired to be forwarded to Fort Enterprise. He then lavishly praises the factors of both rival companies for their help, as if trying to heal recent wounds. On 5 March Back's party set off across Great Slave Lake on the last leg of their journey north. Back stopped at McVicar's house on Stony Island and doled out a dram to each of the people there, noting that this was 'an easy way of attaching Canadians to your interest, the effects of which were visible in both sexes'.

The privations of his journey, and his disappointment over Greenstockings, encouraged him to notice local girls, of whom he patronizingly wrote: 'each seemed to strive who should render me the most attention, the one provided the best fish, the other the finest meat. But when I perceived a pleasant looking girl basting and turning the roasting joint, the matter was immediately decided in my mind and was just as soon communicated to the brown object that occasioned it who nothing loath presented her jasperr'd face for a salute, a ceremony which I performed with becoming gravity.'

Back and his companions took three days to reach Fort Providence where he stopped briefly before setting out north, following the canoe route. Feeling very fit, he occasionally broke into a run. While crossing a rapid he fell through the ice and nearly froze in the extreme cold, but this didn't freeze his spirits on reaching Fort Enterprise. He had snowshoed 1,104 miles during four and a half months away, sometimes passing two or three days without tasting food, 'sleeping constantly in the woods without any other covering at night than a blanket and rein deer skin, with the thermometer always low – 40 minus zero [to] 57 minus zero [°F] – suffering hunger, pain, fatigue, and anxiety for the very purpose of providing the Expedition with the means of proceeding, and without which it could not have gone on'.

Franklin was clearly pleased with the performance of Back, who says: 'I was gratified with his full approbation of my conduct' – as well Franklin should have been after such a remarkable winter journey. He offered Back the chance of returning to York Factory and taking a ship northwards to Wager Bay, in the hope of meeting Parry's expedition coming along the Arctic Ocean from the west (they knew nothing about the problem of the Boothia Peninsula intervening). Franklin's apparently magnanimous gesture appears double-edged. He wanted to compliment Back openly, yet also he wished to get his abrasive junior out of his hair, the two having grown increasingly at odds. Not surprisingly, Back declined, even though he knew Hood was cuddling Greenstockings nearby.

CHAPTER 9

The Hyperborean Sea

1821

View of the Arctic Sea, from the mouth of the Copper-mine River, midnight, July 20, 1821. Drawn by Back, engraved by Finden.

On 8 May 1821 a large housefly heralded spring at Fort Enterprise. Franklin remarked that it 'spread cheerfulness through our residence and formed a topic of conversation for the rest of the day'. The change of season also gave hope that cabin fever would lift. However, it was another six weeks before the expedition could head north towards an ice-free Coppermine River.

On 4 June Dr Richardson led a group to Point Lake; it comprised fifteen voyageurs variously carrying loads, driving dog teams, or hauling one of three sledges, each loaded with a refurbished birchbark canoe. Accompanying them were two Indian hunters, and the wife of one of them.

The party to follow would number three officers – Franklin,

Back, and Hood – together with Hepburn, Wentzel, the two Eskimo interpreters, Augustus and Junius, and three Canadian voyageurs each carrying a sixty to eighty-pound load; the officers had a daypack apiece of 'at least 20 lb'. At the outset they were short of food and depended entirely on the skill of their Indian hunters – a precarious position for so large a group ignorant of what they would find in unmapped country, apart from reputedly hostile Eskimos.

Pierre St Germain warned Akaitcho's Indians of dangers they should expect on the Arctic Ocean. Franklin, on discovering this, threatened that if he spread further dissent, or interfered in any way with the progress of the expedition, he would take him to England and put him on trial. To which, St Germain replied: 'it is immaterial to me where I loose my life whether in England or accompanying you to the sea, for the whole party will perish.' Difficult, tough, and cheeky though he was, St Germain, the best interpreter, also proved to be their most successful hunter. He became a favourite of Richardson, which speaks well for his character. Akaitcho's brother White Capot who was also with them, remembered Samuel Hearne passing through the country fifty years before. Dr Richardson refers to White Capot as the hermaphrodite – but this tantalizing snippet is all we know.

At first the party crossed barren hills and lakes on tundra that they already knew from their winter exploration of Little Marten Lake and Big Lake, as far as Point Lake, which formed the wide headwaters of the Coppermine River. On returning 'something fagged' after spending most of the night searching for a strayed voyageur, Back tried to cross some open water. 'I forthwith placed myself on a piece of loose ice,' he writes, 'and with my gun began to push towards the shore. But when, about half way, a part of it broke off and left me gradually sinking on the other . . . I made what was intended to be a desperate leap to reach another floating morsel. But my frail friend glided from under my feet, when I got a sound ducking.'

Anyone who fell through the ice was in danger of hypothermia, frostbite, or both, since there was no firewood for drying themselves, merely shrubs and caribou moss, barely sufficient to make a small fire. Just crossing the half-frozen swampy tundra, or walking on ice covered with spring overflow, led to constantly wet moccasins. Prolonged exposure to cold and wet such as this, even at moderate temperatures, causes the feet to feel permanently cold and numb, known as immersion foot. This may turn into frostbite. Back tells of the voyageurs being 'so affected with rheumatic pains and swelling of the joints from continual exposure to wet that it was with the utmost difficulty they could place one leg before the other'. Dr Richardson also described their suffering from chafing and chapping because of 'erythematous inflammation of the insides of the thighs attended with much hardness and swelling'.

On one occasion Franklin was warming himself by standing so close to the fire that the back of his moosehide trousers singed and became hard as a board. While his boss stood there, Back excised the burned piece, and patched the hole with leather using a sailmaker's palm and needle, only to discover that he had sewn Franklin's trousers to his underwear.

Recent spring rain percolated between vertical hexagonal columns of rotten metamorphosed ice crystals, forming honeycomb-like 'candles'. With nothing to bind them the candles collapsed with a tinkling sound and sharp spikes of candled ice cut the men's wet slippery moosehide moccasins through to their feet. Meanwhile large plates of ice cracked and rumbled.

Several became snowblind from the sun's rays burning their eyes by reflecting ultraviolet light off snow, or penetrating hazy cloud – another hazard of spring travel on ice. Swollen conjunctiva completely covered their eyes, so they were effectively blind. Dr Richardson treated those affected by putting a few drops of laudanum (tincture of morphine) into their eyes twice a day. To prevent snowblindness, Augustus and Junius could have told them how to fashion traditional Eskimo goggles from a piece of wood with two horizontal slits to see through.

Back portrayed the scene in a watercolour *Setting out on Point Lake,* and also in words in his journal:

> . . . bounded on each side with high and almost perpendicular rocks whose green summits were capp'd with large stones, and whose vallies displayed at certain distances a few solitary clumps of pines, claimed the first attention, whilst the

continued ranges of receding blue hills, which lost the eye ultimately in the grey dimness of the atmosphere, was scarcely less attractive. Our own cavalcade possessed the centre, and what with the total innovation of transporting the canoes in such a manner, the singular appearance of the men and sledges, the positions and dress of the officers as well as the deep contrast between the perpetual silence of the place and the animation of the party, afforded a most perfect view of a voyage of discovery.

At the west end of Point Lake they entered Lake of the Red Rock, from where flowed the main Coppermine River. Already they were out of dried meat – let alone anything fresh – and had begun digging into pemmican earmarked for the Arctic Ocean. One of the new trading guns exploded in the hands of a young Indian, the sixth such accident since leaving Slave Lake. They were also short of ammunition and gunpowder, essential for hunting caribou. Akaitcho repeatedly asked for more, but he grumpily agreed to accompany the expedition in order to help make peace with the Eskimos. As soon as the river thawed they launched the canoes, but they still had to watch out for floating blocks of rotten ice. Now they were among hills, which Back likened to Salisbury Crags in Edinburgh.

It was as though the season had changed from winter into summer in just half an hour. After a winter of hibernation, aquatic larvae hatched into swarms of adult mosquitoes, with the females voracious for blood meals. On windless days these tormentors thrived so thick that the men could hardly see even a few yards ahead in spite of veils, gloves, or bandannas.

The voyageurs ran their first rapid, having lightened the canoes so they would not dig into standing waves and take on water. They were in their element, and felt good to be on the move again. As they got up speed their long hair (grown to protect them from mosquitoes) flowed out behind them. They ran four miles of dangerous rapids, 'in which the bows and steersmen,' Back tells us, 'displayed not only great dexterity, but uncommon presence of mind avoiding with much caution both rocks and shoal'.

One canoe grounded in the middle of a series of rapids running between high clay cliffs. As a result it did some damage which the voyageurs quickly repaired with spruce gum. The canoes were also in danger of breaking their backs, because they had no proper pole sheathing laid along the bottom to spread the weight of cargo. Henceforth Franklin ordered the bowmen to scout each rapid, and the crew to lighten the boats, especially of precious items like ammunition, guns and scientific instruments. His canoe would thereafter take the lead.

Back's painting of Rocky Defile Rapid shows two canoes navigating large standing waves, and a foaming current running between brick-red felspar and sandstone cliffs. 'The overhanging craggy rocks,' he writes, 'the danger of the canoes in running it, the adjacent towering hill and the distant view of the Copper Mountains formed a most impressive scene.' In this long stretch of whitewater no one could have helped a canoe in trouble.

Once again the great herds of game animals they had expected did not appear, so the men had to feed hand-to-mouth on a caribou here, a muskox there. But the flesh of muskox has a strong flavour that the voyageurs disliked. On the rare occasions when there was a surplus of meat, the men made pemmican, enough for only a couple of days at a time. Now that the Indians were approaching Eskimo country they became increasingly apprehensive, never went unarmed, and even slept with daggers handy. Franklin went ahead, but he ordered the Indians to stay in camp so as not to frighten any Eskimos they might meet, as he was hoping to persuade the Eskimos to hunt for them. Back, referring to their 'mulish companions', says: 'we could not place much reliance on men who had agreed on the same thing but 12 hours before, and who had with unparalleled thoughtlessness and versatility of disposition broken their faith to us almost as soon as our backs were turned. Indeed they commenced to be so troublesome that we wished them fairly away.'

Franklin sent Augustus and Junius ahead carrying presents of axes, mirrors and beads. Each was armed with a pistol hidden under his clothes. From a high rock, Augustus shouted to some Eskimos who stood across from the rapid. Surprised at hearing their own language, they paddled to a nearby island but kept their distance, despite offers of presents. Hepburn, who had gone along with the two interpreters, saw the sea for the first time from the top of the hill.

In 1771, at Bloody Fall and nearby Massacre Rapid, Samuel Hearne's guide Matonabbee and his gang of Chipewyan and Copper Indians slaughtered twenty-two Eskimos while they slept and plundered their copper. In Hearne's book on the expedition, he describes 'one young girl, about eighteen years old, twining and twisting round the spears like an eel'. Even though Hearne – armed with a bayonet, a spear and a brace of pocket pistols – was not actually at the massacre himself, he knew exactly what Matonabbee had carefully planned. Yet Hearne excuses himself by claiming: 'I stood neuter and saw the cruel massacre which was soon accomplished, the inhabitants being all asleep.'

Back's painting of Bloody Fall shows whitened bones and fractured skulls strewn around the foreground. He does not deny the massacre, but he disputes Hearne's account, based on the evidence of old White Capot who was there fifty years before. 'The most interesting part of which I imagine to be unfounded,' writes Back, 'as one of our guides [White Capot] who accompanied him [Hearne], said that he was two days march from them at the time [of the attack].' White Capot pointed out the island where one of them got 'his wigh freshened', presumably meaning either that he was scalped, or that his skull was smashed. Back's disbelief, however, relies on the slim memory of one old man. Subsequently, enmity certainly persisted between Indians and Eskimos across the entire northland.

Added to their anxiety about Eskimos was the difficulty of the terrain they were traversing, increased by dramatic and dangerous rapids. Back describes their rough ride through Escape Rapid: 'The canoes passing through this dreadful chasm at the amazing velocity of 9 or 12 miles per hour were frequently hurled into the most imminent danger, here a huge back recoiling wave broke over us and concealed the bowsman from our sight, then a treacherous eddy, bubbling around hidden pointed rocks, half whirled us to immediate destruction.'

A brief fracas occurred when some of the expedition's Indian hunters ran into a party of Eskimos returning to their camp at Massacre Rapid. Franklin and Richardson went to calm the storm and met an old Eskimo, Terreganoeuck. He wore a hooded caribou skin jacket, knee breeches and tight leggings sewed to his moccasins that were soled with sealskin and stuffed with feathers – a very different dress from their own hunters. He showed his pleasure at the presents the officers gave him by first touching them on each shoulder and, if the item was particularly special, by rubbing it on his head.

From the top of a hill behind their camp the officers had a view about nine miles away of the sea, which appeared to be full of islands and choked with ice. Richardson found some copper ore there. Terreganoeuck told them that normally a passage remained open along the coast where there were plenty of fish, but not many animals. He said they would likely run into small groups of Eskimos. He gave everyone a piece of dried meat and promised more from a stock in his camp some distance away. But it was too rank with large worms and 'horrid effluvia' for the Britons to eat, regardless of their hunger. Terreganoeuck also offered Augustus one of his daughters as a wife, provided he agreed to remain with the band. Augustus, however, had other plans – kind bid though it was.

On 18 July the river water tasted brackish, which suggested that they were near the mouth of the Coppermine where it mixed with tidal Arctic Ocean saltwater. Wentzel, having provided sterling service to the expedition, left to return to Fort Providence next day, along with four discharged voyageurs. His orders were to check food caches en route in case the expedition returned up the Coppermine in the fall, and to collect the canoe left at Point Lake. At Fort Enterprise he would gather all the officers' journals and papers and forward them to England as soon as possible. He planned to pay off Akaitcho's hunters with a promissory note to the NWC for Weeks at Fort Providence. Wentzel wanted to make sure the Indians would be around in September and October when the expedition, now comprising twenty persons, expected to return.

Not surprisingly such seat-of-the-pants travel worried the Canadian voyageurs who had never canoed on open sea. They were evidently reluctant to venture onto the icy ocean in two birch-bark canoes for fear they would drown. With good reason they doubted the strength of the hulls, which had no stiffening keel.

Nevertheless the officers were buoyant at the prospect of raising sail, so familiar to navy men trained on square-sailed ships, and they even speculated that they might be in time to catch the homebound HBC ships that same autumn. Franklin, on behalf of the Royal Navy men, welcomed the ocean 'which was more congenial with our habits than the fresh-water navigations and their numerous difficulties we had hitherto encountered'. Seaman John Hepburn was ecstatic at the prospect of being in his own element again.

St Germain and Jean Baptiste Adam were terrified of going on and starving, since they only had food for three weeks and 1,000 balls of ammunition. They asked Franklin for their own discharge, but he refused because they were the only two reliable hunters. Seals appeared for the first time – a ready source of food, especially vitamin C. However, the hunters could not get close enough to shoot the seals while they napped on ice floes. Seals, if shot in water, just sink out of sight. Several other voyageurs threatened to quit with the dangerous prospect of crossing the Barrens short of supplies. Thereafter Franklin ordered a careful watch on them lest they skulked off. After all, such behaviour was unacceptable since they were conscripted men, compulsorily enlisted under navy rules. Whether the voyageurs understood these rules is another matter.

On 21 July 1821 the expedition left the mouth of the Coppermine and, as Back puts it, 'embarked on the Hyperborean Sea, nothing loth'. Franklin's name for the Arctic Ocean – the Polar Sea – was a little less poetic, but both obscured what it held in store. Grassy meadows sloped to sand or gravel beaches that showed little sign of tide. Abundant bushes of Labrador tea provided a popular drink which Franklin thought – incorrectly – might prevent scurvy. Sea ice surrounded many offshore islands on which icebergs were stranded. The party came across one of Terreganoeuck's caches raised above ground on a driftwood frame. They helped themselves to several sealskins for making new boot soles, and in exchange left beads, awls and a small kettle.

After pushing east through brash ice round a prominent point, they found the coastline changed to craggy rocks. The men set sail in a light breeze that soon changed to gale force which proved too much for the canoes, so they tucked into the safety of Port Epworth inlet. When the storm calmed, fog obscured the way ahead and masses of brash ice threatened to puncture the fragile canoes.

Rounding Cape Barrow's steep cliffs they sheltered in Detention Harbour for fear of being crushed between ice and fog-shrouded rocky hills. Back's painting *Canoes off Cape Barrow* shows two tiny canoes paddling against breaking waves close against massive cliffs, which drop sheer to ice-choked sea, and men fending off drifting icebergs. Not surprisingly the canoes were damaged and needed gumming. Carrying enough spruce gum for the long treeless journey ahead was a serious concern as they were already short of the precious stuff.

Franklin refers to 'the peril of our situation and the dreariness of our prospect'. Verses 8 and 9 of a poem Back wrote about 'our unfortunate Voyage' are gripping:

> Cold was the sight – now many fears arise
> And the Canadians – their sad fate do mourn
> All fancied miseries glare before their Eyes
> And many supplicate their safe return
>
> Raising their foamy heads – huge curling waves
> Break furiously against our weak Canoes
> Then opening deep – present wide yawning graves
> At once to terminate – our unhappy woes

Every day along the coast Back complains of mosquitoes. While mosquitoes were eating the men, the men had less and less to eat. They discovered that two ninety-pound bags of pemmican had gone mouldy from being soaked with saltwater, and their beef was rotten, having been badly cured. And still there was no sign of Eskimos on whom they hoped to rely for hunting.

The voyageurs increasingly voiced their fear of starving, or being crushed in ice and, worried that they might become fractious from inactivity, and 'to prevent them from chattering and discussing the dangers of the Service', Franklin ordered them to portage the canoes round cliffs at the mouth of Detention Harbour – Galena Point (so named because Richardson found veins of lead sulphide there). 'They must be treated and humoured exactly like children,' Back writes, 'for as long as the [food] lasts you may lead them anywhere. It is quite indifferent to them whilst there is *de quoi à manger*' – something to eat. Faced with having to force a passage through the ice, the men ceased grumbling and excelled at leaping from pan to pan fending off the canoes.

Franklin named a group of offshore islands after Back's home town of Stockport – to its great civic pride. Beyond lay Bathurst Inlet, one of the deepest indentations in the entire Arctic coastline. At the foot of Arctic Sound seawater tasted less salty, suggesting fresh water nearby. They found the mouth of a shallow river, which Franklin later named after Hood. It was not, however, the Burnside (Anatessy) as they believed from both Blackmeat's and Boileau's description and charcoal drawings on the floor of Fort Chipewyan.

Back noted plentiful animals, but the hunters were rarely skilful enough to shoot them, or else they used precious ammunition to pepper them unnecessarily. He foresaw the expedition being unable to complete its objective of mapping the coast solely because of lack of food. The expedition camped on Algek Island, one of the Barry group. Basalt cliffs formed the western side, and green swards sloped to the east with numerous deep inlets. Intricate terraces of raised beaches looked like the tailings of a dredged placer mine.

Dr Richardson described the geology of the islands in his temperate, but enthusiastic, way: 'On the northern end of the island there is red amygdaloidal rock which contains many beautiful pebbles [agates] and some small beds of jasper. The greatest part of the pebbles are formed of concentric layers of calcedony with drusy cavities, but some of them approach to nearly pure carnelian.' Driftwood for fires had become scarce, confirming that they were entering a deep inland bay, littered with islands. Many subsidiary bays led off it, which was confusing at sea level.

The expedition was now about to make a fateful move. They passed to the east of Quadyuk Island, the southern tip of which hides any view of Elliot Point (site of the present day Bathurst community), and the only place from where they could have seen a sandy delta that issues from the mouth of a large river to the west which was the Anatessy, now named Burnside. This omission was to prove critical on their return because the banks of the Burnside (which drains Contwoyto Lake where they were aiming) would have been much easier for tracking canoes than the steep sides of the Hood River, which they eventually chose.

Proceeding southwards, the officers mistook the tiny Amagok River for the Burnside and discounted it, correctly, as a possible inland route. At the foot of Bathurst Inlet a sizeable river entered from the south. Franklin named it after Back, 'as a mark of friendship for my associate' – a doubtful compliment in the light of the previous winter's shenanigans; it was later renamed Western River. The Back River, as we shall see, is now the name of the more southerly Thlew-ee-choh-dezeth, which Back descended fourteen years later – its first descent.

In the usual rain, fog, cold and frequent storms the canoes now turned north and followed the eastern shore of Bathurst Inlet. The hunters shot a muskox and a brown bear, and Back notes, 'seals numerous', but still no luck in killing any. Heavy swell gave a rough wet ride in the canoes which, 'being excessively sharp forward', Back observed, 'there is nothing to oppose the water, so that in a moderate sea they literally pitch bows under.' Undoubtedly a sturdy craft in the style of a York boat would have been more suitable in these waters. The voyageurs complained to the officers with undisguised insolence that the canoes were likely to be stove in by waves and break apart or swamp under them. However, their Royal Navy bosses, to whom the dangers appeared minimal, ignored their whining. The officers pretended not to listen, displaying an arrogance that could only antagonize an already unhappy party.

Pemmican reserves were now down to the last bag, a source of constant worry, but killing a couple of bears assuaged the men's hunger and raised their spirits with the hope of being able to eat their customary six pounds of pure fat a day, and made them 'paddle cheerly'.

They were now leaving Bathurst Inlet and entering open ocean – George IV's Coronation Gulf. They spent four days paddling round the perimeter of a large opening – Melville Sound – thinking it might be the missing link in a North West Passage which would lead eastwards to Hudson Bay. But no such luck. As they left Bathurst Inlet and tried rounding Cape Flinders to rejoin Coronation Gulf and the Arctic coast proper, they were shrouded in fog which regularly hangs over straits of the Arctic Ocean, especially when there is open water. Once past Cape Flinders they turned north where the coast was flat and barren, with only shallow shelving beaches on which to camp.

On heavy open sea again the canoes shipped lots of water, despite close-reefed sails. One became waterlogged, and fourteen ribs of the other were each broken in two places. The voyageurs lashed them together but bark began to separate from the gunwales. The men now became openly mutinous because, according to Back, Adam and St Germain had – not for the first time – poisoned their minds so they despaired of ever seeing home again.

Nevertheless, Richardson sympathized, and wrote: 'They deem any attempt to proceed farther as little short of madness.' His own opinion was: 'In order to insure a fair prospect of a safe journey across the barren grounds, our voyage along the coast must speedily terminate.' One wonders if he communicated these thoughts to his boss, because that evening, 15 August 1821, Franklin held a powwow with the officers. He announced a change of plan: the expedition would not retrace their route up the Coppermine but would follow the Hood River and then cut overland direct to Fort Enterprise. His reasons were: lack of food, disintegrating canoes, rebellious voyageurs, the impossibility of reaching Hudson Bay, and the distance still ahead across the Barrens with winter rapidly approaching. Needless to say, the men were elated on being told the voyage was nearly over 'for they were all heartily tired of one that presented nothing but misery and fatigue.'

More tide rise and fall showed that they were well along the seacoast. The shore was so flat and shallow it was difficult to beach heavily waterlogged canoes. It was a bleak campsite with no shelter for tents, which were flattened repeatedly by gale-force winds, sleet and snow. Sparse vegetation grew between exposed rocky plates inland. Hunting was futile because the men lacked cover for stalking animals, and the land was so featureless that one hunter got lost and spent a freezing night out. Even though driftwood was plentiful there was little food to cook on the fire. For supper the cook served thin soup, the last of the dried meat, and a little pemmican from one remaining bag.

It was 18 August 1821 – their last camp before turning round.

Franklin, Richardson, and Back walked a further ten miles where the coast trended eastwards as far as they could see. They called it Point Turnagain. Although the expedition was desperately short of food, Franklin wasted five full days wandering aimlessly round this barren part of the Kent Peninsula. His vacillating was especially strange since he had already decided to quit and head for Fort Enterprise before being caught by winter. Hereafter we are spared (until his next expedition) Franklin's sycophantic naming of every prominent geographical feature after marginally prominent friends, patrons and sponsors.

Back sums up his disappointment, shared with his fellow officers:

> Thus ended the progress of an Expedition which we had fondly expected would have set at rest all future discussions on the subject of a passage to Hudsons Bay. It was now the season, but more particularly the want of food, that stopped us. Though it may be said, that had we been more successful in procuring dried provisions during our abode at the winter establishment, or the Indians proved less deceitful. It will not be advancing too much to assert, that we had surely reached the The-low-de-zeth [the mouth of the Back River which is in Chantrey Inlet 300 miles further east] at least, and as that is a known resort of the Esquimaux, in all probability we should have been enabled through their means to have accomplished the full purpose of our mission. Be this as it may it must be obvious that we had incontestably proved the practicability of succeeding, and it is only to be regretted that after the time and fatigue incurred in proceeding so favourably to a distance which in a direct line would have taken us to Repulse Bay that the inclemency of the season and our own peculiar misfortunes should have obliged us to retrace our way.

The party turned round and paddled south following the east side of Bathurst Inlet so as to avoid crossing open sea in Coronation Gulf. They had great difficulty in landing through the rolling surf at Point Everitt, which Back drew under the title *Expedition landing in a storm, Aug. 23 1821*. Their passage across to Arctic Sound was no breeze, judging by his vivid drawing of *Canoe broaching to in a gale of wind at sunrise* off that same point when, under a full press of sail, a huge wave broached their canoe and they narrowly escaped sinking. Despite these hazards he found time to describe how they watched the sun's rays casting 'a beautiful yellow tinge over the white foam of the dark green sea'.

Despite the gargantuan efforts of the steersman, Back criticizes his sailing technique: 'He like all Canadians was so wedded to river customs, that is of making every rope fast (halyards, sheet and all) and was so obstinate in maintaining them against all innovation, or reason to the contrary, that we incur'd the greatest risk imaginable of being upset every time the sail was hoisted.' He does not explain why naval officers, once on the ocean, did not take command and give sailing orders.

Following this episode, seas became rougher and, because they were awash and leaden with a dead weight of shipped water, the canoes were about to break in two. One did split its bow. As they passed through Barry Islands the hunters killed five caribou and the men picked lots of berries. With full stomachs their spirits rose and they began to sing at the prospect of quitting the dreaded *Mer du Nord*.

And so again they entered Arctic Sound into which emptied the Hood River – their hoped-for highway home.

CHAPTER 10

Deathly Retreat South

1821

Wilberforce Falls, drawn by Back.

After gumming the canoes, the expedition set off up the Hood River on 26 August 1821. On top of a nearby hill the men placed a Union Jack to alert the Eskimos of their presence, and to show where they had left some gifts. The current was swift up to the junction with the James River. Voyageurs tracked the canoes upstream using a long line, with one man standing amidships fending off the bank with a pole.

After about five miles they reached the mouth of a canyon. Exploring on foot, they found a waterfall nearly 250 feet high with water pouring in two levels over both sides of a massive spit – Wilberforce Falls. Back sketched it and wrote: 'we could see the upper fall, rushing over the steep between immense rocks and falling with stunning noise into a narrow basin below, whilst the

spray rose in clouds about it, this drove violently in one white foam
to the lower fall, which was curiously divided by a pillar in the
centre, but here the sight was lost in mist and spray that rose from
the falling and overwhelming force of this stupendous torrent . . .
Altogether it was by far the grandest scene of the kind in the
country.' One can walk out to the very end and sit astride the rock
that divides the falls, with spray drifting all round and a bottomless
vertical drop below each foot. From a hill above the falls the
prospect upstream appears to be continuous rapids cutting through
gently rolling country.

Franklin was discouraged. He ordered the voyageurs to cannibal-
ize the two damaged canoes to make two smaller ones, each large
enough for fording rivers or setting fishing nets. It took them three
days to rebuild the shattered craft with pliant birchbark but spruce
gum to seal new seams was now in dangerously short supply and
with no immediate prospect of replenishing it.

The party set off on 31 August with each voyageur carrying a
ninety-pound load comprising ammunition, nets, hatchets, ice
chisels, astronomical instruments, clothes, blankets, three kettles,
and two canoes, plus a few books and bibles. The officers carried
'such portion of their own things as their strength would permit'.

Next day new fallen snow made walking painful and laborious,
especially for those carrying canoes. High winds repeatedly blew
the men over so they dropped the boats, causing further damage.
They walked over a mix of muskeg swamp and exposed rocky
gneiss, where loose stones cut soft moccasins to shreds. This
brought renewed rumbles of dissent from among the men. Fit ones
wanted to take a single canoe and forge ahead with light loads in
hope of finding Indians and rallying help; weaker ones urged the
officers to keep the party together at all costs. The banks of the
Hood River were sometimes steep, unlike those of the Burnside so
near to the south, where surrounding hillocks rise gently. The
upper reaches of the river lay due west, whereas their intended
course was southwest. Franklin wanted to cross the river with two
canoes lashed together, but one boat was so badly damaged in a fall
that the men broke it up for firewood.

With information garnered from the voyageurs Back suggests
that Benoit intentionally planned to fall down and smash the canoe

when his turn came. In his journal he launches into an uncharacter-istic tirade against the chicanery of the knavish Canadian voy-ageurs, saying he would fine them and withhold their wages for bad behaviour. Back himself appears to be under the pervasive duress of cold and hunger. Indeed, having only a single canoe remaining sabotaged any possibility of splitting the party, which, as it turned out, might well have saved some lives. Of this crucial event Back says: 'but now this plan was rendered abortive, and perhaps to that circumstance alone many of our future miseries may be inferred.'

They set off south towards Contwoyto Lake walking, appro-priately, in Indian file with the second man taking compass bearings and calling out directions to the leader. Considering how close they were to the north magnetic pole it is surprising that their compasses were of any use at all. The character of the land improved for walking – smooth rolling hills with long valleys enfolding masses of small lakes – but it was still not much fun for voyageurs carrying huge loads.

A gale blew and it snowed heavily, as if overnight they had stepped from summer into winter – from warm days with abundant crowberries underfoot, into sterile cold and snow with no prospect of food. It was so unpleasant that they all stayed in bed, cold, hungry and miserable. On standing up, Franklin fainted – evidence of early starvation – but he revived after drinking a little soup.

Water left in the kettle froze, and the cook served the last of the pemmican. Their only remaining food, portable soup and arrow-root, according to Dr Richardson, 'allayed pangs of hunger for a time but was considered by the voyageurs as a poor substitute for the eight pounds of solid animal food, their customary daily allowance. Indeed after three days fasting there was not one of them that would have been satisfied with less than 20 pounds of deer's meat at a meal.'

They were now reduced to eating the bitter and unpalatable lichen *umbilicaria* (genus Gyrophora) known as *tripe de roche*. Back remarks: 'misery makes us acquainted with strange tastes as well as bedfellows. This voyage perfected me in both.' One wonders if here he is referring to his fellow officers from whom he seems to have become steadily alienated, although no one will come out into the open and say so. In fact, although tripe de roche caused severe stomach gripes, it may have contained just enough vitamin C to delay the effects of scurvy from which they all must have been suffering without noticeable symptoms.

The nights were so cold that their wet clothes froze on them. They made just enough fire to thaw their socks and moccasins, which they took to bed under their blankets to prevent them freezing. In the morning they were 'stiff as planks'. After a difficult crossing of the Cracroft River they reached the outlet of Kathawachaga Lake where the Anatessy/Burnside River runs eastwards. Back surmised about this river (almost correctly): 'I should think it is the same that falls into the southernmost part of Bathursts Inlet viz Backs River.' Using the newly gummed canoe, a voyageur ferried across one person at a time lying flat in the bottom of the leaky craft. Franklin describes it as 'an extremely ticklish' manoeuvre.

Travelling now became even more dangerous, and utterly miserable. Loaded men often fell into recently snow-covered hollows between sharp and slippery rocks. If anyone had twisted an ankle – or worse broken a leg – no one could have carried him over that ground. It would have meant leaving him to his fate – 'melancholy indeed', as Richardson wrote. Back notes in his journal, 'we became so stupid that we stumbled at almost every step', signs not only of exhaustion, but also of hypothermia. The country became more hilly and difficult as they approached Contwoyto Lake. Their spirits rose a fraction when they killed a muskox, their first meat for a week.

They had to backtrack westwards to find the rapids at the lake outflow where hunters killed two caribou. St Germain and Belanger le Gros paddled the canoe carrying Franklin holding a box containing his papers and journals in which were written all his observations of astronomy and meteorology. In midstream Belanger lost his balance and fell out of the canoe; Franklin and St Germain leaned upstream trying to right it – a common and disastrous mistake. The canoe capsized but they hung onto it while swimming and pushing it to shore.

Meanwhile the freezing rapid swept poor Belanger away. Only after several attempts did he manage to hang onto a throw-rope made of lashings and slings. As his fellows hauled him ashore 'almost lifeless' his head went under water so he was in danger of drowning. As Back tells us, they undressed Belanger and wrapped him in blankets placing one person on either side of him, each naked in order to provide warmth – exactly the modern procedure recommended for treating hypothermia. Belanger revived after an hour, although he could not feel his legs for several days afterwards.

The loss of Franklin's papers for this portion of the journey, in what he named Belanger's Rapids, led to his having to rely on the journals of his fellow officers in writing his own *Narrative of a Journey to the Shores of the Polar Sea*. Its turgid verbose prose is almost word for word somebody else's account of the journey under his own bombastic banner. He frequently uses chunks from the journals of Back and Richardson to whom he usually gives due credit.

An entry in Back's journal sheds light on the officers' priorities: 'some of the goods were got across to Lieut. Franklin whose bed was sent over directly we had recovered Belanger.' It seems strange to carry a camp bed across the Barrens (unless it was just a bedding roll), when most of the party was near starving to death. One must remember, however, the rigid hierarchy under which the Royal Navy men laboured. It tallies with what Dr John Rae (much later) named 'useless items' – crested solid silver plate, forks and spoons, and a medal – found by Eskimos beside some of the men who, in a desperate flight from their icebound ship, had dragged their boats south across the ice at the end of Franklin's deathly 1845–48 expedition. Franklin rarely consulted the expedition's junior officers, who had little say in major decisions. He does mention dumping the sextant, dipping needle, azimuth compass, magnet, a large thermometer and a few books in the Barrens, but he makes no mention of the bed. Even Richardson, in order to lighten the loads, with heartbreak got rid of his precious collection of rocks and plants – some of which he knew were new to science.

Their course now trended southeast, which was not the direction where they were aiming. 'But it was supposed to be for the best and we followed it,' Back confides resignedly to his journal, 'and in this measure lay all the distress that shortly befell us.' He is referring to their route passing too far east along the shore of Eda Lake and diverging from the usual route of the caribou migration. This is Back's first open, undisguised criticism of his boss.

The men ploughed through deep wet snow, marching headlong against a squally wind that cut right through their wet clothes and created severe wind chill. With only tripe de roche to eat, each man carried a piece of singed caribou skin to chew on. 'We were generally shivering all the time,' Back says, 'for the blood runs coldly through the veins of a starving man half worn out with fatigue.' Nevertheless, when the officers were eventually too weak to gather tripe de roche, Franklin tells us that Hepburn 'animated by a firm reliance on the beneficence of the Supreme Being, tempered with resignation to his will, was indefatigable in his exertions to serve us, and daily collected all the tripe de roche that was used in the officers mess.' And Hepburn did not even eat with them, but messed throughout the expedition with the voyageurs, as was only proper for a simple seaman.

When the party eventually made camp they lit a fire of caribou moss to dry out their frozen moccasins. They ate supper of lichen, following which each man wrote up his notes and journal. Franklin read evening prayers. Then they wrapped themselves each in a damp blanket which thawed with their own body heat and allowed only fitful sleep. Oh misery! The voyageurs talked openly of starvation and even threatened to dump their loads and take off south on their own, a plan scotched by having no one to guide them. Soon discontent turned to outright mutiny. They dropped the canoe — almost certainly deliberately — which was broken beyond repair.

They now reached the east side of Eda Lake where they again took the wrong direction, being forced to veer eastwards so they ended up almost making a circle to reach the rapids that drain Lake Providence into Point Lake. Franklin sent Back ahead to scout a crossing of these headwaters of the Coppermine River. This would be, they hoped, the last lap to Fort Enterprise.

Those remaining in camp found the bones of a caribou killed by wolves. In the fall the bones are full of fat, which would have made a nutritious soup. However, to render them soft enough to eat, they cooked them over a fire which reduced them almost to charcoal. Likewise they scorched several old moccasins whose untanned uncooked leather would have had nearly the same food value as raw meat. Back was so weak he had to walk with a stick because his shoulders and loins were painful – quite a concession for one so tough. Never plump, he became quite scrawny from losing so much weight.

On 25 September the two hunters temporarily saved the day by killing five caribou beside the lake, which thereafter gained the name Lake Providence. Everyone lay up for a day gorging themselves, which brought on agonizing cramps and vomiting, a story typical of starved men overeating. Next day, feeling a little better, Back set out along with St Germain, Adam and Beauparlant to hunt and search for wood to build a raft. They reached two rapids draining north into Point Lake – named Obstruction Rapids – where they spent the next fateful week trying to cross. This delay would prove catastrophic.

Even Back's 'halfbreeds' mutinied saying that, sorry though they were for the officers, they would now follow the caribou south to save their own lives. Back threatened to dock their wages, but they took no notice. Also they asserted that the Canadian voyageurs were bad men who were *capable de les tuer pour manger* – capable of killing them to eat.' This was a veiled hint at cannibalism.

St Germain took charge of building a raft to cross the rapids. The men collected willows, which they tied into faggots along with their bedding. These they sewed into pieces of painted canvas salvaged from dismembered canoes. The voyageurs now regretted their impatient folly at breaking them, but they willingly began collecting gum from nearby dwarf spruce. The raft had so little buoyancy that it could only carry one man at a time, and steering was hard with only one remaining paddle and a tent pole. Solomon Belanger had failed in several attempts at rafting across, so Richardson, malnourished though he was, volunteered to swim over, dragging a line. He jumped into the water and cut his ankle to the bone on a rusty old Indian knife lying in the mud (he omits to mention this in his own journal – a measure of the calibre of the man). He became exhausted midstream, so he tried turning on his back to swim but he could not kick his legs in the near-freezing water. He collapsed and sank, apparently lifeless. Hurriedly the men hauled him to shore, seated him beside the fire, and rewarded him by wrapping him in a blanket. Nevertheless, for five months afterwards the left side of his body lost feeling, remained weak, and lacked full strength.

The voyageurs, seeing the naked and emaciated doctor, exclaimed '*Ah, que nous sommes maigres* – Oh, how thin we are.' Richardson writes: 'During the whole of our march we experienced that no quantity of clothing could keep us warm whilst we fasted, but on those occasions on which we were able to go to bed with full stomachs, we passed the night in a warm and comfortable manner.'

On 4 October 1821, a week after they arrived at Obstruction Rapids, St Germain paddled across the river in his makeshift raft with a line, and hauled the whole party over one at a time. The men's spirits suddenly perked up and they each shook hands 'cordially' with the officers. St Germain deserves great credit for his untiring work in getting the party across the river. Without him they all might have perished.

The whole party was now reduced to eating the stomach contents of their last caribou, and chewing on their old moccasins and some antlers. Franklin ordered Back to go ahead to Fort Enterprise with St Germain, Beauparlant and Solomon Belanger le Gros (Belanger le Rouge stayed with Franklin) to find the Indians and summon help for the dying party.

Two days later the despondent and gloomy stragglers were struggling. Two voyageurs, Crédit and Vaillant, had collapsed and could go no farther, despite Richardson's encouragement. They must have died shortly after. Hood – never robust, and now reduced to a shadow – was unable to eat because of bowel cramps caused by eating tripe de roche. Junius had wandered off and was never seen again.

A desperate situation required desperate action. Franklin decided to split the party further into three. Back had already gone ahead. Franklin set out for Fort Enterprise with the residue of the partially fit men all carrying lightened loads. The fort was only thirty miles away as the raven flies, and there he hoped to find food and some Indians who could return to help their starving friends. Richardson and Hepburn stayed behind to look after the dying Hood, together with Michel who, despite his comparatively good condition, had accepted Franklin's offer to any man who felt he could not make it, to remain behind with the officers.

About to quit Obstruction Rapids on 4 October 1821, Back writes: 'Having received my orders from the Commander I took leave of my companions and set out in search of relief.' The lives of the remaining eleven men now depended on Back, St Germain, Beauparlant, and Belanger le Gros tracking down Akaitcho's hunters. Akaitcho's hunting ground was a large, featureless area of mixed Barren Land and forest bordering the treeline south of Fort Enterprise. Deep snow made travel hard for already exhausted and starving men. Back had to walk with the aid of a crutch, which hurt his wasted shoulders.

Because tripe de roche was scarce their first night's supper was Labrador tea and a pair of caribou skin trousers. Next day they ate a leather gun case and some old moccasins. A particular delicacy was an old caribou skin infested with warble fly oestrus larvae – a source of protein. At night the men huddled together for warmth, but even so they woke up chilled to the bone.

At the spot where they had cached canoes the year before they cried out, 'Mon dieu, nous sommes sauvés – my God, we're saved.' For a second time, Belanger broke through the lake ice and was nearly submerged, but his companions hauled him out using their belts knotted together. Near the treeline they found brushwood and scrawny pine to make a fire and dry Belanger out.

Passing Slave (or Dogrib) Rock, with Fort Enterprise almost in sight, they had the eerie feeling it was deserted – which, to their horror, it was. They had hiked more than forty miles in five days. The whole fort was a shambles. Wild animals had sheltered in the storerooms, doors were off their hinges, and window parchment was destroyed.

To add to their chagrin there was no food cache, as promised by Wentzel, and no note from him telling them where to find the Indians. In fact, as Wentzel told later, before following Franklin's orders to take all trunks and papers south, he had written a message in pencil on a wooden plank explaining to Franklin his own difficult circumstances. Back, however, had not found it and was unaware of what Wentzel had endured in just getting to Fort Enterprise.

While returning from the Coppermine, Wentzel had eaten nothing but tripe de roche for eleven days. He had met Akaitcho, who complained of the hardships all his Indians were suffering, especially after three hunters – all relatives of his – had drowned when their canoe capsized in Marten Lake. Their families had become so unhinged with grief that they threw away their clothes, and broke their guns, so they were unable to hunt. Nevertheless, Akaitcho promised to continue laying down caches of caribou meat, and to stay around his hunting area near Fort Enterprise, although he had lost all hope of seeing the crazy white men ever again.

Back and his hungry escort gobbled any raw scraps of putrid meat they could find lying around. Then they sat down to contemplate their sad state. Back decided to rest for a day to make new mittens and repair snowshoes. Then, if they saw no Indians, they would go on another 130 miles to Fort Providence, knowing all the time that their starving companions expected them to have found help already. As it turned out, within hours of Back leaving Fort Enterprise, Franklin arrived there and was dejected at finding the houses so desolate.

To the south, ice was still thin on lakes and rivers just recently frozen during a cold snap. At the head of Roundrock Lake, only three miles from Fort Enterprise, St Germain broke through and had to be thawed out yet again. There was still no sign of Indians, despite Back's party spending nearly two weeks – from 14 to 30 October – near Akaitcho's hunting camps in the triangle between Winter, Snare, and Reindeer Lakes.

Back decided that his group was too weak – and rapidly worsening – to try to go farther south to Fort Providence. So he sent Belanger with a note addressed to Franklin asking what he should do. Back suggested they should all return to the fort, regroup, and see if they might have more success at hunting there. This idea, however, would mean more starving mouths to feed at one place. But perhaps the prospect of dying in company was better than dying alone. Back also complained that St Germain had become uncommonly sulky and mulish, and was feckless at hunting even though he was proven the best hunter.

Belanger, the messenger, arrived at Fort Enterprise nearly frozen, having fallen through the ice a third time. Franklin noted: 'My companions nursed him with the greatest kindness . . . they now no longer betrayed impatience or despondency but were composed and cheerful and had entirely given up the practice of swearing to which the Canadian voyagers are so lamentably addicted.'

The dwindling party weatherproofed the houses of the fort as best they could and gathered scattered old skins and bones for food. Franklin set off with Benoit and Augustus hoping to follow Back, but he soon broke a snowshoe and, exhausted by struggling without them, decided to return to the fort.

Now half the remaining party – Franklin, Adam, Peltier and Samandré – was at Fort Enterprise. Augustus and Benoit had gone on to look for Akaitcho or Back. Richardson and Hood were playing out a tragic melodrama near Starvation Lake. Franklin tried to help Peltier and Samandré collect tripe de roche, but they were too weak to tear down a storehouse for fuel. Adam was too ill and swollen to be of use. In the evening of 29 October 1821 Richardson and Hepburn stumbled in with the stark news that Hood, Michel, Perrault, and Fontano were dead; Crédit and Vaillant had already died.

After resting, Richardson made incisions in Adam's grossly swollen abdomen and scrotum to drain oedema fluid which had accumulated owing to starvation protein deficiency. Adam's condition was made worse because he had eaten large amounts of salt he found in a barrel. Peltier and Samandré were unable to eat because of agonizing raw throats; they both slowly gave up and died.

A few miles south of the fort, while Beauparlant waited with Back and St Germain for Belanger to return, he tried to cut firewood, but he could hardly see because his face and eyes were so swollen from starvation. About himself, Back noted: 'The want of food and weakness had now so changed my appearance, that on looking in a glass, I scarcely knew myself. My shoulders were as if they would fall from my body, my legs seemed unable to support me, and in the disposition I was then in, had it not been for the remembrance of my friends, and the reliance they placed on me, as well as the persons of whom I had charge, I would have preferred remaining where I was to the miserable pain of attempting to move.'

Even though Back was starving, the above passage – from his

original parchment-bound journal secured with two brass clasps –
is written in his meticulous copperplate hand as evenly spaced as
ever. The steady handwriting in Richardson's holograph journal,
easier to read than Back's, also shows no sign that he was close to
death. He still used ink, even though it must have been nearly
frozen; and he continued to collect plants, the imprints of which
show pressed onto the yellowing page.

Beauparlant was in bad shape. He asked Back and St Germain to
take their axes and go ahead to prepare camp in a clump of pines
nearby (still only a few miles from the fort). Selflessly he said he
would follow at his own pace. In a stand of spruce Back and St
Germain found a gathering of ravens feeding on frozen heads and
shoulders of half a dozen caribou left behind after wolves had taken
their fill. 'Oh merciful God we are saved!' they said spontaneously
as they tucked into their first proper food for two weeks. Pre-
dictably this gave them agonizing stomach cramps. Back was
convinced that without this food he would not have lived another
day. At nightfall they fired a shot; Beauparlant returned fire, so
they presumed he was alive. As Beauparlant did not turn up next
morning, Back sent St Germain to look for him. Soon he returned
with Beauparlant's bundle, and said, 'Ah! monsieur, il est mort – Oh!
sir, he's dead.' Back's faithful servant was lying supine, frozen limbs
extended.

Belanger returned exhausted from Fort Enterprise with news
that Franklin and five others were there. Having again nearly
drowned in a rapid, Belanger was too weak to tell the whole tragic
story of what he had learned of Hood and the others. A week later
Back sent St Germain and Belanger to bury Beauparlant. He wrote:
'[I] would willingly have accompanied them to perform the last sad
duties, but that I had not the funeral service, having been obliged
to leave even my Prayer Book to lighten my load.' He adds, as if to
excuse his absence, that he was by far the weakest of the three, and
the soles of his feet were deeply cracked and painful.

Back's party had now been wandering haphazardly for three
weeks around Akaitcho's hunting ground only a few miles south of
Fort Enterprise. For the next few days he and his companions
survived on discarded caribou heads that they found in the snow.

From them Back carefully collected two packets of dried meat and sinew 'sufficient to last for eight days at a rate of one indifferent meal a day'. This food he put aside for their long delayed hike of 130 miles to Fort Providence. He estimated it would take them about fourteen days, six of which would be foodless.

They saw a pack of wolves following a herd of caribou but could not get close enough for a shot. When not looking out for caribou, or abandoned heads, they sat around making sledges, refurbishing snowshoes, darning socks, and mending clothes. They had enough wood for a good fire, and Back even washed his shirt for the first time in many weeks. Added to his other miseries, he now became severely constipated, so passing even a pellet stool was agony. The aurora borealis scintillated in the very cold nights, and wolves howled eerily nearby.

Back and his companions saw snowshoe prints several times. At first they presumed they were those of Franklin and his remaining men having overtaken them. But soon they realized that Indians heading south towards Fort Providence had made them. Back now became utterly disillusioned and convinced that they were the only expedition members still alive.

On 3 November Back sent St Germain ahead on his light pair of snowshoes to look for Indians. The next day St Germain found Akaitcho's camp on Upper Carp Lake, just south of his hunting triangle. A boy from Akaitcho's camp appeared like a genie in front of Back bringing from the chief fat caribou meat and tongues and an invitation to meet him next day. The boy also brought a confused, and barely decipherable, note from Franklin sent from Fort Enterprise saying he thought they could kill enough caribou there to last a month.

Back met Akaitcho and thirty of his Yellow Knives at their camp, whereupon they shook hands and smoked a calumet pipe together. Benoit and Augustus had arrived there the day before following a hard two-week walk from Fort Enterprise. Next day Akaitcho sent meat, shoes and a blanket with a rescue party – comprising Boudelkell, Crooked Foot and The Rat – who achieved the prodigious feat of covering fifty-five miles in two and a half days. When the Indians arrived at Fort Enterprise, Richardson tells, they 'wept on beholding the deplorable condition to which we had been reduced'.

Back's mission was over, but at considerable cost to his health. Meanwhile his companions remained many miles north at Fort Enterprise, still in dire straits.

CHAPTER 11

Things which Must Not Be Known

1821–22

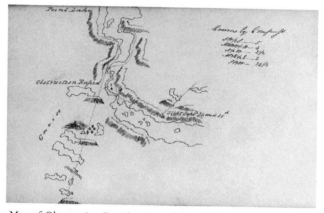

Map of Obstruction Rapids and environs, showing the expedition's
route 24 Sept.–5 Oct. 1821, by Back.

While seated round the fire at Fort Enterprise dividing a partridge
he had shot, Richardson, himself emaciated and with a long beard,
remarked on the hollow sepulchral voices of the other survivors,
and asked them 'to make a more cheerful tone if possible'. Unaware
of his own timbre, he told his own sad story in the same key and
his official narrative to the Admiralty has all the formal reserve one
might expect. Sadly absent is an account in his original personal
journal, which is blank from 7 to 29 October 1821. It might have
given us a more accurate, unedited story of the strange events of
those two fateful weeks at Starvation Lake.

On 10 October Richardson and Hepburn had pitched their tent

in a thicket of small willows beside the lake where tripe de roche was plentiful. Hepburn collected sticks of green willow, which made a feeble fire at best. Then they settled down under the same blanket to share their meagre body warmth with the ailing Hood. Meanwhile they read to each other religious tracts, which 'proved of incalculable benefit'.

Michel arrived with a note from Franklin which said that, since Michel and Belanger le Rouge could not keep up, they would stay behind with Richardson. The note added that they should move the tent to a stand of small spruce a short distance from their present camp. Michel claimed he had lost his way and spent the night in the snow only a mile away, while Belanger had impatiently forged ahead alone. The officers were duly grateful to Michel, who brought a hare and a partridge shot that morning.

Next day Michel guided Richardson and Hepburn directly to the spruce stand. Although nothing appeared peculiar at the time, the Iroquois's accurate knowledge of the local geography did not jibe with his story of having gone astray the previous day. Michel said he would stay put, asked Richardson and Hepburn to leave the hatchet, and promised to join them next morning. Meanwhile they exhausted themselves moving across some of their heavy gear. Since Belanger did not appear, they presumed he was dead.

Next morning Michel did not show up, so Richardson and Hepburn moved the rest of their camp, following very slowly in their previous day's footprints. Hood staggered behind them, utterly debilitated and near death. Michel arrived in the evening bringing some meat, which he said was part of a wolf that he had found, gored by a caribou's horn. To the Britons the meat had an unfamiliar taste.

According to Richardson's forthright report to the Admiralty, they 'implicitly believed this story then, but afterwards became convinced from the circumstances, the detail of which may be spared, that it must have been a portion of the body of Belanger [le Rouge] or Perrault. A question of moment here presents itself; namely, whether he actually murdered these men, or either of them, or whether he found the bodies on the snow.' Certainly Michel did not appear as undernourished as his companions.

Richardson knew that any mention of cannibalism would shock

the British public because eating human flesh, even *in extremis*, was utterly taboo, hence his delicacy in sparing the details. Today eating dead companions still holds horror, even though admitted to in some stories of survival after shipwreck or disasters in wilderness and mountains.

Richardson pieced together some clues about Michel's strange behaviour. He never reported that Perrault, as well as Belanger le Rouge, had turned back; he asked for the hatchet when normally a hunter would use only his knife to skin an animal, but he would need a hatchet to cut up frozen meat; and he had become increasingly surly, erratic and evasive while he stayed away from camp all day, refusing to hunt, cut wood, or sleep in the tent at night. When Hood chided Michel for his selfishness he replied, 'It's no use hunting, there are no animals, you had better kill and eat me.'

Franklin's after-the-fact interpretation of these events was that Michel had killed Belanger. After Perrault had turned back Franklin watched him heading for some willows that hid the smoking fire which was probably being stoked by Michel. Michel then killed Perrault, who had witnessed his crime, in order to cover his traces.

Sunday, 20 October 1821 was a cataclysmic day. Richardson went to gather tripe de roche, leaving Hood sitting in front of the tent beside the fire. Every time Hood tasted tripe de roche he suffered fierce stomach cramps. He complained of cold and weakness, and could barely sit up. Richardson later wrote in a letter of consolation to Hood's father: 'Our sufferings were never acute during the march, the sensation of hunger ceased after the third day of privation, and with the decay of strength the love of life also decayed. We could calmly contemplate the approach of death.' And so for a time did Robert Hood, while Richardson read to him from scripture. Richardson saw him last arguing angrily with Michel. Hepburn was not far away cutting down a tree. Richardson takes up the story:

> I heard the report of a gun, and about ten minutes afterwards Hepburn called to me in a voice of great alarm, to come directly. When I arrived, I found poor Hood lying lifeless at

the fire-side, a ball having apparently entered his forehead. I was at first horror-struck with the idea, that in a fit of despondency he had hurried himself into the presence of his Almighty Judge, by an act of his own hand; but the conduct of Michel soon gave rise to other thoughts, and excited suspicions which were confirmed, when upon examining the body, I discovered that the shot had entered the back part of the head, and passed out at the forehead, and that the muzzle of the gun had been applied so close as to set fire to the night-cap behind. The gun, which was of the longest kind supplied to the Indians, could not have been placed in a position to inflict such a wound, except by a second person.

Richardson confronted Michel and accused him of killing Hood. Michel denied it vociferously. Thereafter he constantly hung around Richardson and Hepburn so as to prevent them from discussing these events in private. They moved Hood's body into a clump of willows behind the tent, and Richardson read the funeral service from the Prayer Book.

On 23 October Richardson, Hepburn, and Michel set out for Fort Enterprise. Each man was armed. Michel was supercilious and paranoid towards Richardson, and constantly muttered threats against Hepburn. Michel tried to persuade them to head to the woods for better hunting, in order to prevent them from going to the fort, where he knew he would have to answer to Franklin for his crime. Richardson concluded that Michel, to hide all evidence, would try to kill Hepburn and himself as soon as he had the chance. The only reason he had not done so before was that he did not know the way south.

While Michel was gathering tripe de roche Richardson and Hepburn agreed they were no match for an armed maniac – Michel carried a gun, two pistols, a bayonet and a knife. For their own safety Richardson decided he must summarily execute Michel as a suspected murderer of Hood, Belanger and Perrault, and the potential slayer of themselves.

When Michel returned to camp Richardson promptly shot him through the head with a pistol. Thereby he alone would take full responsibility for waiving the legal formalities of a trial. He justified his action by presuming that when Michel was supposedly gathering lichen, in fact, he was priming his gun. Had Michel shot Richardson and Hepburn he could then arrive at Fort Enterprise as the sole survivor, and say the others had fallen behind and died.

The deed done, Richardson and Hepburn set off for Fort Enterprise – still a horrific forty miles away for two weary starving men. In his Admiralty report Richardson writes of one day: 'During the last few hundred yards of our march our track lay over some large stones amongst which I fell down upwards of twenty times, and became at length so exhausted that I was unable to stand. If Hepburn had not exerted himself far beyond his strength and speedily made the encampment and kindled a fire, I must have perished on the spot.'

When he took up writing his journal again Richardson always referred to Hepburn as John – a token of gratitude, respect and friendship for his subordinate who, when both their lives were in peril, had behaved as a staunch friend. Five days later they reached Fort Enterprise. Their hideous long beards seriously offended the smooth-chinned Indians at the fort.

The story of murder, cannibalism, and retributive summary execution was to have profound and resounding consequences both in Canada and in Britain, understandable though the circumstances were. Rumours were rife among Indians throughout the country, fuelled because, of all the expedition personnel, only one officer had died, compared with nine out of eleven voyageurs, and one Eskimo interpreter. What Richardson would tell the Admiralty was a selective version of these facts, omitting the more gruesome details.

At Fort Enterprise the Indians cared diligently for the ailing survivors, who still faced the gloomy prospect of seeing out another winter before they could hope to reach Hudson Bay and get a passage home. All were still feeble and suffered gut-wrenching cramps from overeating to satisfy their ravenous appetites. With rest, however, they began to improve, and being saved from death made them appreciate their good fortune. Bleak though their future still was, Richardson even noted: 'The view down Winter River, at all times beautiful, was uncommonly so today.'

After two weeks the last expedition members left Fort Enterprise

THINGS WHICH MUST NOT BE KNOWN 149

on 16 November 1820 having, as Franklin noted: 'experienced a degree of misery scarcely to be paralleled'. The Indians gave the invalids their own snowshoes until they could make temporary ones. They waded through deep snow beside the stumbling men and supported anyone who fell. Richardson was still weak, swollen, and unable to walk unaided. Both he and Franklin constantly remark on the 'utmost tenderness' shown by the Indians, who 'prepared our encampment, cooked for us and fed us as if we had been children; evincing humanity that would have done honour to the most civilized nation'. Moreover these were the very people about whom the officers had made much harsh criticism in earlier days.

Back, meanwhile, was at Akaitcho's camp feasting on caribou for the first time in a month and arranging to pay for the Indians' promissory notes that Weeks had refused to honour at Fort Providence. They longed to see this unpopular man reprimanded by 'the Chief' (Franklin). Almost at the same time as the union of the NWC and HBC became known, news came from England that Franklin had been promoted to commander, and both Back and Hood to lieutenant – sadly forty-seven days posthumously for Hood.

Back reassured Akaitcho that presents promised to the Indians, but never forwarded from points south, would be sent on to them later. Akaitcho, who had been remarkably patient and stoic, said something along the lines of: 'The world goes badly. All are poor. You are poor. The traders appear to be poor. I and my party are poor likewise, and since the goods have not come in we cannot have them. I do not regret having supplied you with provisions, for a Copper Indian can never permit a White man to suffer want on his lands without flying to his aid. I trust, however, that we shall, as you say, receive what is due to us next autumn. And at all events,' he added with good humour, 'it is the first time that the White people have been indebted to the Copper Indians.'

Back took leave of Akaitcho and walked on to Fort Providence with St Germain and Belanger. Back was disappointed to discover that no expedition supplies had been forwarded there from Fort Chipewyan. The niggardly Weeks held written instructions from his superior, McVicar, only 'to afford such assistance as was convenient to him, or as otherwise would not interfere with the interests of the trade'. So Back decided to cross Great Slave Lake to Moose Deer Island where he knew some expedition supplies were stored. Too exhausted to walk, he rode on a sledge on the lake for an uncomfortable four-day-ride over snow ridge sastrugi caused by constant winds. McVicar, usually the most accommodating of all the fur trade factors, was in charge at Moose Deer Island. Back found the stores he expected and had them sent immediately to Fort Providence, including some presents for Franklin to give to Akaitcho.

The expedition had suffered moments of discord – even acerbic exchanges – with Akaitcho. Now, however, all the party appreciated the profound debt they owed the Yellow Knife (Copper) chief and his fellow Indians in caring for them in distress. When Franklin and Richardson left Akaitcho, the doctor wrote: 'We felt a deep sense of humiliation at being compelled to quit men capable of such liberal sentiments and humane feelings in the beggarly manner in which we did.' During the survivors' difficult walk south the Indians stopped frequently to rub their hands or faces when telltale white patches appeared on their freezing cheeks. Franklin was particularly prone, being so chubby – now less so than in better-nourished days.

Back welcomed them to Fort Resolution on 19 December. 'We met our friend Mr Back,' Franklin wrote, 'to whom under Providence we felt our lives were owing.' He describes Back as 'a traveller of sterling and heroic cast' and congratulates him on his toughness, resilience and courage in pushing on ahead and dispatching supplies that saved their lives.

During the next five months, Robert McVicar, the HBC chief trader, fed and nursed the party back to health. They stayed with McVicar until the rivers unfroze, when they could continue their journey to Hudson Bay.

Compared with their previous year's travails the return journey to Hudson Bay was uneventful. It seems cavalier, however, to dispose so tritely of a seven-week wilderness canoe passage which still entailed much hard work and danger. They started from Fort

Resolution on 27 May and reached York Factory on 14 July 1822. Governor George Simpson welcomed them and relations were much more cordial than on their previous meeting. One hopes that Simpson ate the unkind words, in his *Athabasca Journal*, about Franklin being unable to walk more than eight miles a day.

'And thus terminated our long, fatiguing and disastrous travels in North America,' Franklin wrote at York Factory, 'having journeyed by water and by land (including our navigation of the Polar Sea) five thousand five hundred and fifty miles.' Add to this Back's winter journey of 1,100 miles.

On 7 September 1822 they embarked in *Prince of Wales*, the same boat in which they had arrived three years before. They landed in England six weeks later and were welcomed as conquering heroes, feted royally, and amply rewarded. Franklin was further promoted to post-captain and elected a Fellow of the Royal Society, the most prestigious of all British scientific societies; Richardson got a plum job as surgeon to the Chatham division of the Royal Marines; and Back was posted as lieutenant in HMS *Superb* to the West Indies station. All these appointments came at a time when active jobs were scarce during the depression that followed the Napoleonic wars, and when most of their advancement-seeking Royal Navy contemporaries were sidelined in semi-retirement on half pay.

But there was a price to pay for fame, and questions about what went on in the Barrens had to be answered. The explorers' stories were published in British newspapers – notably Richardson's sanitized version of events which appeared in the winter of 1822–23. It originally reported that all expedition deaths were from natural causes – conveniently glossing over the fate of Michel. In Canada different versions emerged.

In all the following exchanges we must bear in mind Wentzel's sore feelings against Franklin's strong criticism of his failure to refurbish Fort Enterprise and supply it with an emergency cache of meat. On 10 April 1823 Wentzel wrote to the Hon. Robert Mackenzie, governor of the NWC, reporting on the expedition's legacy: 'The surviving officers have left in the country impressions not altogether very creditable to themselves amongst both the trading class of people and the native inhabitants.' This letter leaves only veiled hints of wrongdoing; details came later.

In a letter of 1 March 1824 Wentzel writes about the officers who 'acted on some occasions imprudently, injudiciously and showed in one particular instance an unpardonable want of conduct. As to the report of some of the Canadian voyageurs having fallen a sacrifice to support others, it is currently circulated amongst the Copper Indians, and is generally credited in this country.' This oblique hint does not actually use the dreaded word cannibalism.

Wentzel goes on to assert that Back, when returning through Fort Chipewyan in 1821, told him there had been dissension among the officers themselves. Back confided to him, 'To tell the truth, Wentzel, things have taken place which *must* not be known.' Wentzel doubts that a true account of what went on will ever be published in England. He says Franklin tried to persuade him to stay longer in the north in order to let any impending storm subside, despite early on in the expedition having invited him to accompany them on their anticipated glorious return to England as reward for his sterling service.

Of Michel's execution without investigation, trial, or defence, Wentzel later wrote: 'I find no delight in exposing circumstances which might be considered *criminal* conduct in one of the officers who has survived and been rewarded . . . conduct for which he richly merited to be punished.' Although at first Wentzel regarded Richardson highly, he appears subsequently to have changed his opinion, which turned to intense dislike following Franklin's harsh and open criticism. But it says much for the respect in which Richardson was universally held, that the Admiralty took no disciplinary action against him.

The author of a satirical skit, written perhaps in the winter of 1824–25, was probably Dr William Todd, resident surgeon at York Factory, who spent several weeks with expedition members while they waited for the ship to leave for England. The skit mimics the bombastic style of Franklin's recently published *Narrative*. The author changed all names and places, but expedition characters appear with pseudonyms: e.g. Franklin is Mildmay, Richardson – Capriole, Wentzel – Quiz, and Back – Bluebeak, who was referred to as 'a distant diffident and modest youth'.

Most significantly the skit refers to the council held at Fort Wampoom – Fort Resolution – where 'it was unanimously agreed that all difference of opinion should be buried in oblivion and that the public were only to know us by the perfect unanimity that marked our proceedings.'

Many years later, in 1855, Joseph René Bellot, second in command of *Prince Albert*, took Hepburn onto the crew of an Arctic search for the lost Franklin expedition. Hepburn, then age sixty-two, became loquacious about his former boss. Concerning their meeting at Fort Enterprise after the Michel incident (which he does not specifically mention), he says: 'their constitutions have been irreparably injured. He [Franklin] had a sort of dropsy on his return; he was all bloated, his hair perished, his nails broke, etc . . . Inarticulate sounds, issuing from the nose like grunts, were their only means of conversation.' Hepburn also said Back was 'not very brave but charming to those from whom he hopes to gain something'. Spiteful though this remark may appear, evidently many of Back's companions found him abrasive. We shall see this particularly when Franklin selects the party for his next expedition.

In Bellot's own analysis: 'The English have a practical way of looking at these things, very different from ours. They call want of judgment the admirable temerity of the man who perseveres in risking his life in a manner almost certain.'

Franklin's first Arctic Land Expedition was a human disaster – eleven out of twenty members perished. Geographically it was a resounding success, having covered a vast swath of northern Canada, although actual mapping of the Arctic Ocean was meagre. Could this disaster have been avoided? The obvious answer with modern hindsight is 'yes' – if Franklin had planned better, if the officers themselves had learned to hunt instead of putting all their trust in native hunters, if they had been less militaristic and shared the burdens of impending catastrophe. But this ignores the rigid social hierarchy which permeated every Royal Navy officer's training, something that would not change over the next century, and would be played out at the opposite pole of the earth by Captain Robert Falcon Scott.

PART THREE

FRANKLIN'S SECOND ARCTIC LAND EXPEDITION

CHAPTER 12

To the North Coast of America

1823–25

North Shore of Great Slave Lake, August 13, 1833, drawn by Back,
engraved by Finden.

Franklin and his fellow survivors returned to England as heroes.
The parties ground relentlessly on. George Back was invited to a
public banquet in Stockport, held in his honour by fifty 'leading
gentlemen of the town and neighbourhood' at the Warren Bulkeley
Arms. The *Stockport Advertiser* reported: 'The gallant Captain Hum-
phreys, R.N. was in the chair, and on his right sat the heroic young
man, so justly the pride of his fellow-townsmen.' It continued with
a eulogy of Back's sufferings and privations. Being a men-only
affair, his father attended along with some school friends whom
George had not seen for fourteen years.

As a party piece, he 'favoured the company in the course of the
evening with several excellent songs, and raised a powerful interest
by exhibiting with great effect specimens of the original airs with
which the Canadians solace their labours as they paddle along the

perilous rivers of North America'. Back had collected, and translated from French, these voyageur canoe-paddling songs, *chansons d'aviron*, and had them published in London as a booklet called *Canadian Airs . . . with Symphonies and Accompaniments.*

The dinner ended with a toast proposed to the health of Lieutenant Back, and prosperity to that undistinguished group of Arctic Ocean rocks, the Stockport Islands. Responding, 'the gallant explorer remarked that he would not say much for their geographical situation. With respect, however, to the productions of the islands, he said, that if we could not import cotton or sugar from them, there was plenty of selenite, silica, granite, and some masses of basalt. He had not perceived many purling streams, but when the sun shone on the tops of the mountains, another Mersey might be produced, but Lord have mercy on those who went there.'

Shortly after this celebration, in November 1823, Back joined HMS *Superb* at Spithead, off Portsmouth, carrying troops of the 12th Regiment bound for the West Indies station. Sea duty was necessary for a lieutenant to qualify for promotion to commander. The ship sailed to Gibraltar where, he comments: 'the Effluvia is horrid, [and] the contaminating breath of Turks, Jews, Spaniards, and the lower orders of the French almost putrify the atmosphere.' Then *Superb* struck west across the Atlantic, called at Tenerife, and a month later anchored in Carlisle Bay, Barbados, where she discharged her cargo of soldiers. Back was specially pleased to be rid of Brevet Major Jones: 'possessed of little education and less manners, his conduct in the wardroom mess obtained for him a general dislike bordering on disgust.' During his stay on Barbados, Back visited a plantation where he saw for the first time slaves at work. He considered them, however, better off than poor Irish. *Superb* also called at three nearby islands of the Lesser Antilles – St Vincent, Dominica and Marie Galante. Then she sailed for home.

Meantime Franklin had been busy courting. After returning from the Spitzbergen expedition, he met Eleanor Porden and thereafter become romantically – if that is not too emotive a word for so pragmatic a man – involved. Eleanor and John were married at the end of August 1823, an incongruous pair if ever there was one. She was a beautiful lively socialite and intellectual, who

regularly attended lectures at the Royal Society with more enthu-
siasm than church – a matter over which they squabbled. A keen
writer with some talent, she had just completed an epic poem
entitled, *Richard Coeur de Lion*, and some verses written in the guise
of an Eskimo maiden imploring Franklin to return to the Arctic.
Even before the wedding she wrote to him doubting their compat-
ibility: 'The question is not, my dear Sir, whether you and I can
mutually esteem each other as friends, but whether we are calculated to live together in the closest domestic union.'

Franklin was an ambitious, focused, stolid, honest-to-God naval
officer, totally loyal to the service. As he once said: 'the highest
object of my desire, is faithfully to perform my duty' – a
philosophy that does not allow much room for romance. Eleanor
wrote him charming light-hearted love letters to which he would
reply thanking her – in the stiff platitudinous prose that character-
izes his writings – for her 'interesting communication'. Bumbler
though he was, nevertheless Franklin had charisma and courage
sufficient to lead men willingly into danger.

Eleanor bore him a child, whom they named Eleanor Isabella.
Captain George Lyon, a fellow officer, remarked about the baby
that: 'it was like looking at Captn. Franklin thro' the wrong end of
a telescope.' Eleanor, the mother, was always sickly; soon it became
evident that she was mortally ill with consumption, as tuberculosis
was known. This did not prevent her husband agreeing to lead his
next major exploration.

While Back was away in the West Indies plans were afoot for
Franklin to lead a second overland expedition to the Arctic. His
first choice of personnel was his friend Dr John Richardson, who
had shown such courage under terrible hardship during the first
expedition. He then appointed two lieutenants, E.N. Kendall and
John Bushnan. Kendall was a surveyor and artist, Bushnan had
served with distinction under John Ross in HMS *Isabella* in 1818,
with William Parry in *Hecla* in 1819–20, and also in *Fury* in
1821–23, but he died 'prematurely' of unrecorded causes, so a
replacement was needed urgently. So where was Back during all
these discussions?

Back was a favourite of John Barrow, but certainly not of

Franklin, with whom his relationship was marked by constant ups and downs. Considering Franklin's repeated assertions of friendship, one wonders why he did not offer Back a position in the first place. Despite having spent so much time together on their former expedition, when Back helped save the lives of Franklin and others, relations between the cocky young midshipman and the bombastic captain were always uneasy and ambivalent. As usual with the British, stiff upper lips prevailed. Servicemen closed ranks, so their journals never mention mutual disharmony, which gives a false impression that all was skookum.

In July 1823 Franklin and Richardson started corresponding about the appointment of junior officers. Even before Back left for the West Indies, Franklin wrote to Richardson: 'Back is still in London and not likely to be employed immediately. I see very little of him. He has called once and written two or three notes.'

They must have discussed the possibility of Back being included in the upcoming party because, in another letter to Richardson, Franklin wrote these harsh words: 'You know I have no desire for his company but do not see how I can decline it if the Admiralty press the matter without being of great disservice to him and publicly making an exposure of his incapacity in many respects.'

At a meeting between Barrow, Parry and Franklin to discuss the makeup of the expedition, they agreed that Back should remain in the West Indies completing his sea service required for promotion. Soon after, Franklin wrote to Richardson: 'I am very happy to tell you that it is quite decided Back is not to be of the party though I made the offer of taking him and so far I have done my duty towards him and his friends.'

In a letter of condolence to Robert Hood's father who had already lost three children in childhood, Franklin had promised to consider a place on any forthcoming expedition for his second son, George. But George was to die of fever while serving in the Royal Navy off the coast of Africa.

Franklin, aware that Back was on his way home in *Superb*, urged Barrow to promote him and thereby to disqualify him for the expedition because he would be too senior to be Franklin's subordinate. Of this he writes to Richardson on 24 August 1824: 'I could not without entirely injuring his professional prospects mention my reasons for declining his Service, and it might be retorted on me why did you permit these to be dormant so long? An explanation on this point would only lead further into the mire. It is useless however to teaze ourselves about his matter until we see how things go.'

Barrow had now given Franklin sole responsibility for appointing his officers. A week later, Franklin followed with a letter to Richardson: '[having] to wait for Backs refusal is a convenient answer to all present applicants, unless one should offer who is in every way qualified.' And again later: 'I really think young Buchan will do as well as any that have offered, but the vacancy will be kept open for Back . . . I cannot learn whether it is Lord Melville's intention to promote him, and am rather inclined to think that he will promise him the step providing he goes with us, as soon as he is fairly on his voyage. This however is mere conjecture on my part and I hope will prove fallacious.'

But clearly the Admiralty had not taken the hint. In Franklin's *Narrative*, written long after the fact, he says: 'The vacancy occasioned by the death of Lieut Bushnan not having been filled up, Mr Barrow early in December offered the appointment to My friend and former Companion Lieut Back then serving in HM Ship Superb at Lisbon and on Christmas Day I had the gratification of seeing him in London ready to join the party. I then shewed him all the documents relative to the Expedition, and he at once evinced his wonted zeal in the service by offering to render me every assistance in his power.'

From this correspondence it is clear that all had not been amicable between Back and his companions on the first expedition. Unfortunately we do not have Richardson's responses to Franklin, but it is obvious that Richardson, who seems always to have been very fair-minded, was in accord with his boss. On another sour note, Franklin wrote to Richardson in December, saying that Mr West, the missionary, had seen Augustus who, 'wearing all his gay clothes armed with sword and pistols wished to accompany him to England to see you and me whom he Says he likes properly, but our friend *B* only a little.'

In January 1825 Franklin received Official Instructions from the

Admiralty, signed by Lord Bathurst, Lord President of His Majesty's Council. He was to conduct an expedition overland 'for the purpose of exploring the North Coast of America between the Mouth of Mackenzie's River and the Strait of Behring . . .' Such an idea had been mooted in 1823 when the government decided there should be another attempt on the North West Passage to be led by Parry, but nothing more came of this.

Besides expanding its exploration, science, and natural history programmes, the government had another problem on its mind – Russia's presence in the Arctic. In 1824 an Imperial ukase, or edict, had claimed the western North American Arctic as Russian territory. Britain was, therefore, intent on re-establishing its sovereignty over its lands up to the Alaska border.

Franklin had proposed to the government a two-pronged attack by sea and land simultaneously. He offered to lead an overland party down the Mackenzie River to explore unmapped parts of the Arctic coast. There he would hope to meet Captain Frederick William Beechey, who would have sailed HMS *Blossom* via Cape Horn, up the west coast of the Americas, and through the Bering Strait (the fifty-three-mile passage between Russia and Alaska) into the Arctic Ocean.

Franklin was ordered to divide his party at the mouth of the Mackenzie. One group commanded by Franklin, and including Back, would then proceed west along the Arctic coast, past Icy Cape, to rendezvous with Beechey in Kotzebue Inlet. The other group under Richardson, along with Kendall, would travel east mapping the coast between the Mackenzie and Coppermine Rivers, thereby linking up with the coastal survey made three years before on the fateful first expedition.

Franklin had strict instructions to turn around 'about the 15th or 20th of August [and return] to the established winter quarters on Bear Lake'. If they met Beechey in *Blossom* they would proceed to England either via the Sandwich Islands, or Canton in China, depending on where they could pick up a ship. The stated objectives of the expedition were 'important at once to the naval character, scientific reputation, and commercial interest of Great Britain'. Should Franklin die during their absence, Back would take command (since Richardson was not a Royal Navy deck officer). His elders and seniors notwithstanding, Back was on board again.

Franklin had done much to prepare for the forthcoming journey using experience gained from three years before. Most significantly, he included several British seamen in order to avoid having to depend on ocean-shy, unreliable Canadian voyageurs.

Nonetheless, Franklin's requisition for stores – sent to the Under Secretary of State, Colonial Department – is utterly random. It jumps from food to gifts for Indians, to scientific equipment, to guns, to clothes, again to gifts for Indians, to tea, to combs and looking glasses. There is no organized gear list such as would constitute the basis for a well-thought-out trip. For his part, Back merely had to collect astronomical instruments, drawing materials, and paper. Everything else had been taken care of.

Franklin had three boats built of mahogany by Mr Cow, master boatbuilder of Woolwich Dockyard, 'to withstand sea & rapids'. Having learned from sorry previous use of frail birchbark canoes on the stormy Arctic Ocean, he wanted these boats to be stable and buoyant at sea, and to carry a large cargo. They also had to be navigable in shallow rivers, yet light enough to be portaged.

Captain Buchan, formerly of *Dorothea*, supervised their construction. One was twenty-six feet long, designed to carry three tons of cargo with a crew of eight; the other two were each twenty-four feet long and carried two and a half tons and a crew of seven. They each had a high prow and stern, similar to a York boat. Steering was either by sweep oar or rudder as circumstances demanded. Twin masts supported loose-footed sails, which hung from yards and were controlled from the stern by rope sheets.

For crossing rivers Lieutenant-Colonel Pasley, Royal Engineers, designed a collapsible 'walnut shell' made of well seasoned thong-whipped ash, covered with canvas. It was nine feet long, four and a half feet wide, and weighed only eighty-five pounds. It could be packed like a large umbrella and assembled in twenty minutes from five or six parcels. On the Thames at Woolwich each boat was tested for performance under sail, oar and paddle; they proved to be faster all round than similar boats built of canvas. Pasley also designed a portable oven.

Expedition food was wrapped in waterproof boat canvas, and made up into ninety-pound packages. It consisted mainly of flour, arrowroot, macaroni, portable soup, chocolate, coffee essence, tea and sugar. They planned to acquire pemmican in Canada.

Each man had two waterproof suits made of material, patented by Mr Charles Macintosh of Glasgow, which consisted of layers of cloth cemented with rubber. This material was also made into covers for boats, bales of food, two tents for the men, a marquee for officers, and four 'life-preservers of belts of water-proof Canvas which when inflated supports men in swimming' (presumably one for each officer – no mention of the men). Richardson designed green and red uniforms for the men, but Franklin pointed out that these were the colours of Russians for whom they might be mistaken, and suggested an 'equally showy' sky blue with red and silver trim.

Later, on some loose pages of a diary, Back noted his own ideas about equipment necessary for the Arctic:

<u>On anyone going to the HBCo's Territories it will [be] prudent to take the following Articles:</u>
Strong warm calico shirts with or without linen collars
    ”   ” drawers (sorry, to the ankle) and under waist-coats with sleeves to match
Good chamois leather under waistcoats and long drawers (large enough for shrinking in washing)
Mufflers (different lengths and thickness)
Angora gloves are very useful to wear *inside* the large 'Mitten' of the country and which often prevent being frostbitten. They are excellent for shooting with in cold weather.
Socks made of good strong blanket to come up above the ankle and intended to be worn with a 'moccasin' when one sock is not warm enough a piece of blanket is folded cornerways over it and a larger moccasin used. The latter will do for snowshoes.
    (Note – It is unnecessary to state that English Boots and Shoes are useless in winter)
Shawls for the Neck
Two good Fur Caps

Good thick cloth Surtout, double-hooded and trowsers for winter
Waistcoats double-breasted

For Summer:
Different patterns of Boat Shirts. Extra collars.
Lighter sort of drawers &c &c but long ones. Light trowsers &c
Leather gloves of different kinds but all strong and lasting
A Veil for the Hat to descend as low as the waist as a guard against mosquitoes
A mosquito net for the Bed
Golashes or large Shoes to slip on over the light Moccasin when crossing a portage or stepping outside the tent &c &c
Waterproof cloak and cape – separate (and never button or clasp either in descending a Rapid)
Cigars take up room therefore have a supply of four or six *Pipes*, one with a long stem
Extra Good Steels and Flints – a few good Knives, one with a lancet &c &c
A good double-barrelled Gun with extra locks, nipples &c
The water is too muddy for fishing with fly though a few Trout were caught.
Sheets for bedding are never used and therefore unnecessary in Hudson's Bay.

Franklin had planned for the expedition to winter at the western end of Great Bear Lake, a three-day march up the Bear Lake River, which drains into the Mackenzie. As the expedition's base camp manager, he asked the HBC to second their chief trader, Peter Warren Dease, who had been with them on the first expedition. Although a former employee of the NWC, the two fur companies had now amalgamated (in 1821) and sublimated their differences. Even George Simpson told Franklin that: 'there was not a man in the Hudson's Bay Company who would not be happy to form a member of the Expedition and share your danger.'

Dease would go ahead to build houses for their winter quarters, and arrange with local Great Bear Indian hunters to gather a supply of meat. Franklin reckoned that the lake would likely provide hunting and fishing necessary to nourish the party, possibly for three years – and this in a country where 'in the oldest Trading Establishment the greatest Anxiety is caused frequently for the Ration of the following day'. The Britons would have had plenty of time to sharpen their own shooting skills (Hepburn was a marksman) and practise living off the land. Nevertheless Franklin evidently still planned to rely on Indian hunters and to travel in a single over-large group – some reasons why half his previous party had perished. Clearly, the example of Hearne who went native and travelled successfully had not made its mark.

The expedition went out to North America in three groups. First, in March 1824, Robert McVicar, who was returning on the HBC supply ship after home leave on the Isle of Islay, took most of the stores and 'sixteen able-bodied men all from Argyllshire'. The second group followed to York Factory in June with more stores and the boats. It comprised two carpenters, four volunteers from England (including Sparks and Duncan who had sailed with Franklin and Back to Spitzbergen in *Trent*) and five Highlanders from Islay.

The third group, bound for New York, left on 15 February 1825 aboard the packet *Columbia*, with a send-off of a jubilant three cheers from thousands of spectators crowding Liverpool's quay. This group comprised Franklin, Richardson, Back and Kendall, plus Thomas Drummond, an assistant botanist from Tayside, and four Royal Marines – one corporal and three privates – and a piper, all volunteers from the Chatham division. Franklin hoped that a southerly approach – from America – on unfrozen rivers and lakes would allow an earlier start than by taking the Hudson Bay route.

Less happy must have been Franklin's leave-taking from Eleanor, his ailing wife of just eighteen months. Their daughter, Eleanor Isabella, was only eight weeks old – but Daddy had important business to attend to in the Arctic. Eleanor and her husband had discussed in detail whether he should sail or not, and she was determined he should. 'It would be better for me that you were gone,' she says, implying that Franklin would not cope well with a dying wife. Her final devoted act was to embroider a silk Union

Jack for him to unfurl on the shore of the Arctic Ocean. She had already ordered her affairs, signed her will, and planned her own funeral service with a reading from I Corinthians XV, verse 55, 'O death, where *is* thy sting? O grave, where *is* thy victory?'

Jane Griffin was a family friend, intimately concerned for Eleanor, and wrote in her journal: 'Captn. Franklin took his last leave of his poor wife . . . He was obliged to settle all his affairs before he went as if she were certainly not to recover & as if he himself would never return.' One week later around midnight, with Franklin then on the high seas, Eleanor died – 'without a struggle or a groan after having been lifted into bed from the sofa'. On the day of her funeral, still unaware, Franklin wrote expressing his confidence in the impending success of his expedition, his hopes for her recovery, and with affectionate chat about their daughter.

Later, at Penetanguishene in the heart of Canada, on hearing the grievous news, Franklin wrote to Captain Beaufort: 'I have this Evening received through the Newspaper the distressing intelligence of my dearest wife's death – the shock is a severe one – but it is my duty to bow with reverence to the wise disposition of the Almighty.' Baby Eleanor Isabella was placed in the guardian care of her cousin, a niece of Jane Franklin, Sophia Cracroft (who incidentally and unaccountably detested Back).

Of 'the melancholy demise of Mrs Franklin' Back wrote in his journal, 'the manner in which our Friend supported himself under this unfortunate and irreparable loss was such that would call for the admiration of all Men, and would be a lesson to most.' That Franklin's fellow officers did not find his behaviour bizarre and callous is a sign of times when Duty to one's country came before everything else – even a dying wife.

Years before, Jane Griffin had cast an eye on Franklin through her friendship with Eleanor before her marriage and during many social events to which she was later invited by the married Franklins. At dinner with them a month before the Captain's departure, she gave him a silver pencil 'with ready-pointed leads having his crest engraved on the seal at the head, & added a pair of fur gloves'. She was more than ready to defend him from those, not of a naval turn of mind, who thought him heartless to leave his wife to die alone, confiding to her diary that 'idle & contradictory gossip' was so rife in London society that her voice 'trembled with agitation not unmixed with anger while I replied to all this unfeeling nonsense'. In due course her reward would see her become the second Mrs Franklin.

Frances Woodward in *Portrait of Jane* describes Franklin as 'a solid, almost bovine, sailorman, suggesting all that is honest and brave and kind but nothing is winning'. This impression is confirmed, as we have seen, by his letters which Woodward admits are, 'toilsomely formed, abounding in impeccable sentiments, platitudinously expressed; they describe rather than transmit affectionate feelings.' Grandiloquent prose is the hallmark of Franklin's journals, in raw contrast to Back's writing which is mostly as sensitive and descriptive as his painting and drawing.

If the above is a fair slant on Franklin's character, it highlights the ambivalent relationship between him and Back. It is hardly surprising that the two men rankled like crumbs between the bedsheets. Back was youthfully handsome, a lady's man who flirted with every wench he encountered, tough and athletic, artistic – in fact, everything that Franklin was not. But these very qualities hardly endeared Back to jealous rivals – and they were many.

The Atlantic passage was uneventful, apart from one sailor being washed from the bowsprit and drowned. In New York the party lodged in Mrs Wilkinson's boarding house near the Battery. The British consul helped them clear the expedition stores through customs, and then they were ready to proceed.

They took a steamboat upriver to Albany, then by coach to Niagara over a rutted, frozen trail about which Back notes 'the advantages of macadamizing public roads'. They travelled by the schooner *Richmond* across Lake Ontario, by ox-cart and wagon to Lake Simcoe, and canoe to reach Penetanguishene, the naval depot on Lake Huron's Georgian Bay where their stores and equipment were deposited a year before.

During this varied voyage Niagara Falls made the deepest impression on Back and his companions: 'An immense chasm 750 feet in circumference, it being shaped like a Horseshoe between two steep Rocks covered with Pine Trees, which still retaining their Autumnal foliage and contrasted to the shadowy green and light yellow foam in the boiling Gulf below have a most somber and surprising effect.'

Back stayed behind at York (present day Toronto) to await the Canadian voyageurs sent from Montreal by arrangement with the HBC. The men eventually arrived in two large *canots du maitre*. Next day after attending mass they had a meal on the commissioner's lawn where 'they gave some decided proofs of their possessing regular North West Appetites, where their allowance is 8 lbs of Meat a day.'

Once afloat, the canoes clung to the northern shore of Georgian Bay, passing the mouth of French River, the main canoe route from Montreal. Along with fog and gales on Lake Superior, the last of the winter ice delayed them. On a piece of wood hung over a door at Fort Mississauga, Back was surprised to notice a rough sketch by his late friend Robert Hood. Persons unknown must have lifted it from the main living room door at Fort Enterprise.

Another bizarre event, harping back to those sad days of four years before, was meeting an Iroquois, the brother of Michel Terohaute whom Richardson had summarily executed on the shores of Starvation Lake following the murder of Hood by Michel. With 'sullen gloom that hung over his dark Features' the Iroquois told Back he understood that his brother Michel was dead, but he did not know the circumstances nor what had happened to wages still due to him. Back reported this to Franklin, who promised to send a letter to the HBC House in Montreal asking them to pay the Iroquois any money owing to the family. Thereafter they set night watches to keep an even closer eye than usual on their packages for fear the Indian might try to take revenge.

The northward inland canoe highway started at Fort William where large Montreal-based *canots du maitre* were exchanged for smaller *canots du nord*, which were more versatile but carried less freight. Franklin and Richardson decided to forge ahead in a light express canoe in order to speed up the Woolwich boats that had gone before them. Franklin left Back with written instructions to take charge of the rear party, along with Kendall, the surveyor, and three laden canoes. They were to meet him at Fort Chipewyan as soon as possible, but to continue surveying rivers and lakes on their route.

While tracking and poling up Barrier Rapid shortly after starting out, the bowman of Back's second canoe let the current catch his bow and whip it round into midstream – a common mistake. The canoe became wrapped round a rock, broke its back and damaged many delicate instruments. However, the men dived to salvage most of the sodden stores, which they laid out in the sun to dry. Subsequently they had several more close calls. The same bowman repeated his mistake once too often on the Winnipeg River, whereupon Back peremptorily fired him.

During passage of many rapids and portages on this early part of the journey the men had to stop frequently to gum cracked birchbark seams of the canoes. Canny voyageurs, according to Back: 'seldom despatch a Canoe thoroughly gummed from Fort William, but leave it to the crew to get over the worst part of the River as well as they can until the reach Lac la Pluie (Rainy Lake) where it is perfectly understood they are to undergo a complete repair'.

While Back was sketching Kakabeka (or Cleft Rock) Falls – which he described as far more beautiful than Niagara – a massive rock slide occurred. He heard 'a long rolling sound which increased to a report [like that] caused by the discharge of a first rate broadside'. Watching trees being thrown into the vortex, he says: 'I took a few hasty steps from it, not wishing to experience that which . . . must have proved instant death to any human creature.'

In the relatively short passage from Lake Superior to Lake Winnipeg, Back notes in unusually tedious detail every corduroy road portage, muddy-bottomed lake, fallen tree sweeper, and whirlpool-sucking rapid. The canoe highway now crossed the height of land, and then passed the Lake of the Thousand Islands to reach Rainy Lake and Lake of the Woods. On Rainy Lake, Back writes: 'it was evident from the gloomy and overcast appearance of the Sky as well as the hushed and silent state of the atmosphere, which left the trembling Aspen at rest that we must soon be pelted by a storm.' Northerners still call them trembling aspen because their leaves quiver in the slightest breeze.

At Great Rock Rapid, before reaching Lake Winnipeg, the third canoe met another near disaster when they lost many books and instruments. Later on this would frustrate the expedition's plans for scientific observations. At this point, Back shows, in the vivid style of which he is so capable, his hard-learned understanding of canoeing techniques:

> In order to arrive at the next [portage] which they could plainly see, it was only necessary to avoid the centre stream that led to the Fall and pull strongly across to the Eddy where the others were unloading. But they had no sooner gained the Rapid within 300 yards of the Fall and from whence the Mist is seen issuing from below, than they became simultaneously possessed with a strange Fear of descending it. Thus panic-struck they were for a moment powerless. Then acting with the desperation of horror they collected their strength and dashed the canoe against a rock near the Eddy, when every Man except one threw themselves either on Shore or in the Water, and received some severe bruises as the reward of their cowardice. But [the Canoe being left with two men aboard] the greatest alarm was not excited by old Vallie's perilous situation, who holding on the Canoe and deprecating the conduct of the others, contrived by admirable exertion to get her into the Eddy where she was whirled against a craggy rock with such force that he was thrown out, and striking the shore fell back into the passing Water which was bearing him to the last limit of existence when, by the greatest good fortune he was extricated from what was thought inevitable destruction at the moment of his approaching the upper Fall. He, poor Fellow, thinking his Fate inevitable, had actually said 'Adieu' to those on shore.

At the very foot of Lake Winnipeg a storm forced them to spend four days at Fort Alexander where the factor, John McDonnel, kept a farm with cows, oxen, buffalo, pigs, and chickens. Men who had been banged about in rapids – some quite severely – there got a chance to recover in 'one of the most comfortable Places in the Country'.

Once back on water the lake lived up to its tempestuous reputation with thunder and lightning, squalls, swells and breaking surf, so the canoes were frequently forced to shelter in protected bays. The men passed their downtime by collecting gull, duck, and pelican eggs, a thousand of which went into making one giant omelette. At the north end of Lake Winnipeg they joined their 1819 route from York Factory to Norway House. They reached the outlet of the Saskatchewan River, up which they had a fairly easy passage to Cumberland House. Rondeau, a voyageur with a previous history of epileptic fits, had a seizure and fell overboard. His colleagues retrieved him, but his convulsions were so severe and frequent during the night that four or five men had to hold him down to prevent him writhing around and hurting himself.

Chief factor Thomas Isbister – whom Back had met on the first expedition, and would meet again on his way to the Great Fish River – was looking after the chief carpenter, Thomas Matthews, who had broken his leg playing football. Dr Richardson had ordered him to stay put for a month in order to let the fractured tibia heal. At Cumberland House Back regretfully left the indefatigable and gentle Thomas Drummond in the care of Isbister and his wife. Drummond was heading off for three years intending to study the natural history of the prairies. Because of dangers from marauding Blackfeet Indians he moved on to the Rocky Mountains where he made the largest collection of birds, plants, and insects that had ever come from that country.

When Back left Cumberland House Isbister presented him with 200 large fish hooks and twine, which later were to prove very useful. In a continuous rapid on the Maligne (Sturgeon) River the men performed well until the last rapid when Kendall's canoe broadsided a rock. The bowman just salvaged the canoe by jumping into the water and hauling it off. He then dragged it to shore and gummed it.

At Otter Portage, Back again proved his skill as a fly fisherman. Using a thick pole with a length of strong cord attached, and a cod hook baited with a chunk of fat or a young frog, as he confides, he landed 'a Jack or a Dorée at every cast'. A cross, erected after Louis Saint Jean drowned there in 1820, was still standing. The party forged onwards to Isle à la Crosse. At Methye River – just before the infamous portage – Back received a note from Franklin saying the advanced party had met the other half of the expedition coming from York Factory. They had taken only a week to carry 116 loads, each weighing about ninety pounds, as well as the boats, across the ten-mile portage. For the Royal Marines and Argyll men this was a stark introduction to northern river travel.

As Back so often did on the previous expedition, he complains bitterly to his journal about the mosquitoes and sandflies, now thriving again in the warmth of burgeoning spring: 'we were tormented by those unceasing labourers after Blood, the Mosquitos, and the Men who had merely a Blanket to cover them were literally groaning with Pain the whole Night.' After sleepless tossing and turning, the men shouted, '*Allons puisqu'ils nous mangoient, il faut chanter* – let's go because they'll eat us, we must sing', and drew away from shore with a paddling song. Eventually they lashed the canoes together and drifted, trying to get some sleep, but those little 'haters of rest' continued plaguing them.

As respite from the bugs Back strolled along a sandy beach and went for a swim, leaving a loaded gun beside his clothes. After a quarter of an hour in the water he emerged to find a wolf watching him from thirty yards away. The wolf frisked about, so Back imitated its frolicking while reaching for his gun. It misfired three times. The wolf, Back tells, 'growing tired of such useless ceremony was quietly walking into the Woods, by which time I had changed the Flint and gave him a parting Shot as he was turning into a thick Bush'.

After an easy run down the Clearwater and Athabasca Rivers the expedition reached Fort Chipewyan – well known to Back from his 1820 winter snowshoe journey. Franklin was waiting for them there, having sent Richardson ahead to Great Slave Lake. Back reports: 'I, of course, delivered to our friend Capt. Franklin the Minutes of our Journey . . . and had the pleasure to receive his entire approbation of my conduct.' He had a little explaining to do, however, over the broken instruments and the parlous state of his canoes. Some Montreal voyageurs were now discharged to return home.

Back wandered round old haunts, remarking: 'There is something indescribably pleasing in revisiting Places that had once been familiar with you and in again contemplating the hopes and fears with which such objects are associated.'

During the descent of the Slave River they had to portage a bad section of rapids below which the Salt River entered. The salt had fascinated Back five years before, so they revisited the salt deposits and took on a good supply of this valuable stuff.

At Fort Resolution the factor, their old friend McVicar, laid on a dance for the men who, as Back put it, 'though they had scarcely ceased paddling for the last 48 hours complained bitterly of being quite knocked up'. After a few glasses of grog they danced until 3 a.m., 'as if they had been preparing a week for it'. Franklin and Back were also delighted to meet two Indian friends (both brothers of Akaitcho), Humpy and old Keskarrah, father of Greenstockings whom Back had lost to Hood. Franklin presented both men with a medal, to their evident delight, and left an even bigger one with McVicar to give to Akaitcho.

The voyageurs were anxious about going farther down the Mackenzie for fear of Eskimos about whom evil stories were circulating. But Back reassured them that they would be allowed to return after reaching Great Bear Lake because 'we did not wish them either to be grilled by an Esquimaux or swallowed by a Bear and therefore Mon. le Capitaine [Franklin] would allow them to return.'

They now cheerfully put up sail and traversed to Big Island at the west end of Great Slave Lake where they began to descend the Mackenzie River.

CHAPTER 13

Down the Mackenzie

1825–26

The western termination of the Rocky Mountains, Mount
Copleston, Aug. 5, 1826. Drawn by Back, engraved by Finden.

For Franklin, Richardson and Back, the prospect of floating slowly
down the wide muddy Mackenzie River was very different from their
situation of five years before when they set off into the Barrens. Then
they followed crystal clear, tumbling rivers through countless big
and small lakes, into country of unimaginable wilderness (as most
Canadians still view it). The Mackenzie is Canada's longest river, in
North America only the Mississippi is longer. It is generally one
mile broad, three miles in some places, and trends north west almost
in a straight line towards the Arctic Ocean. It flows in the lee of the
Mackenzie Mountains, which, in part, separate present-day North
West Territories from the Yukon. Eastwards, beyond a smaller chain
of hills (now named the Franklin Mountains), tundra stretches across
the roof of Canada to the shores of Hudson Bay. Halfway along the

Mackenzie, just to the east of the main river, was their intended wintering site on the massive inland sea of Great Bear Lake – as large in area as its vast southern neighbour, Great Slave Lake.

On 2 August 1825 the main expedition launched the boats, Richardson having already gone on ahead in a canoe. With summer winding down and fall in the air berries were abundant. Stunted spruce and poplar on either bank showed that they were heading into the high north. The air was thick with smoke from fires that commonly rage through the boreal forest in summer. Started mostly by lightning strikes, these conflagrations are part of nature's cycle of destruction and renewal, generally best left to burn themselves out. With space to breathe, undergrowth revives and fresh willow shoots provide nutritious browsing, especially for large animals like moose.

The men rafted the canoes together and drifted with the strong current. With sails raised, they made good time to Fort Simpson where the wide Liard River joins the Mackenzie from the west. There they learned from the factor, Edward Smith, that Richardson was only a day ahead. Back writes: 'the turgid and muddy River curling into large Eddies or circling Whirlpools hurried us past the soft or dark green bank of either side.' He mentions the 'porcelain blue' tint of the distant Rocky (Mackenzie) Mountains, through which the Nahanni River carves spectacular gorges.

After only five days on the Mackenzie they reached Fort Norman, upstream from the mouth of the Great Bear River, issuing between jagged limestone hills. This fort became their depot for supplies, which included forty-two bags of pemmican and the plethora of other stores intended for the following summer's journey. There they met their Eskimo interpreter friend, Augustus, who willingly agreed to accompany them again on their journey north. Evidently his traumatic experiences of four years before, which would have deterred many lesser men, had not put him off. During his absence, Augustus had lent his wife to the brother of his friend Junius who died on the last expedition. This gesture was to placate Junius's relations, who were seeking revenge because they suspected Augustus of using witchcraft.

That same season Franklin intended to proceed to the mouth of the Mackenzie. He took Augustus with him in order to give presents to any Eskimos they might meet. Thereby he hoped to make friends and smooth a passage for the main expedition the following summer.

Back received written orders from Franklin to take three canoes to Great Bear Lake, loaded with supplies for building winter quarters. When completed, he would discharge the main party of eighteen voyageurs to return in two canoes to Great Slave Lake where they would winter, since it was too late in the season to make the long journey back to Montreal. Richardson would take a boat to map the eastern end of Great Bear Lake, and explore a possible return route for his party from the Arctic Ocean by way of the lower Coppermine. Peter Dease would remain with Back at the newly named Fort Franklin in order to set up a fishery and to supervise Indian hunters in laying down a store of meat. Again the expedition would depend on others for much of their food. It was as if they had learned nothing from previous experience.

Ascending the Great Bear River against a current required much tracking and poling. On reaching the lake the men immediately saw on its north bank the houses of a fort built the previous winter by the sixteen Argyll seamen under Dease's supervision. They got busy again inside the fort completing a third house which would become the officers' mess.

Fish became the mainstay of their diet. Fish nets set at the lake outflow, which kept the river free of ice, each day produced about a hundred whitefish – some weighing fourteen pounds – and fifty trout, one of which weighed fifty pounds. The hunters were less successful because recently local Indians had embarked on a spree of murdering each other after a Yellow Knife warrior had absconded with, and subsequently killed, a Slave girl. This catalysed a tit-for-tat of slaughter, which Back notes, 'for savage Barbarity stands unequalled'.

The aftermath of distrust was still smouldering when Back occupied the fort, though he took pains to forge his customary good rapport with the Indians. He hired as an interpreter and hunter, François Beaulieu, a mixed blood Indian who was now chief of the Yellow Knives. A colourful character, renowned for terrorizing the Dogribs and Slaves, Beaulieu had accompanied Mackenzie overland to the Pacific Ocean in 1793. He had met Franklin in 1820 and suggested wintering at Great Bear Lake rather than near the head of the Yellowknife River. He once had three wives, but became monogamous when baptized at age seventy-nine; he was still hunting at eighty-five, and died at a hundred.

Both Franklin and Richardson returned from their reconnaissances within a week of each other. During seventeen days absence Richardson had reached the farthest eastern point where a river (which he named after Dease) entered Great Bear Lake. There, only about three days march from the Coppermine River, they cached a canoe for their return the following year.

During their absence, Franklin, Kendall, and Augustus had tasted saltwater from the Arctic Ocean. They had also seen black and white whales spouting, together with plenty of seals – a good portent for food. The Woolwich boats were much more sturdy, and faster, than canoes and in the ocean sailed well with their loose-footed sails, which could easily be double-reefed in a gale.

On their way they met some Loucheux Indians, or Squinters – referring to 'the people who avoid the arrows of their enemies by keeping a look out on both sides', a useful trait because they were generally at war with Eskimos. The traders knew them as Sparkling Eyes, but Alexander Mackenzie called them Quarrellers. Nowadays they are known as Gwich'in. Some Loucheux women took a fancy to Augustus and, Back notes, 'caressed him exceedingly and denoted their joy at anything he said by repeatedly rubbing their hands up and down their thighs'.

At the mouth of the Mackenzie the officers dressed up in full Royal Navy uniform, thereby hoping to impress Eskimos. Not seeing any, however, Franklin left presents at each of their camp-sites. The expedition reached Whale Island and Garry Island, which lay off the mouth of the Mackenzie Delta. There Franklin raised the silk Union Jack embroidered by his late wife, Eleanor, who had given instructions that it was not to be unfurled until the expedition reached the Polar Sea. In a box placed at the foot of the flag he left letters and 'a statement of our proceedings' in case Captain Parry should pass by in *Fury* on his final attempt to navigate the North West Passage. In fact at that time he was icebound in Prince Regent Inlet at Fury Beach on the east side of the Boothia Peninsula. The men also launched a waterproof box containing a copy of their letters into the sea. Franklin collected some bituminous coal, which he put in his pocket where it corroded a copper powder flask – fortunately without exploding. Then they all turned round to track upriver to Fort Norman, and thence to their new winter quarters on Great Bear Lake.

Fort Franklin – as it was newly named – was built on a sandy bank where the old NWC post used to stand. The site, chosen by Dease, looked naked because all nearby trees had been previously cut down for lumber. Omitted from Back's drawing of the fort is a stockade, which gave protection from drifting snow (rather than marauders). The men upturned the boats on a bank above the lake and covered them with branches to let snow drift over and insulate them.

The hall, measuring forty-four by twenty-two feet, was a substantial log building chinked with mud. It had a chimney, a floor of whipsawed plank, wooden doors and parchment windows (later replaced by six panes of glass ordered from Fort Chipewyan). The men decorated it with flags, and mounted caribou heads on a wall where Back painted a Crown & Anchor. Officers' bedrooms led off the hall – one for Franklin and Richardson, one each for Back and Kendall, and one for Dease and his family. Behind the hall stood a kitchen. There were also two bunkhouses for the men, two storerooms, a blacksmith's shop and an observatory with a tall flagpole nearby. Certainly it was more comfortable than Fort Enterprise, even in the latter's heyday in the winter of 1820–21.

They all celebrated completing the fort with a party. Present were British seamen, Scots Highlanders, French Canadian voyageurs, Indians, an Eskimo (Augustus) and only three women. The men paraded in single file behind the piper, fired a musket volley, and then each received a dram of grog. Until the wee hours of the morning they danced cotillions and reels to the music of violins and bagpipes, and played party games like blind man's buff and hide the handkerchief. Back put on a puppet show.

Nights were closing in, and Back records in his journal: 'The manner of passing a Winter in this Country is usually of such dull uniformity and so destitute of any novelty to enliven it, that a recapitulation of daily occurrences would be equally as tedious, as it must necessarily be prolix.' Since trees were scarce near the fort, men were sent some distance across the lake to cut timber. They were then split into two parties and sent off to build huts at different fishing spots where fish abounded. But there were too many people at the fort to subsist solely on fishing. As in 1820, the hunters were singularly unsuccessful, and the same old story emerged of Indians not having enough food for both their large complement at the fort, and all the hangers on.

Highlights of the short daylight hours were skating and games of ice hockey (possibly the first international event). Every alternate evening from seven to nine o'clock officers held school for the men, who were divided into small groups for tuition in reading, writing and arithmetic. Richardson gave a series of eleven weekly geology lectures, probably over the heads of most attendees. The officers wrote up their scientific observations each in his special field of interest. Back finished off his sketches, using colour notations he had added in pencil in the field, when time and temperature did not permit a completed painting.

For relaxation, officers played chess, and men joined in party games. They all spent Sundays 'in quietness and devotion'. Franklin read divine service both morning and evening, as was his regular habit (even when starving on the Barrens). Every man had to attend and, believe it or not, they 'evinced the most rigid attention to the holy doctrine, and the Day closed in Harmony and Peace'.

Throughout the winter they were visited by various groups of Indians, besides those 'lethargic, improvident, miserable and lazy' Dogribs, who permanently hung around the fort hoping to be fed. Some Hare Indians arrived with a sick child, who soon died despite Richardson's attention. Back was touched by how, towards the grieving mother, they 'observed an unusual silence that bespoke their sympathy better than all the useless attempts of condolence that worldly Erudition could invent'. Nevertheless infanticide was not uncommon among some Indian women, especially Dogribs, during a severe winter when food was scarce. Back calls it 'one of the most revolting and bitterest Crimes against Nature'.

The winter so far was less cold than the former one at Fort Enterprise, and auroras and parhelia were particularly vivid. Christmas and New Year rolled around and were excuses for another party, with the whole complement of the fort present — fifty-eight persons, including women and children. The Indians were especially intrigued by a game of snapdragon where players tried to snatch raisins out of a bowl of burning brandy, and eat them while still alight. A package of letters, newspapers, and magazines arrived from England, but Indians had rifled some of them on the way. The news they bore raised everyone's spirits and, Back says, 'gave a fresh Fillip to our little party'. Though hardly light reading – *Quarterly Review*, *Edinburgh Philosophical Journal*, *Literary Gazette*, *Mechanics Magazine* – they gave the officers something new to talk about and staved off incipient cabin fever, common in those who winter in cold, dark latitudes.

By February 1826 they were running low on food. Dried meat was finished, and fish stocks had dwindled to three or four herrings per man per day; dogs got none. Some men were sent down to Fort Norman to collect pemmican, arrowroot and portable soup. This mirrored the desperate food shortage at Fort Enterprise that developed in spring of 1820, despite Franklin's careful planning and his previous experience of unreliable Indian hunters. However, caribou returned to the neighbourhood in March, and Beaulieu kept sledges continually busy fetching meat. At the same time St Germain, who was hunting successfully at Fort Norman, asked for more men to help him.

At Great Slave Lake some Red Knife Indians told McVicar that the previous autumn they had stumbled on a saw pit where squared logs lay around, a saw hung from a tree, and axes were strewn on the ground. Also they claimed to have found the carcass of a caribou killed with buckshot. The Yellow Knives deduced that this was evidence of Europeans since saws and buckshot were not trade items, and neither Eskimos nor Indians used buckshot. If they were correct, Franklin questioned, who were they other than some of Captain William Parry's crew wintering in Bathurst Inlet?

This hearsay led to endless speculation about the chances of Richardson and Kendall meeting Parry the next summer as they cruised along the Arctic coast towards the mouth of the Coppermine. Richardson even made a bowl of treacle punch and celebrated the news by drinking a toast to the health of Captain Parry. But McVicar scotched debate by saying, correctly, that the whole story was a fabrication of Indian rumour mongers.

April was now well advanced, and with daily thaws the country was beginning to show signs of spring. Richardson and Kendall set off with dog teams to survey the south side of Great Bear Lake. The carpenters refitted *Lion* and prepared *Dolphin* and *Union*, the three Woolwich boats which had both been laid up for winter. They then laid the pine keel of a new twenty-six-foot boat *Reliance*, and made timbers for it from birch trees cut at Fort Norman. The blacksmith forged nails of iron, instead of copper, and made other ironwork from spare axes and chisels melted down over a charcoal brazier. Some men made new sails, masts, rigging and poles for the coming voyage; others sewed trousers and warm clothing. Back writes: 'there now appeared every possibility of our quitting Fort Franklin in as perfect a state as we should have done from one of His Majesty's Dock yards.'

By May ducks, swans and geese were returning to patches of open lake water, along with Back's bane, mosquitoes, against which he once more rails continually. Willows and dwarf birch were in bud, and dark woods 'exchanged their cold sombre hue for a beautiful lively green'.

At Franklin's suggestion two voyageurs, Felix and Vivier, volunteered to join the crews now that two boats each were ready for both parties for the coming summer. In June, Back composed a letter to his brother Charles, using cross-writing which, although almost unreadable, created an elegant effect. In it Back uses bombast one might expect of Franklin, rather than the poetic, straightforward prose of which he is capable. He talks of the past winter as 'wrap't in a Halo of unanimity and happiness . . . without a murmur, aye, even without an insinuating Hint of discontent'. Of the coming expedition, he says they are 'relying firmly on the support of Almighty Providence, we shall encounter the Trials of this voyage with the Zeal and Spirit of our profession, and I trust with Honour to our beloved Country'.

Brothers usually write to each other in a more down-to-earth style. But Back's obsequious formality may have something to do with his political manoeuvring: 'Of my promotion I say nothing,' he writes, 'uncertain as I am of great Men's favours, for the two Maxims of any great Man at Court is "Always to keep his countenance and never to keep his word."'

The parties got ready to quit Fort Franklin, but even then – just past the solstice – large chunks of ice still blocked the Great Bear River. Peter Dease stayed behind in charge until their return, they hoped later that autumn. On reaching the junction with the Mackenzie they observed that spring runoff had raised the river six feet. This caused such a strong current that men had to track the boats in soft clayey mud nearly thirty miles upriver to Fort Norman (the present fort is at the river junction). There they loaded supplies for the coming months together with gifts for any Eskimos they might meet. They passed the place where permanently burning bituminous wood-coal emitted flashes of fire, and columns of smoke and steam rose from fissures in the ground.

On 28 June 1826 the crews left Fort Norman and set off in high spirits down the Mackenzie, nursing vicious homebrew hangovers after another wild boozy party. Nevertheless, they proudly paraded their new sky-blue and red waterproof uniforms (thanks to Mr Macintosh) with 'two appropriate feathers' – use uncertain. His Majesty's Row Boats – decorated with ensigns and pendants – were bound once again for the Polar Sea. *Lion* and *Reliance* carried Franklin and Back respectively, together with fourteen British seamen, Augustus, and two voyageurs. Richardson and Kendall followed in *Dolphin* and *Union* with ten men and Ooglibuck, another Eskimo interpreter. During winter the carpenters had built a barge solely to carry the bulk of freight downriver as far as the braided delta of the Mackenzie.

The men hoisted both mainsail and foresail to help push the boats, along with the current, down the river. At that point it was from two to four miles wide, and with many islands midstream. A huge volume of water flowed through steep limestone hills on either side, the higher ones to the west rising towards the Mackenzie Mountains.

The boats shot the rapids of the Ramparts without trouble, high meltwater having ironed out whitewater that appears later in the season when river levels drop and protruding boulders create rough rapids. Back describes 'innumerable fantastic forms resembling Turrets, Archways and the ruins of old Castles', where the upwards incline of horizontal limestone strata gave an optical illusion of going downhill as though approaching a large waterfall. This was, he says laconically, 'well calculated to create alarm to novices'.

At Fort Good Hope they met a party of Loucheux Indians. Franklin asked one of them to draw in the sand a map of where they were going, because he was unsure which of the myriad channels of the delta to follow. The map, however, left him none the wiser since the Loucheux themselves were obviously not sure of the local geography.

The river sped between 250-foot perpendicular cliffs of the Narrows, and the boats raced on through with it. They then approached Red River with the Richardson Mountains lying to the west. Recently a brief but bloodless quarrel had broken out there between Loucheux and several hundred Eskimos who were bartering furs. Since the British were entering the heart of Eskimo country, they all checked their guns, powder, and ammunition because, as Franklin noted: 'Vigilance and precaution are never to be omitted in intercourse with strange tribes.'

Franklin decided to split the party in two at Separation Point where the river began to braid into two channels. Richardson and Kendall's boats would follow the eastern branch, Franklin and Back's the western. They stashed the freight barge in some bushes in case they should lose any of their boats and need it in emergency on their return. Also they left a kettle and a towline for tracking upriver to Fort Norman.

Before taking leave of each other, the whole expedition drank a glass of grog and danced to bagpipes, not knowing whether they would meet before 'being again united in Old England'. Franklin's crew were hoping to meet Beechey in *Blossom* near the Bering Strait and, if successful, return with him to Britain via China. It was an emotional, but buoyant, parting in one of the most remote places on earth. Each man, recalling the tragic events of four years before, must have wondered what Fate held in store.

CHAPTER 14

Eskimo Affrays

1826–27

Portraits of two Eskimo interpreters by Back.

The expedition now ventured onto the Arctic Ocean, this time in strong boats provisioned for three months instead of, as previously, in birchbark canoes with inadequate supplies. The contrast to 1821 must have felt profound to all who had partaken in that disastrous journey. Sails helped push *Lion* and *Reliance*, with Franklin and Back respectively as skippers, along the winding braided western channel of the Mackenzie River. Usually the men slept under an awning of sails in or near the boats; the officers occupied tents and always posted a sentry. Whenever they came to a prominent point, Franklin left a visible hoard of gifts. On mid-stream islands they observed lobsticks – Eskimo signals made of trees with the lower branches lopped off leaving only a bushy tuft on top. Soon they were shrouded in fog, which typically clings to the Arctic coast. Whenever they lit a fire ashore to warm a brew of pemmican, the permafrost under the fire thawed creating a muddy morass.

On 7 July *Lion* and *Reliance* passed a large Eskimo camp situated on an island, but because the water was so shallow they had to stand a mile offshore. Augustus shouted greetings to the Eskimos in their own language, which is common across the Arctic. Three old chiefs launched kayaks, paddled out towards the boats, and stopped within speaking distance.

The Eskimos first asked if the visitors were friends. Augustus reassured them they were, and invited them repeatedly to come closer so as to accept presents. He explained that the White Men's purpose was to discover if the channel was deep enough for the passage of large ships, which would bring to the Eskimos all sorts of gifts. At this news the three chiefs whooped with joy and offered to barter their knives, and also the ornaments piercing their cheeks and encircling their arms.

The river was soon alive with a flotilla approaching from every direction. Franklin stopped counting after seventy-three kayaks and five umiaks (larger boats holding six to eight women each, plus children). Their occupants crowded round the boats offering to barter their bows and arrows, and spears, which had so far remained hidden in their kayaks. During the ensuing pandemonium Franklin and Back enquired about the coastline ahead, but with exciting trade afoot the Eskimos were in no mood for such mundane discussion.

The atmosphere was becoming fraught among the growing crowd of Eskimos, who now completely surrounded the expedition boats. The tide was ebbing, and Franklin ordered his men to put to sea so they could escape if necessary. At which point *Lion* ran aground on a sandbar, so Back passed a rope from *Reliance* to pull her off. The Eskimos helped drag her free but warned the officers that the whole bay was equally shallow.

During this manoeuvre one of *Lion*'s oars accidentally upset an Eskimo paddler, who fell headfirst into the mud and nearly drowned. The crew quickly pulled him out and put him into their own boat while they emptied the water out of his kayak. Augustus noticed him shivering with cold, so wrapped him in his own greatcoat. Realizing that *Lion* was full of trade goods, the Eskimo demanded everything he laid eyes on, and became angry when refused. Franklin ordered all gear to be stowed out of sight, including a furled Union Jack, which the man evidently fancied. Meanwhile one of *Lion*'s crew reported that the Eskimo was hiding under his shirt a pistol stolen from Back. Having been detected, the Eskimo jumped into the water, taking with him Augustus's greatcoat and the pistol.

The tide was ebbing fast and several young Eskimo men waded out in the now knee-deep water. They surrounded the boats and stole anything they could grab, even trying to cut buttons off the sailors' uniforms. Franklin ordered ashore two chiefs who were sitting in *Lion*, on the pretext that the expedition had to leave in order to meet a ship which would return with many more goods for barter. At first the chiefs seemed pleased and invited the officers to land so as to carry on further business. They then jumped out of the boat and ran up the beach to tell their companions about possible forthcoming riches.

Once free of the shoal, the sailors dragged *Reliance* and *Lion* towards the beach. Three large Eskimos jumped on board *Lion*; one sat on either side of Franklin, a third in front of him. They seized Franklin's wrists and pinned his arms so he could reach neither his gun nor his dagger. Many of their armed fellows surrounded the two boats and pilfered anything they could find, handing the loot back to women on the beach. Back and his crew on *Reliance* tried amicably to stop them but were overpowered by greater numbers. One chief drove away the marauders, who cut the anchor buttons off Franklin's waistcoat and carried off his writing desk and a cloak.

Meanwhile *Lion*'s crew sat on the canvas cargo cover and beat off with their rifle butts the prying hands of Eskimos, who this treatment barely bothered. Franklin, released from bondage, went ashore with Augustus to try to calm the situation. But Duncan, the coxswain, recalled his boss when a horde of knife-brandishing Eskimos renewed stealing from *Lion*, passing trophies back to their companions. Duncan tied the box of astronomical instruments to his leg so, if the Eskimos wanted them, they would have to drag him away too. Franklin was worried lest they lose the oars or masts, guns, ammunition and knives – any of which would be disastrous to their onward journey. Finally several Eskimos jumped aboard and tried to disarm the crew. Back persuaded the chief to drive the intruders off *Reliance* and to go to Franklin's aid on *Lion*.

Marine Wilson, ever quick on the draw, was about to fire his musket at an Eskimo, who promptly sliced through his coat and waistcoat, nearly cutting down to flesh. The Eskimos were about to seize Franklin's gun, when Back ordered his crew to take aim. The intruders panicked, fled up the beach, and hid behind a pile of driftwood. This afforded both crews an opportunity to refloat the boats and row away. Despite this prolonged standoff, and the duress of it, the British officers remained restrained and did not fire a shot. Had they done so the Eskimos would eventually have over-whelmed, and undoubtedly slaughtered, all of the party.

The Eskimos meanwhile jumped into their kayaks in pursuit, but backpaddled when Augustus shouted to them that Franklin would shoot the first man who came within range. During this fracas, which lasted well into the evening, the Eskimos took the mess canteen, kettles, a tent, blankets, and shoes, and the jib sails, as well as some gifts, which they would have received anyway. The chief, having returned the stolen writing desk and cloak, returned and sat on Back's knees repeating to his fellow Eskimos the warning 'Tima (peace)'.

A quarter mile beyond the point the boats grounded again. In case of another attack, the crew lashed the gunwales together side-by-side and sat, guns cocked, waiting to be refloated by the rising tide. Some Eskimos came down to the beach and invited Augustus ashore for a discussion. He accepted, but chided them for their bad behaviour and warned them that the British crew would fire if they were attacked again – and next time their guns would kill. Franklin ordered the Eskimos to return the large kettle and the tent as a show of goodwill. This done, Augustus joined them in some wild dancing and singing. But several valuable stolen articles were still missing, particularly a kettle of gum, which was badly needed to repair boats along the treeless coast.

A few crewmen went ashore to build a fire and make hot chocolate, which they offered to some curious Eskimos, who promptly spat it out. By midnight a rising tide refloated the boats so the men could haul them to a safe spot six miles along the beach. The officers posted watch while the exhausted men slept till nearly midday. Then they began repairing sails and rigging damaged in the ruckus. Back noticed 'the horizon darkened by canoes' of another band of Eskimos paddling towards them, so he ordered the boats to be launched into the comparatively safety of deep water.

The leading kayaker held out the kettle, and called out that, in exchange for gifts, he would return these and other stolen goods following behind with the women. Not trusting the Eskimos, Franklin told Augustus to order them to stay away. But they came on regardless, so Franklin fired a warning shot across the bow of the leading kayak, whereupon they all turned round and returned to their camp. Thus ended an anxious day – perhaps the most eventful of the whole expedition – of which Augustus was the undisputed hero.

A breeze got up and *Lion* and *Reliance* ran swiftly along the shore away from aptly named Pillage Point. Back noted how such 'An open Sea and a fair Wind' is every sailor's dream. Soon the men faced a barrier of ice pushed into pressure ridges thirty to forty feet high, and stretching way out into the ocean. Some Eskimos told them that the westering shore was usually choked with ice all summer, and that the present barrier would only shift with a rare southerly wind. They advised the British officers to travel along the coast by dog team because pack ice could easily crush the boats. Franklin admits in his journal that it was a mistake not to follow their advice.

So the expedition made fitful progress along the Arctic coast, owing to barriers of drift ice, gales, and fog. In addition, landing was difficult on shelving shingle and shallow muddy foreshore. Inland the ground, being swampy and tussocky, was hard to walk over. They passed Points Sabine, King, Kay, and Stokes before reaching Herschel Island, which stands off the narrow strip of northern Yukon coast. Far inland the Richardson and British Mountains were constantly in view.

All along the coast small groups of Eskimos appeared apparently out of nowhere, and were always manifestly pleased to accept gifts. However, their limited knowledge of local geography was of little help in planning any advance. They warned Franklin and Back about their evil eastern neighbours with tattooed cheeks, and offered to escort them to the mouth of the Mackenzie on their return journey. Meanwhile the Eskimos were going to sea to hunt whales and seals.

In fits and starts dictated by the position of the sea ice, the expedition wended its way along the Yukon coast. Whenever they passed a point they found Eskimo huts built of driftwood stuck in the ground with roots upright. Judging by their knives and beads, the Eskimos must have travelled far to the west to trade with Russian middlemen, who had been on the Alaskan coast since 1784.

Augustus dressed up in his ornaments and his 'properly chief coat' in order to impress the Eskimos. Later he put on a marine's uniform and strutted about in front of an astonished audience, greatly improving relations between them and the expedition. According to Back, the Eskimos were so impressed by Augustus conversing with them, that 'on expressing his desire to have a "Wife", the boon was immediately granted and he was gratified in his amorous inclinations the same night.' Lucky fellow. During pillow talk Augustus successfully negotiated recovering the horn protractor, which Back had seen an Eskimo woman pick up during the earlier melee. Augustus was absent without leave longer than expected – even allowing for his newly acquired bedmate – and eventually he turned up with the precious instrument at 4 a.m., 'much fatigued with his long walk'.

For ornamentation, the Eskimos pierced the septum of their broad noses with a sliver of white bone or shell, and set a large blue glass bead in a circular piece of ivory, which protruded from either side of their lower lip. They dressed in caribou or seal skin breeches and jackets (hooded and with a long skirt behind), and sealskin boots. From a distance Back – as usual – noted the young women's pretty faces, but observed that they were short in stature, and fat. Back made some sketches of the Eskimos, who thought he had a magic pencil. In fact, he was using a camera lucida, a cunning device that uses a four-sided prism to bring the object, or view, and the drawing paper into the same apparent plane. The observer can then see, apparently lying on the paper, an image which he can trace. However, it is extremely tricky to use because, by looking over the outer edge of the prism, the observer has to place his eye so that half of his pupil received the scene while the other half looks directly down at his pencil on the sketch book to which the instrument is mounted firmly on a brass rod stand. But it would also have had to be anchored to some secure surface – a difficult task in the Barrens. Back, as a midshipman artist, would have learned and practised this technique, and frequently used it when sketching, especially landscapes. He also impressed the Eskimos by using a magnifying lens to set alight a wood shaving.

Despite fall approaching, Back still deplores the mosquitoes, even building a fire inside his tent to smoke them out. The men frequently saw seals, which would have been an invaluable addition to their diet, but they were too far off to shoot. 'Some Seals and a Wolf were seen but none of us were expert enough to approach them,' Back reports. 'We fired at 3 or 4 Seals but killed none,' and again: 'a few Seals were seen but were too cautious to come within shot.' Where was Augustus, who certainly should have known how to hunt seals? Surely not busy all the time with Eskimo ladies? Even more surprising is that the British officers *still* had not learned to hunt. It was just fortunate that on this journey they were not starving.

At Demarcation Point, longitude 141° West, the boundary between Russia (now Alaska) and Great Britain (Yukon), they hoisted the Union Jack on a pole set in a cone of driftwood, and left a message buried in a tin at its foot, reporting the expedition's progress. But that progress was mighty slow and laborious owing to the ice that, more often than not, closed any open leads, so the men were 'obliged to try a thousand different methods to attain the miserable pittance of a few yards'. Only a rare south wind could blow the ice pack offshore, so they frequently had to jump into freezing water and drag the boats across muddy shallows. Constant immersion in cold water caused painful chilblains and rheumatism in their joints. The dreary scenery was matched only by Franklin's dreary encomiums as he named every geographical feature, significant or not.

At Point Manning Augustus hailed an Eskimo camp, whereupon a 'jolly plump Female arrayed in that simple and primitive garb which adorned our first parents' appeared from one of the tents, followed by swarms of naked Eskimos, both women and armed men. This must have enlivened the day for a bunch of sex-starved British seamen, 'much fatigued' after pulling at the oars for nineteen hours straight.

The men hauled the boats up on the beach near Lion and Reliance Reef so the carpenter could do some running repairs. In the distance they could see the Romanzoff Mountains (named after the chancellor of the Russian Empire). Thereafter the sailors navigated skilfully along that dangerous shoaly coast through gales, heavy seas and surf, often in dense fog among broken pack ice. The boats had performed incomparably better on open ocean than had the birchbark canoes.

Geese were flying south in V-formation, a sure sign of the onset of winter; caribou of the Porcupine herd which migrates from Alaska across the northern Yukon would follow at the first snow-flake. This inhospitable coast was no place to be stranded for a winter, and Franklin's Admiralty Instructions stated plainly that if he was unsure of reaching Kotzebue he should turn around between 15 and 20 August. It was now 16 August and they were only halfway between the mouth of the Mackenzie and their intended rendezvous with Beechey in *Blossom* at Icy Cape (which Captain James Cook had sighted in 1778).

To everyone's relief, Franklin ordered turnaround at Return Reef just beyond Prudhoe Bay. Across Gwydyr Bay they could see yet another point jutting into this featureless coastline; Franklin named it 'after my excellent companion Lieutenant Back'.

Doubtless swayed by memories of his disastrous retreat of five years before, reason won out at a point 'beyond which perseverance would be rashness'. The western party had travelled 374 miles without finding a single harbour suitable to shelter a large ship, a fact that did not bode well for a North West Passage route.

In fact, simultaneously, Beechey had sent forward from Icy Cape a barge commanded by his mate, Thomas Elson, who reached beyond Point Barrow after numerous brushes with shipwreck.

As Franklin wrote: 'Could I have known . . . that a party from the Blossom had been at a distance of only one hundred and sixty miles from me, no difficulties, dangers or discouraging circumstances should have prevailed on me to return [to the Mackenzie].'

At Foggy Island, just east of Point Anxiety, the men built a cairn of driftwood surmounted by a flagpole, and at the foot of it buried a round tin box with another letter for Captain Edward Parry, should he pass this way heading for China. It also contained a large silver medal embossed with George III's head, and a halfpenny donated by Royal Marine Corporal Hatton. Below a hoisted red flag they left various ice chisels, knives, and small presents, free for taking by any passing Eskimos.

Next morning they got away from Foggy Island 'with the most sincere wishes never to behold it more on this occasion'. With a following wind they made good speed, despite having to run well offshore through the same drift ice as before. Navigating through the narrow, fog-shrouded channel behind Herschel Island was a nightmare, since they knew there were reefs and shoals on either side.

The boats ran double-reefed in a 'perfect gale' and heavy seas off King Point. 'The most severe storm came on that we had almost ever witnessed,' wrote Back (not usually prone to exaggerate), 'which was terrible to behold against the contrasted horror of the sky.' Franklin described the waves: 'raised as I had never before been exposed to in [an open] boat'. Violent, whistling squalls of sleet and snow churned the sea into white foam, and the boats were in danger of being swamped by waves breaking over the stern. The men had to bail constantly as they headed for the safety of shore. Such storms were common in the fall when Eskimos usually sheltered in the mouths of big rivers, the only calm places along the coast, also suitable for hunting whales and seals. Both officers praised unsparingly their cool and fearless crews.

All along the coast small family groups of Eskimos hailed them, no doubt hoping the foreigners would land and offer more of the same gifts they had distributed so liberally on their outward journey. At one camp Augustus went ashore to greet some families he had met previously. These people told him how they had met some Eskimos from the Pillage Point fracas, who had apparently become agitated on seeing the crew brewing hot chocolate after the celebration dance. They openly regretted having allowed their quarry and its treasures to escape. On finding them stranded, they planned to kill the whole party, including Augustus. However, they could not agree on whether to murder their blood brother because, if they did so, White Men might stop coming with gifts. Having decided not to spare even Augustus, they offered the kettle as a ruse showing their willingness to return the stolen trophies. Apparently this was merely a delaying tactic, since they intended to attack next morning, having recruited more of their fellows so they could surprise the white men and overpower them. But Franklin had judged the situation shrewdly and not been taken in.

Both boats' crews landed beyond Point Sabine and pitched camp. The men recognized some 7 July pillagers, one of whom was even wearing Vivier's leather trousers, which he swore he had bought from some Indians. The officers, no longer trusting any Eskimos, ordered a round-the-clock guard on their camp.

Two Eskimos returned in late afternoon warning that two or three miles away a large war party of Mountain Indians (different from Loucheux) armed with guns and bows had gathered, apparently planning to attack the expedition that night. The Mountain Indians, who did business annually on Herschel Island, were anxious lest the expedition should threaten their monopoly of trade with Russians in Alaska.

Because they were vulnerable to attack in a shallow bay most of the seamen, guns at the ready, spent the night in the boats with the gunwales lashed together, while only a few men went ashore to cook an evening meal. When the tide eventually let them get away, water in the narrow channel was still so shallow that the men had to drag the boats for about three miles with their legs immersed in freezing water.

Now abreast of Pillage Point, they pushed on into the Mackenzie Delta's main western branch where seal and whale hunters had assembled. Soon they were among willows in autumnal tints of gold and yellow, and evergreen pine and spruce they had not seen for a couple of months. They made a false detour a short way up the Peel River before realizing that it was flowing out of the Richardson Mountains and was therefore not the main Mackenzie. *Reliance* entered a small channel and broke its pintle on a submerged fallen tree.

At Separation Point the crew found, still untouched, their cached boat and gear hidden in the willows. They left a letter and a bag of pemmican for Richardson, in case his party had been unable to return to Fort Franklin by way of the Coppermine and the east end of Great Bear Lake. By tracking, rowing, and occasionally sailing, they made good time past Fort Good Hope and the Ramparts, where a strong current caused them 'a hard fag'.

Tracking up the Great Bear River took four days. On 21 September 1826, they sailed across the lake towards Fort Franklin with flags flying. There they met Kendall, who told them that he and Richardson had arrived three weeks before, and that the doctor had gone ahead to Great Slave Lake to complete his natural history studies. Their journey eastwards along the coast had been a complete success – and without a single accident. Of both parties combined three months absence, Back later wrote: 'Our united discovery is about 1,700 miles, and the [total] distance travelled will be near 10,000.'

Dease had evidently met little success in getting the 'indolent Indian hunters' to lay down any store of meat for the coming winter. But instead of attending to this, the officers set about winterizing the Fort Franklin house in order to make themselves more comfortable. In October they received a packet of mail from England telling of Parry's safe return, and of Back's promotion to the rank of commander.

They all settled down to hear Kendall's account of his and Richardson's journey in *Dolphin* and *Union*. The eastern party had the advantage of running before the prevailing northwesterly winds, which gave them a comparatively straightforward passage apart from the ubiquitous 'hazard of being overset by pieces of buoyant ice which frequently broke off from the bases of the floes'. Two icebergs nearly crushed *Dolphin*, and Back adds: 'In the language of the whalers, the ice is said to calf.'

Richardson records in his journal a similar contretemps to that of Franklin and Back's party at Pillage Point. Some Eskimos followed their boats in canoes, closed in on either side of them, laid hold of the gunwales, and lifted the oars out of the water so the crew could not row. The British officers and the coxswain beat them off. Undeterred, however, the Eskimos then tried to steal anything they could lay their hands on 'with all the coolness of a practised thief'. The crew primed their guns, but fortunately did not fire. On another occasion Kendall slipped and fell on his knife, which pierced his chest over his heart. Luckily it only hit a rib and the wound healed in a few days.

Richardson's naming of places was as toadying as Franklin's: 'bestowed the name in honour of . . . received the appellations of . . . was distinguished by the name of . . .' – and so on. Evidently he deeply admired his boss and wrote: 'having served under Captain Franklin for nearly seven years in two successive voyages of discovery . . . the hold he acquires upon the affections of those under his command by a continued series of the most conciliating attentions to their feelings, and an uniform and unremitting regard to their best interests is not less conspicuous. I feel that the sentiments of my friends and companions Captain Back and Lieutenant Kendall, are in unison with my own.' Coming from a man of Richardson's proven integrity, this tribute appears profoundly genuine. Whatever one may think of Franklin's method – or lack of it – he undoubtedly had an uncanny ability to lead his men willingly to the ends of the earth.

The party reached the mouth of the Coppermine well ahead of schedule and all felt happy about the ease of their voyage. Since both Kendall's chronometers had frozen and broken during the previous winter, he relied on dead reckoning – courses and distances checked by compass bearings each time they changed direction. By the much more complicated method of lunar observation he estimated latitude and longitude every week or so – weather, clear skies, and moon permitting. Nevertheless he produced a map that was out by only twenty seconds over a thousand miles of uncharted coastline – equal to two and a half miles overall.

They started up the Coppermine and soon came to Bloody Fall, where they ditched the boats that had served them so well. Each man set off on foot carrying a seventy-pound load, including the walnut shell coracle designed by Captain Pasley for crossing rivers. By any standards it was still a mighty hike back to Fort Franklin.

They passed Escape Rapids and rounded the bend made by the Coppermine Mountains; then they left the main river at Rocky Defile and struck westwards, following the Kendall River to Dismal Lakes, and crossing the height of land to the headwaters of the Dease, which they had scouted the previous summer. They reached the mouth of the Dease, where it flows into Great Bear Lake, on 24 August, two days before the elapse of their planned rendezvous with Boileau, who had paddled from Fort Franklin in a large canoe. During seventy-one days away they had covered 1,709 miles.

Now the whole expedition had to hunker down for another winter before returning home. Ahead, next spring, still lay another major transcontinental canoe journey – rugged by any standards. Few modern adventurers can truly imagine the toughness of these men, the harsh conditions they lived under, and the distances they covered over unexplored and hostile land and water. Back disposes succinctly of the rigours of the coming winter: 'The occurrences at the house are so destitute of novelty that they may be summed up in the account of the daily fishing or the number of Ribs, Sides, and Legs of Rein Deer that we received, which as they were not palatable to us cannot I should think be interesting to any body else.'

A Christmas party enlivened the winter's boredom with a 'comic piece' written by Back, and a three-night run of his puppet show. New Year was ushered in with another boozy party and a dance.

In Franklin's summary of the expedition's achievements, he writes of his 'deep obligation to Lieutenant Back for his cordial co-operation and for his zealous and unwearied assiduity during [their sea voyage] progress . . . daily delineation of the coast, numerous drawings and collection of plants'. In a personal letter to Back he writes: 'I am happy to have the opportunity of thanking you for your uniform kindness to me personally . . . and of expressing my fervent hope that your Services May be rewarded by promotion.'

Franklin also wrote to the Under Secretary of State at the Colonial Department, Downing Street, hoping that 'Lieut Back and Mr Kendall in particular [will obtain] the promotion which in my opinion those officers most justly merit'. Considering Franklin's and Back's awkward start to the expedition, this recommendation is obviously heartfelt and genuine. They must have made up a lot of ground together on the Polar Sea when, nevertheless, they had plenty of opportunity to fall out because of living close to each other for so long. They appear to have settled down to a mutual tolerance at least, friendship at best.

Back was evidently satisfied with the achievements of their absence of two years and seven and a half months. He expressed his 'unqualified opinion of the existence and practicability of the Passage along the Coast and of my readiness to offer my assistance for the completion of it'.

Back received written instructions from his boss to escort the party to York Factory, Hudson Bay, and thence to England; Franklin was going home via Montreal and New York in reverse of the outward journey. After this unequivocally successful enterprise, they returned to a much quieter reception than that of four years previously when they were the surviving heroes of a consummate disaster.

PART FOUR

INTERLUDE ASHORE

CHAPTER 15

Tour of the Continent

1830–32

Grand Canal, Venice.

In 1830 George Back's spirit was low since he had exhausted all leads to a job of any sort in the navy, let alone gained promotion to captain. On top of the physical strain that he had endured in two consecutive Arctic expeditions, he became unwell and melancholy from continuing disappointment. To avoid dwelling on misfortune and to keep his mind active, he decided to go on a cultural tour of Europe, in order, as he confides to his journal, to 'reap such advantages, as we are told are to be had by travelling among our neighbours'.

The nineteenth-century Grand Tour often had a dual purpose. While the most advertised aim for tourists was to soak up culture and improve themselves in the arts, they frequently also sought sexual adventures. Back gives no indication that the latter was on his agenda; nevertheless, it turned out so.

He kept a detailed journal in a leather-bound notebook written in his immaculate regular spidery copperplate hand. He used no paragraphs, breaks, nor spaces for dates (which are not even underlined). Throughout he frequently breaks into lengthy passages of French (and later, Italian), having evidently kept up a high standard in the language he learned twenty-two years before in prison just across the border of Belgium, where his European journey began.

On 3 August Back set off down the Thames in the cross-channel packet bound for Ostend. It was a rough crossing, during which a timid fellow passenger asked Back, who was tucking into a hearty dinner, whether he thought going out into the 'hump of the sea' was prudent. To which Back comments: 'the most splenetic Man could not have answered no.'

While travelling to Bruges by horse-drawn stagecoach, or diligence, he caught the eye of a young Flemish lady sitting opposite him, 'pretty enough to have served as a model for Rubens'. He asked if he could help lift down her picnic hamper. However, her gluttonous eating manners, especially with lamb cutlets in sauce, soon turned his ardour to disgust. 'For once,' he remarks, 'I saw a handsome creature leave my society with satisfaction.'

On leaving Ghent he sat next to a jolly, pockmarked, rosy-cheeked girl who kept asking the driver to stop for her urgent bladder. Climbing back onto the coach, she wedged herself between Back and his recently acquired travelling companion, Atkinson. Her pockets were full of apples, which dug into them at every jolt of the carriage. With typical midshipman humour, Back tells of the practical jokes – not detailed – that they played on her, 'particularly such as affect the digestive organs'.

Back records visits to numerous churches where he notes his surprise at the indiscriminate mingling of both sexes at mass, and he describes minutely many undistinguished paintings. He passed through Brussels, which had just broken away from the Kingdom of the Netherlands and declared its independence. He crossed the Rhine at Cologne and entered Germany.

In Koblenz he suffered his first attack of piles, which would recur and vex his entire journey. He was so uncomfortable that he asked to see a physician, who ordered medicines and a dozen leeches, saying he would immediately send a woman to apply them. Back presumed she would be an experienced older nurse. However, to his surprise, after an hour, 'in came a well-dressed middle aged Woman with her hair in two large curls, followed by a young Girl, both carrying jugs, towels etc.'

'Which is the Gentleman who desires to be bled?' enquired the nurse, rolling up her sleeves.

'*C'est moi, madame* – It's me,' Back replied. Realizing she meant business, he blurted, '*mais, Mon Dieu, ce n'est pas possible* – but, my God, this can't be.'

Atkinson, who was still in bed, sent the women away, so Back never did get the prescribed treatment, but they both had a good laugh at the thought of Back exposing himself to so decent a woman. Soon he felt better and they continued their boyish pranks, emptying their chamber pots out of the window to shouts of 'gardyloo', and other exchanges of scatological humour. At the same time, his journal prissily refers to the lavatory as 'the room which delicacy forbids me to name'.

Nevertheless, before long his piles returned – as did the nurse. When she applied leeches, Back flinched at her first grasp of what he calls 'the very antipodes of my brain'. He paid her over the odds, and stayed in bed all day feeling miserable. Thereafter, he notes, the chambermaids looked at him 'in a most roguish way'. This uncomfortable event featured large in his memory, even compared with his Arctic privations.

But the problem had not gone away completely, and plagued Back again at an inn near the St Bernard Pass in Switzerland. He sent a lad to fetch some *médecine*, but instead the lad called the *médecin*.

'Sir, you want a physician?' asked the doctor, 'where is the problem?'

'*Ici, en bas*,' replied Back, pointing, 'Here, down below.'

'Perhaps you will allow me to inspect,' said the doctor.

'What for?' Back asked petulantly. Whereupon he discharged the doctor, and ordered some vinegar from the cook, who was upset at Back's suggestion that his fundamental problem might be due to his diet. Almost in the same breath he refers in his journal to a Swedish travelling companion as 'very hypochondriacal'.

Much of Back's account of his continental journey comprises prolix descriptions of his fellow travellers, occasionally interjected with flashes of humour. He most frequently comments on the females next to whom he finds himself sitting. One nice girl who dozed off made frequent body contact with Back as the coach jolted; she suddenly awoke and demanded that the *conducteur* let her change places. On another occasion he was wedged in between two women, one fat, the other thin, which 'did not fail to communicate from my brain to the digestive organ' – an unusual reaction. The females consequently 'fell out of humour' with him.

Back becomes lyrical about crossing the Alps, especially the view of Mont Blanc, 'the icy Queen . . . which appeared in all its grandeur'. He notes how most of the countrywomen had goitrous necks, which he mistakenly attributes to poverty rather than iodine deficiency.

On crossing into Italy several occupants of his coach had a contretemps with the border police. Back's response was: 'an Englishman with a passport, who will not thrust himself into every squabble that chance throws in his way, is perfectly safe and generally respected.' *Plus ça change!* Back's journey continued to Venice where he visited all the tourist attractions by gondola – St Mark's Cathedral, the Bridge of Sighs, and numerous palaces and churches with paintings, which he describes in tedious detail as though he were preparing a definitive guidebook.

In Italy the inns were as awful as those in France. In one of them, Back portrays: 'beds in ridges like Mountains, the dinner execrable, and what preyed most on the delicacy of my friend [male], there was no getting to the *comodo* but by going through the Hall full of both sexes'. Whereupon, with amazing control, he decided to wait till morning.

Back met an Italian grand duke in his palace at Fiesole, in the hills above Florence. They passed two and a half hours discussing polar exploration, during which the duke, to liven the conversation, sent a servant to collect polar books from his library. On listening to a minstrel singing after dinner, Back let down his customary guard and wrote with feeling: 'for a few minutes I forgot the

Admiralty, and every mundane disappointment, wishing for no other talent but the skill of that poor Minstrel.'

In Back's journal, written in Naples, appears one of his most telling entries, reported with tight-lipped British reserve, as if writing an official report for the navy. He starts this paragraph writing with dark ink and a sharp new nib, though the emotion overtakes grammar towards the end.

Little misunderstandings however stale took place between xxxxx and myself which perhaps only rivetted us closer than before, though at some moment I would have given the world to have been quit of her presence, but such importunity and perseverance were beyond my resistance and more than I could have supposed any lady would have used; insomuch that my resolution yielded to them; from the conviction that only the strongest attachment could possibly induce anyone to place herself in a situation that if discovered must damn for ever in the Eye of the World. Yet it was our unhappy and a dissimulating life, and whatever were my other feelings still [illegible] involved gratification, predominated as the day of my departure came on. It was on the 24th of September 1831 that I took my last walk with xxxx under the shady grove of Ilex and Myrtle in the extensive and elegant garden of the Villa Reggio. All the passed was forgiven and new confidence restored.

Back's love affair – presumably with a married woman – allows a glimpse of a man with genuinely sensitive feelings, albeit couched in such cautious language. Back continued his travels fifteen miles south of Naples to witness Mount Vesuvius erupting. A renowned local guide, Salvatore, led a party of clients to visit the Hermitage on the slopes of the volcano, inhabited by one solitary monk. Roped to the guide, Back climbed the volcano, 'by following the Indian method of treading precisely into the footsteps of my predecessor' – a throwback to his Canadian travels.

On reaching the rim of the crater, Back expostulates: 'But oh! who can describe the sight that met my gaze on arriving at the summit – light and darkness, Fire and Thunder, and forky lightning darting amid the gloom.' In the centre of the crater was a small cone from which, at intervals, belched a stream of burning larva and red sand that slowly flowed towards where the party stood. A rumbling made the ground around the crater tremble, as it did some of the more timid clients.

Back descended into the crater with the guide, and they bivouaced there with, as Back confesses, 'thoughts of being blown into atoms by an eruption'. During the night he sat on his cloak, but soon smelled burning; he writes: 'I remembered that I had been in the chill and frigid regions of the Pole, had wintered with the Savage in his desolate haunts, had suffered the frost-biting blast that arrests the blood, and had lived when those with me had perished of famine, and there at that moment I had burnt in the Crater of a Volcano.' This is the second, and last, time that his journal refers to his polar experiences.

At the summit of Vesuvius, Back writes, in the vivid style of Milton:

> the orb of day burst into view and shed a brilliant tinge on the neighbouring Vallies . . . Then indeed on looking down into the abyss below, all its demoniacal horrors were visible at once. It seemed like a tempestuous sea suddenly petrified, 'confusion worse confounded', Wave after wave, Mass upon mass, jagged, splintered and broken, then long even surfaces like large slabs, or the surface of molten led, tinted with brownish yellow, sulphuric and pale livid green, the fizzing of smaller volcanic Apertures, and the Thunder like eruption of the cone in the Centre.

Then he bursts into a long lyrical passage in French, followed by some equally fluent Italian.

The party descended from the volcano and went to visit Pompeii where Back comments prudishly: 'nothing can be more disgusting than the obscene Statues and gross indecencies that have been found [there].'

Back continued to lead the social high life with theatre outings, dinners, and balls. However, he found Neapolitans standoffish – meaning their reluctance to ask him to dance – which he attributes to being a lone foreigner. His wrath gathers, especially towards the ladies of Naples whom he condemns as being illiterate, unfriendly

Wilberforce Falls on the Hood River, by Back

The Mackenzie Delta, painting by Kendall from Franklin's
Second Land Expedition, August 1825

The confrontation on the Mackenzie, 7 July 1826:
Esquimaux coming towards the Boats in Shoal-water Bay, by Back

The Esquimaux pillaging the Boats, by Back. Miraculously, no blood was shed.

Winter Houses of Esquimaux, 12 July 1826, by Back

Launching boats on what is now the Yukon coast of the Beaufort Sea,
painting by Back, 19 July 1826

The long paddle home, upstream: *Rapid in the Mackenzie River*, by Back, September 1826

Portage on Hoarfrost River, by Back, 19 August 1833

Two sketches by Back made in the Chantrey Inlet, at the mouth of what is now the Back River: this is Victoria Headland, done July 29, 1834

Expedition's Boat Beached probably at Cape Beaufort, Chantrey Inlet,
August 17–18, 1834

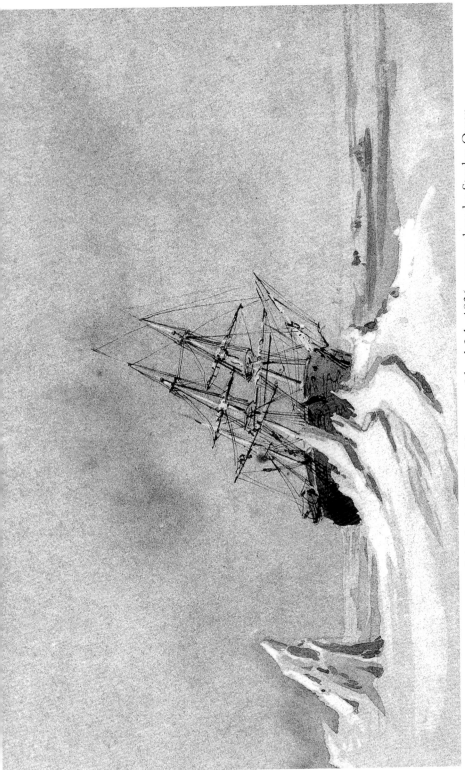

HMS *Terror* stuck in the ice off Southhampton Island, July 1836, watercolour by Stanley Owen

The Arctic Council planning a search for Sir John Franklin, painting by Stephen Pearce, 1851
(from left to right: Sir George Back, Sir William Parry, Edward Joseph Bird, Sir James Clark Ross, Sir Francis Bauforte,
John Barrow, Sir Edward Sabine, William Baillie Hamilton, Sir John Richardson, Frederick Beechey)

and untrustworthy, and having dirty habits (unspecified) among themselves. Finally he rants: 'they do everything too upon calculation, and to get inside of their Houses in the daytime is near to impossible for someone is always on the look out to frustrate your purposes [unspecified].'

Next he rails against the country as a 'Paradise inhabited by Devils', and against its denizens: 'the habits of the habitants of the lower orders are so indecent and so offensive as to be disgusting to our sex, what then ought they not to be to the other?' He went to Rome but, to his disappointment, he could not attend an audience with the Pope because he had not brought his uniform.

Back had been on the road seeking culture for a year and a half; it was obviously time he returned home. This was precipitated by hearing a rumour that brought his journal to an abrupt end and sent him rushing back to London post haste.

PART FIVE

THE GREAT FISH RIVER EXPEDITION

CHAPTER 16

Return to the Barrens

1833

View of the Barren Lands, August 17, 1828. Drawn by Kendall,
engraved by Finden.

In 1832, while George Back was in Naples improving himself in the
arts, and incidentally squiring Mrs xxxx, he had heard a rumour of
anxiety mounting in Britain over the fate of Captain John Ross and
his nephew James. They had not been heard of since setting out
three years before to find the North West Passage. People were
speculating: was their ship *Victory* locked in Arctic ice? Were they
all either in deep trouble – or dead? The bait was too enticing for
Back, still a commander on half pay, aged thirty-seven, and with no
proper Royal Navy job in the offing, and with little prospect of
advancement unless he could think up some dramatic venture to
draw attention to himself. So he hurried home and offered to lead
an expedition in search of Ross and company.

Dr John Richardson had been the first to suggest an overland search expedition, but the Admiralty turned him down because he was not a Royal Navy officer. Nevertheless, they still adopted his idea. Richardson was then director of the gigantic Royal Naval Hospital at Haslar, Portsmouth, where he developed its library and museum, pioneered the use of general anaesthesia on sailors, and improved standards of nursing, especially for psychiatric patients.

George Ross, brother of John and father of James, purloined Richardson's plans with an eye to the chance of thereby making his name. He was also a civilian, so he needed an Admiralty-approved sailor to lead the expedition he was planning. Back was the ideal person. The Admiralty accepted George Ross's proposal to travel overland to Fury Beach where the other Rosses were thought to be icebound, living off stores stashed by Parry in 1825 after he abandoned *Fury*. Back decided on an approach by way of the Thlew-ee-choh-dezeth, or Great Fish River, about which he had learned during Franklin's first land expedition. The Chipewyan Indian, Blackmeat, had then drawn in the sand a river flowing from the east end of Great Slave Lake into the Arctic Ocean.

It is uncertain why Richardson did not offer to accompany Back, with whom he had already shared two previous expeditions. Perhaps that itself was the very reason. Although Richardson is not overtly critical of Back, he evidently found him a prickly and irritating companion. Nonetheless, he generously continued to give Back unstinting help and advice during the planning of the Great Fish enterprise.

The Arctic still fascinated the British public; less so the Admiralty. Yet its recently knighted second secretary, Sir John Barrow, was still scheming to send his 'Boys' north to fill in blanks on the map, especially the few remaining uncharted sections of the North West Passage. Money for mounting expeditions was now scarce since, shortly after Franklin's second expedition, Parliament had repealed an Act of 1818 offering Arctic explorers handsome rewards for significant discoveries.

The necessary cash for the Great Fish River Expedition came through a direct grant of £2,000 from the Lords Commissioners of the Treasury, £3,000 contributed by John Ross's friends, and £800 subscribed spontaneously during a meeting at the Horticultural Society's rooms. The HBC promised 120 bags of pemmican, two boats and two canoes – all free of charge. This was a remarkable turnabout from their previous niggardly attitude.

Lots of people applied to join the expedition, and gratuitous offers of bright ideas and advice were plentiful. A Wiltshire gentleman, J. Lacy, suggested using a one-man balloon for scouting the route ahead – a perfectly sensible theory when applied to the tundra where the view from even a small hillock is endless and from an airplane spectacular. He also proposed flying one or two kites to pull a small car or sledges on frozen rivers – less practical, however, with a prevailing north wind and uneven ground.

Mr H. Clarke, from Winchelsea in Sussex, wrote: 'I am a surgeon, strong and in good health – have middling pluck – am a pretty good shot . . . and perfectly acquainted with the dangers and privations incident to such a life . . . I am not unacquainted with Nat: Hist: – consider myself a pretty good chemist and play the Key-Bugle like an angel, and in a manner that would astonic the Esquimaux Bears. Moreover my services as an Accoucheur might be acceptable to the Esquimaux women.' He was not chosen; but a young doctor, Richard King, was.

King was appointed to the expedition as surgeon and naturalist. He had been apprenticed to the Society of Apothecaries in London, became a student at Guy's Hospital, and then was made a member of the Royal College of Surgeons. He was an abrasive character, variously described as waspish, egotistical, blunt, impetuous, prickly – qualities not destined to make an amenable companion for Back, even though the latter had mellowed considerably with age, and had grown in wisdom if not in stature.

Besides Dr King, Back hired only three men from England, two of whom he knew from the previous Franklin land expeditions; two were shipwrights. The rest he would recruit in Montreal, or from HBC posts in the interior of Canada. He planned to build a base camp at the east end of Great Slave Lake. During the first autumn he would explore to the northeast, and search for the origin of the Thlew-ee-choh using canoes (as suggested by Richardson). He planned to rely on Indian guides and hunters again – had he still not learned his lesson of their fallibility?

After wintering on Great Slave Lake the carpenters would build boats 'combining the qualities requisite for both the river and sea navigation'. Back has been criticized for his choice of such heavy craft. However, with two firsthand experiences of the type of boat capable of handling storms on the Arctic Ocean, he should not be faulted when one remembers the near-disastrous use of canoes there.

At an audience in the Royal Pavilion, Brighton, King William IV discussed all these plans with Back. His Majesty, when Duke of Clarence, had served in the Royal Navy on the American and West Indies stations, and thereafter he rose through successive ranks to become Lord High Admiral – hence his nickname, the Sailor King. Also present was his niece Victoria, destined to succeed him as queen in 1837. She subscribed to the expedition's finances and presented Back with a case of mathematical instruments and a pocket compass – which was to prove a lifesaver.

Detailed Official Instructions came down to Back in a letter from Lord Goderich, Secretary of State for the Colonies, since this expedition was to be under the auspices of the Colonial Office rather than the Admiralty. If Back could reach the wreck of *Fury*, where Ross might still be stranded, he should do so; failing this he should map the coast west toward Point Turnagain. However, Back was unsure if the Great Fish River entered the Arctic Ocean east or west of the Boothia Peninsula. The Official Instructions were adamant that on no account was his journey to the Arctic Ocean to jeopardize his party's safe return to their winter quarters, and he must turn around between 12 and 20 August. They concluded with: 'Your proceeding afterwards [reaching the Polar Sea] must be much guided by your own judgment.'

Back's preparations were exemplary, based on his wide previous experience. Among myriad stores, cocoa and macaroni featured high, 'than which few things are better suited to such undertakings'.

Back left Liverpool in the packet *Hibernia* on 17 February 1833. He arrived at New York 'after a somewhat boisterous passage of thirty-five days, during part of which the ship was entangled amongst ice on St. George's Bank'. Back was given a hero's welcome and customs officers waived their dues. Serenaded by the cheers of several hundred well-wishers, he was ushered onto the steamboat *Ohio* bound for Albany in upstate New York. The seven-week journey to Montreal followed exactly his 1824 route.

In Montreal Back stayed first at Mr Goodenough's Exchange Coffee House on St Paul's Street, before moving to a nearby hotel owned by Francisco Rasco, one of the city's Italian hoteliers. The officers of the British garrison – 79th Highlanders, 24th Warwickshire, and 15th Yorkshire Regiments – quickly descended on Back, vying with each other to entertain him. However, it was from Captain Anderson's 6th battalion of Royal Artillery that he enrolled four volunteer gunners.

On 24 April, in the auditorium of Rasco's Hotel during a musical soirée given by the Bohemian Brothers Hermann, pine branch decorations caught fire and the hotel burned to the ground 'in a scene of awful grandeur'. Many guests, most of them ladies, escaped by the back stairs. Some jumped through upper windows with their petticoats flaring like parachutes. It was Back's last night at the hotel (a new Rasco's Hotel was built within a year, and its elegant façade is prominent in Old Montreal today). Fortunately he had just sent most of his baggage and scientific instruments to Lachine for packing in canoes due to leave next day. Nevertheless he lost his only working barometer, two others having been damaged irreparably during the sea voyage.

While in Montreal, Back suffered headaches over expedition personnel. Two Scotsmen, hearing jeremiads about the perils in store, took fright and nearly absconded, whereupon Back peremptorily packed them off north out of earshot of doomsters. James Keith, HBC officer at Lachine, advised Back that he might find better men among the *hivernants* wintering at one of the northern depots.

The local men, a mix of old-hand voyageurs and greenhorn, pork-eating *mangeurs de lard*, took fright at the evil omen of the hotel fire, and threatened to quit. Some men were still drunk when Back arrived at Lachine next morning accompanied by Colonel Macdougall of the 79th. Others were so hungover they meekly climbed into their canoes and, amid a cacophony of cheers and musket shots from the farewell crowd, paddled away into the wilderness croaking out voyageur canoe songs. Fortunately, Paul, the chief Iroquois guide, was a skilful boatman who reputedly knew every dangerous rock in the rapids between Montreal and Hudson Bay, and tolerated no nonsense from his crew. Nevertheless at the junction where the Ottawa River turns north off the St Lawrence, he allowed the men to go ashore at a small church to pray to their patron saint for protection in the rapids ahead.

The route north was now quite familiar to Back and his party reached the north shore of Lake Superior without incident. The HBC factor at Sault de Ste Marie, Angus Bethune, had told Back that, because of delays due to heavy ice on Lake Superior, his stores sent from England had been forwarded only three weeks ago. The supplies were now a mere eleven days ahead of him, so it was urgent that he should meet Governor Simpson who had authority to get things moving faster.

At Norway House, Back recruited at exorbitant expense several essential crew, notably two excellent steersmen, James McKay and George Sinclair, both of whom distinguished themselves later in the expedition. He had less luck with two voyageur middlemen he had known before. In one case his wife, 'a good strapping dame', on hearing that her husband had signed on, cuffed him round the ears so roughly that he took refuge in a friend's tent; the other's sweetheart, 'an interesting girl of seventeen', burst into tears and clung sobbing to her new-found lover. So Back had to look elsewhere for crew, and by good fortune found Antoine de Charloit, a skillful Iroquois boatman.

Back sent King ahead in the freight canoes, or bateaux, with fifteen men and most of the gear, while he stayed behind to ensure supplies were forwarded – another lesson from 1821. Back gave King specific orders not to touch any of the sixty bags of pemmican in his care. Afterwards King wrote indignantly that, should the lives of any of his men be at stake, he would not hesitate to use the pemmican if he could not reach the wintering grounds without doing so. Using a fast canoe, Back caught up with King, overtook him to go ahead and smooth out arrangements, and ordered him to follow with the boats. Historians have unfairly criticized Back for leapfrogging thus, which King himself used as an example of the superiority of canoes over his 'cumbrous' boats.

Being in the wilderness again evidently made Back feel quite content. When his men requested to make camp, he remarked:

'they had been nearly eighteen hours labouring at the paddles and I could not refuse them a little rest.' Looking round his tent he saw with nostalgic pleasure a bundle of three blankets rolled in an oilcloth; a table made from a box on which lay a teapot, some dried buffalo meat and pemmican; and in the corner his instruments and a gun with all its bits and pieces. What more could a man want, apart from some warm company between the buffalo blankets?

The ubiquitous and voracious mosquitoes were, nevertheless, one of the few things about Arctic travel the otherwise impervious Back repeatedly complained of. He was evidently delighted that his companion, King, 'being indifferent to the attacks of English insects of every description, had fondly imagined he should be invulnerable to those of America'. But he was not, and his bite-puffy face became barely recognizable.

At Fort William, as was customary, they exchanged their freight *canots du maitre* for the lighter *canots du nord*, more suited to northern rivers than to heavy seas that build up on the Great Lakes. Back was delighted with the two canoes – newly built for the expedition by order of Governor George Simpson – which he would use as far as Great Slave Lake.

The voyageurs repacked the cargo wrapped in ninety-pound *pièces*, which to prevent grumbling about favouritism they distributed by drawing lots using twigs of different lengths. At Savannah Portage an express mail canoe caught up with them, so Back sent a letter to Simpson saying he hoped to find a shortcut to Great Slave Lake, which the governor had suggested might lie at the east end of Lake Athabasca. Later, he discovered that no such practical shortcut existed, and as a result took the usual route north.

While Back awaited the arrival of Simpson at Fort Alexander, situated at the foot of Lake Winnipeg, one of the best Montreal voyageurs asked to be discharged because 'he was sure [they] should all be starved to death'. Back obliged, preferring to be rid of one lily-livered man early rather than late, when a canker of discontent might spread among his fellows. But he was unimpressed by 'such pusillanimous weakness [that] was irreconcilable with an enterprise like that in which we were engaged, which demanded an entire sacrifice of home comforts, and an enthusiastic and unreflecting ardour in the prosecution of its objects'.

Simpson arrived on 10 June, in such poor health that he was heading directly for Lower Canada. Nevertheless he reassured Back by letter – which was to act as his decree – 'that all our [HBC] resources are available to you; that our craft will be at your service, and our stores at your command'. He also wrote to Alexander Roderick MacLeod and Simon McGillivray letting them choose who of them should accompany the expedition. To whoever it should be, he promised early promotion to chief trader, and a pay raise. This was a sea change from the tetchy encounters between Simpson and Back at Fort Chipewyan in 1821.

Thomas Simpson (cousin of the governor), then a humble HBC clerk at Fort Alexander, wrote of Back: 'he seems a very easy, affable man, deficient I should say in that commanding manner with the people, so necessary on this savage country. From my soul I wish them every success in the generous and humane objects of the expedition' – meaning the finding of the lost Rosses. After the expedition he praised its achievements as 'greater than any of us in the North expected'. However, when Back published his own account of his expedition, Thomas Simpson called it: 'a painted bauble, all ornament and conceit, and no substance . . . Back, I believe to be not only a vain but a bad man.' Undoubtedly turncoat Simpson's grapes were soured by his own failure as an explorer – in fact, he became a competent one later on.

Back's crew on leaving Fort Alexander comprised an Englishman, a Hebridean Scot, two Canadians, two métis and three Iroquois; of them he wrote: 'Babel could not have produced a worse confusion of unharmonious sounds than was the conversation they kept up.' Before arriving at a trading post they would dress in their finery of silver bands, tassels and coloured feathers in their hats. A large crimson silk company flag hung on a pole in the stern of their craft.

As usual Lake Winnipeg was stormy. Back writes, in admirable descriptive prose, that it 'resembled one rolling sheet of foam, which contrasted strongly with the dark sky to windward; the mosquitoes had vanished; six or eight gulls, unable to sustain their flight in search of food had huddled together on the lee side of a projecting sand-bank; and two crows, wearied with exertion, sat perched on the waving branches of a tall pine, unscared by the approach of intruding feet. It was altogether an impressive scene of picturesque and melancholy wildness.'

They passed Cumberland House and Isle à la Crosse without incident. Crossing Methye Portage la Loche proved just as tough as on each previous occasion so, at the end of the day, the utterly exhausted men threw themselves on the ground and lay inert for an hour. Back enthused over the view he painted in 1821: 'there is something appalling in the vastness of a solitude like this.' Being familiar with the scene, however, he admits that he was not as impressed as his companions who were seeing it for the first time.

Near Fort Chipewyan they met Alexander MacLeod – one of Governor Simpson's nominees for expedition assistant. On hearing of his secondment to the expedition, in spite of being on his way to Lower Canada, both recuperating from poor health and incidentally escorting a valuable cargo of furs from his post in the Mackenzie District, MacLeod put everything on hold, and signed on. Back was delighted to have his trusted friend as base camp manager on this present adventure. He immediately wrote to the HBC requesting the supplies – mainly materials for building their wintering house – promised for the next year, 1834.

Not surprisingly, the guide complained that his canoe was overloaded to the gunwales, having fourteen bodies aboard instead of eight – including MacLeod, his wife, three children and their servant, who Back also immediately recruited. The guide's fears were soon vindicated when the canoe hit a sunken rock, and he had to put ashore for gumming. In the space of half an hour at the Salt River, Back's men packed and loaded five bags of pure white salt. There they met a small canoe loaded with eight Slave Indians – men, women, children and dogs, 'packed heads and tails like Yarmouth herrings, half naked, their hair in elf-locks, long and matted, filthy beyond description, and all squalling together'.

On returning to camp they found MacLeod surrounded by a cluster of Indians. He had spent the entire previous night trying to get them to draw a rough map of the rivers arising from near the east end of Great Slave Lake. Their consensus, and that of all the Indians consulted before, was that two great rivers ran northeast across the Barrens – the Teh-lon (Thelon) and the Thlew-ee-choh (Great Fish) – both of which arose so close that the smoke from a fire at one could be seen from the other. The Teh-lon was broad, tranquil and wooded throughout; the Thlew-ee-choh was narrow, shallow, full of dangerous rapids and falls, and treeless. At Norway House the Grand Jeune Homme, an Indian from Fort Resolution, said he doubted if boats, or even large canoes, could descend it. But no one seemed to know whether both these rivers emptied into the Arctic Ocean, or if the Teh-lon discharged into Hudson Bay (which indeed it does at Chesterfield Inlet). They assured Back that if he chose the Thlew-ee-choh, no Indians would endanger their lives by accompanying him. Nevertheless, Blackmeat had observed that it emptied into the Arctic Ocean, which, to Back, seemed as likely as the many other vague opinions he was getting from sundry passing Indians.

On 8 August 1835 the expedition arrived at Fort Resolution, on Great Slave Lake. After seeing to expedition business, Back ordered MacLeod and King to follow with the heavy bateaux loaded with gear and supplies, while he set off in a small canoe to scout the east arm of the lake for a suitable base camp site. He passed through Taltheilei Narrows, a spectacular passage between the Pethel Peninsula and the north shore of the lake. This gateway to the eastern end of the lake never freezes because of the current. They found a waterfall at the mouth of the Mountain River where Indians used to leave their canoes when hunting in the Barrens. Thereafter it was unnavigable because one steep rapid succeeded another as far as the treeline. The Hoarfrost River entered farther on, also with a waterfall near its mouth – Beverly's Fall. Their Indian guide, Maufelly, assured them they should follow the Hoarfrost to reach the source of the Thlew-ee-choh.

Back wrote a letter to MacLeod, instructing him and five of the men to build wintering houses near the mouth of the Ah-hel-dessy (Lockhart) River. Back told him he was going to explore access to the Thlew-ee-choh, so not to expect him until some time in

September. He sent the letter with a voyageur, La Prise, who was returning to Fort Resolution because his contract was up. Then Back's party of four followed Maufelly up the Hoarfrost River gorge, deeply cut by falls and rapids, which leads into the heart of the Barren Lands.

CHAPTER 17

Hunger at Fort Reliance

1833–34

Sussex Lake, source of the Thlew-ee-choh-dezeth, August 28, 1833,
by Back, on a stone by Haghe.

After a long and arduous climb carrying their canoe and supplies up the forested banks of the Hoarfrost River, Back's small party emerged onto open Barrens where it straightened out like a highway for several miles leading northeast. Despite the difficulties encountered he was quite lyrical about the 'turbulent and unfriendly' river: 'Nothing, however, can be more romantically beautiful than the wild scenery of its course. High rocks beetling over the rapids like towers, or rent into the most diversified forms, gay with various coloured mosses, or shaded by overhanging trees – now a tranquil pool, lying like a sheet of silver – now the dash and foam of a cataract.'

In the evening, while contemplating the stillness of the landscape, Back remarks how it seemed, 'a type of that best period of the life of man when the turbulence and energy of youth [precedes] the calm sobriety of ripened age'. If Back was reflecting here on his own career, he was certainly now more mature than the brash young man of the 1820s who did so many remarkable – even heroic – deeds, which Franklin tardily recognized.

It was past the middle of August, when winter at that latitude was not far beyond the northern horizon, so Back had to move fast before the rivers iced over. Although geese might soon start flying south, not so mosquitoes and sandflies that drove the men demented with itching and scratching until blood streamed from their faces. As ever, Back vituperates: 'There is certainly no form of wretchedness . . . as the torture inflicted by these puny blood-suckers . . . for a time [the voyageur] may go on crushing by thousands . . . at last, subdued by pain and fatigue he throws himself in despair with his face to the earth and, half suffocated in his blanket, groans away a few hours of sleepless rest.'

Beyond Cook's Lake, the 'cool, fearless and collected' bowman, De Charloit, navigated the fifteen rapids that flowed from Walmesley Lake. At the top, after much tracking, the canoes inevitably required a halt for gumming and patching. From a nearby hill, Maufelly pointed ahead to a sheet of water, which he said would lead them to other large lakes they must pass to gain the height of land where they would find the source of the Thlew-ee-choh. Back named it Artillery Lake 'out of respect to the distinguished corps to which some of my crew belonged'. Samuel Hearne had crossed forth and back just below the treeline near Artillery Lake on his journey to the Coppermine River in 1771. None of these geographical features had English names until given them by officers like Franklin and Back – and they had many sponsors to satisfy.

Beyond Ptarmigan Lake they reached Clinton Colden Lake, only a short distance from the headwaters of the Hanbury River. The Hanbury leads into the Thelon, which empties via Baker Lake and Chesterfield Inlet into Hudson Bay – definitely not where Back planned to end up. In the evening, after passing through Thanakoie Narrows into Aylmer Lake, Back climbed a prominent sandhill and felt 'deeply impressed with the intense stillness of the scene: no living thing was seen or heard; the air was calm, the lake unruffled:

it seemed as if nature had fallen into a trance, for all was silent and motionless as death.'

The modern aeronautical map shows the contorted shoreline of these big lakes, broken by a multitude of inset bays, projecting points, and countless islands. Finding the main course of the current in such a vast body of water is extremely difficult. Under extraordinary difficulties, Back was making maps that would still be a boon to any lost aviator or canoeist. Chief Factor James Anderson, who twenty years later made the second descent of the Great Fish River while on a search for Franklin's lost expedition, disdained Back's maps as: 'so small a scale as to be *utterly/perfectly useless*' (repeated three different times), and 'a snare and a delusion, I trust never to be guided by such a map again.' These comments reflect more on Anderson than on Back. But one must remember that the volume and difficulty of a river varies widely during the course of a season owing to rainfall and snowmelt; one paddler's easy passage over well-pillowed rocks is another's boat-bottom-crunching nightmare. Eventually Anderson, in his 1855 account, gives Back grudging credit: 'We are guiding ourselves by Back's Journal – his description of the route is so minute and correct that it is needless for me to say anything,' and, 'his descriptions of the scenery is most correct – it is beautiful indeed.'

Being well north of the treeline, they had to cook on fires of caribou moss laid between two parallel walls of stone which created a draught. Caribou were scarce, but provided enough meat for their present needs. Ice was beginning to form on lakes, so the bowman had to use an axe to prize open a lead wide enough for the canoe to pass. The men also made leather gunwale fenders to prevent ice scraping the sides.

Maufelly was now quite lost and made wild guesses as to their whereabouts and the direction they should take. At last, on 29 August 1833, some low hills appeared at the most northerly bay of Aylmer Lake, which Back named Sandhill Bay. This oriented Maufelly who, with renewed confidence, pointed the way to the Thlew-ee-choh. Beaten caribou tracks indicated, as they do today, the migration path across a narrow neck of land that separates Sandhill Bay from a small nameless lake. From the top of a sandy hill – where Back himself must have stood – one can see a whitewater rapid in a river that flows northeast. From this height of land waters drain south to Great Slave Lake, and – after a turbulent passage Back was yet to experience – north into Chantrey Inlet and the Arctic Ocean.

Back sent the Indians to look for the river itself. When they did not turn up in the evening he became anxious and followed them, found the river, and confirmed that it flowed north. With justifiable delight he threw himself down on the bank and 'drank a hearty draught of the limpid water' – a restrained expression of joy for such a major discovery. Meanwhile the guides had reached the shore of a small lake which they were convinced was the very origin of the Thlew-ee-choh River. Back named it after the Duke of Sussex, the expedition's vice patron and chairman. When the Indians returned to camp and reported that the river was large enough for boats, Back broke out a little bottle of grog that he had stowed away for the occasion and they all had a celebratory swig.

The canoe was in bad shape from its rough passage through water already full of floating ice chunks, and from overnight frosts which caused the brittle birchbark to split. So it badly needed patching and gumming. Nevertheless, Back was determined to scout at least the first part of the river. Soon they passed a creek on their left where a huge sheet of ice arched – and still does – across its mouth. This *aufeis*, or winter ice, occurs in an area of permafrost where stream water overflows, or seeps from the ground. Sheet upon sheet of ice builds up, and becomes so thick it does not melt, even in summer.

The outflow of Muskox Lake gave rise to a four-mile stretch of rapids. Back decided to turn around there, partly because the canoe was so rickety from recent buffeting, partly because winter was nearly upon them. He had found *his* river, and knew from its volume that it was navigable. However, he deduced, from the appearance of distant blue mountains, that there was 'abundant reason for supposing that we should have no lack of rapids and falls'. Little did he realize that eighty-three serious rapids awaited him, some several miles long. He estimated they were now 109 miles south of the toe of Bathurst Inlet; in fact, he was only out by three miles, the measured distance being 106 statute miles as the snowgoose flies.

On the return journey Back again extols the technical skill and grace of steersman De Charloit in running their shattered canoe down the rapids north of Ptarmigan Lake: 'Nothing could exceed the self-possession and nicety of judgment with which he guided the frail thing along the narrow line between the high waves of the torrent and the returning eddy' – an elegant description of canoeing technique.

Two hunters of Akaitcho's band, whom Back knew from Coppermine River days, arrived looking emaciated because caribou were so scarce. He gave them presents for their chief and his brother, Humpy. Then he allowed Maufelly to visit his wife, 'who had favoured him with a child in his absence'. The only condition was that he return by next morning – which he did, accompanied by one of the former Fort Enterprise hunters. Such chance encounters in the Barrens emphasize the range over which these northern Indian bands roamed following the caribou, their source of livelihood. A widespread network of bush telegraph linked them over vast distances of featureless country where only the shapes of lakes and an occasional low hill helped them navigate.

Back reached the treeline at Artillery Lake where the first scraggy dwarf spruce appeared, and grew steadily larger as they paddled south. The landscape intrigued him, especially the area ravaged by forest fires east of Artillery Lake:

> It was a sight altogether novel to me; I had seen nothing in the Old World at all resembling it. There was not the stern beauty of Alpine scenery, and still less the fair variety of hill and dale, forest and glade, which makes the charm of a European landscape. There was nothing to catch or detain the lingering eye, which wandered on, without a check, over endless lines of round backed rocks, whose sides were rent into indescribably eccentric forms. It was like a stormy ocean suddenly petrified. Except a few tawny and pale green lichens, there was nothing to relieve the horror of the scene; for the fire had scathed it, and the grey and black stems of the mountain pine, which lay prostrate in mournful confusion, seemed like the blackened corpses of departed vegetation. It was a picture of 'hideous ruin and combustion.'

High overhead flocks of geese winged their way southward in wavering formation, 'as if anxious to escape from the wintry horrors of the north'. Back and his men were then only twenty direct miles from Great Slave Lake. The water from Artillery Lake tumbled down the Ah-hel-dessy (Lockhart) River which, Maufelly warned, had an evil reputation among Indians. De Charloit confirmed this by nearly capsizing during a brief paddle in some desperate rapids. So they decided to cache the canoe and set off on foot carrying 120 pounds each through contorted country that lay south of Parry's Falls, as yet heard but not seen by them because the falls lie in the bottom of a deep canyon.

As they dropped off the high Barrens they were tormented by sandflies, so Back tried to fumigate his tent with wood smoke. Maufelly remarked how different Back was from his old chief, Franklin, who, quoting Tristram Shandy's Uncle Toby, had Maufelly but known, would never kill a fly or a mosquito, but just blew them off his skin, saying, 'The world is wide enough for both [of us].'

Near the lake shore the clanging strike of a woodsman's axe guided them to a bay where MacLeod was supervising men constructing some houses, grandiloquently (and later ironically) named Fort Reliance. The fort stood on a bank of sand and gravel twenty feet above the lake. For protection from prevailing southerly winds it was set back in small trees, which Back described as, 'looking more like a park than part of an American forest'. This beautiful place, carpeted in foot-crunchy caribou moss, commands wide views of the east end of Great Slave Lake. A few hundred yards west is the mouth of the Ah-hel-dessy, now tranquil after its turbulent descent through a multitude of falls in its short course.

Sandflies had also plagued MacLeod's men so badly they had to stop work until they could smoke them out by continuously burning fires of green wood and pine branches. De Charloit and some men, when they had recovered from their bites, climbed back up their recent trail to collect meat they had cached. Returning by a slightly different route they found a stand of large knot-free trees suitable for boat planking – a vital discovery since Back had already contemplated having to fetch wood from far away down Great Slave Lake.

On 16 September King arrived with the two bateaux laden with cargo all in good order. He had suffered the usual problems of northern river travel, but had indeed done well for a *cheechako*. Now that the whole expedition was assembled, Back divided them into two parties and gave them regular tasks like sawing planks and squaring logs for framing the houses. But this Elysian scene did not portend the rigours of the winter ahead.

Fort Reliance began to take shape, and the expedition men camped in tents nearby while completing the building. Three houses were arranged round a small square. The main house measured fifty by thirty feet; leading off a central hall were four rooms, each with its own fireplace. The men collected stone to build chimneys – the flues of which still stand – from a nearby outcrop of frost-fractured granite. A lean-to tacked onto the back of the house apologized for a kitchen. The walls of squared logs were plastered with a mix of mud and clay, together with dry marsh grass and sand dug from the beach at the mouth of the Lockhart River. By then the weather was so cold that mortar froze as soon as it was applied. The roof of wood shingles, tamped with mortar and mud, sloped from a ridgepole. Windowpanes were made of moose skin parchment.

King noted that they could have managed with a much smaller building that would have needed less wood to heat, and fewer hungry woodcutters eating precious pemmican. In his own account of the expedition he continues throughout with the same usually mild, but occasionally harsh, snide remarks about the expedition and his boss – never tantamount to open criticism, which would have been akin to mutiny.

On a gentle rise a hundred yards distant the carpenters, Thomas and William Matthews, built a twelve-foot-square observatory facing the four cardinal points of the compass. They used only tenon and mortise jointing without a single nail or other piece of iron that might disturb the magnetic needles of the instruments. Dead centre of the room they set a large tree stump with a table placed exactly level on top. Poles outside supported weather vanes and various instruments, the whole area being fenced for protection from animals.

On 28 October 1833 Back immediately started making notes and sketches of an unusually spectacular aurora borealis:

While occupied in taking the transit of a star, I perceived the coruscations streaming from behind a detached and oblong dark cloud in a vertical position at E.b.S. They issued along an undulating arch 38° high, and spread themselves laterally in beams north and south. Another arch, brighter and narrower than the former, suddenly emerged from W.b.N., and passed between a nearly horizontal black cloud and the stars, which were then not visible through the Aurora. I immediately looked at the [magnetic] needle, and found it slightly agitated, but not vibrating: on returning, I was surprised to see the dark horizontal cloud to the westward not in the same shape as before. It had now taken a balloon form, and was evidently fast spreading towards the zenith. On looking to the eastward, I perceived that a dark cloud there was altering its appearance . . . and we saw the dark broad mass from the westward gradually expand itself, so as to meet the other, which was likewise rising, at or near the zenith. The effect of the junction was a dark grey arch, extending from E.b.S. to W.b.N. across the zenith, and completely obscuring the stars, though at each side of the arch they were particularly clear and twinkling. In the meantime the Aurora assumed every variety of form; such as undulating and fringed arches . . . with flashes and beams at right angles to them . . . In a few seconds, the part of this nearest the horizon assumed a zig-zag form, like forked lightning; and immediately the western extremity sympathized, undergoing momentary transitions which defy description. Such convulsions at the extremes soon affected the centre of the arch, which becoming gradually fainter and fainter, at last vanished entirely, leaving the stars to shine forth in all their brilliance.

The observatory caused an unexpected problem for Indians returning from the Barrens. They were half-starved having been unable to get close enough to kill any caribou which, owing to very mild weather, had not begun to follow their migration paths out of the tundra into forests. The hunters imagined that secrecy surrounding the observatory – the officers being the only people allowed inside it – was the cause of their hunting failure.

Two of the voyageurs themselves, hearing commands at intervals – 'Now!' 'Stop!', then silence – imagined the officers were performing devilish base rituals on each other. The Indians were certain that the instruments affected the caribou, so stirred themselves from their lethargy and went off to hunt. They quickly shot a tough old bear, which, though better than nothing, did not go far in feeding hungry families.

A trickle of infirm old Indians gathered around the fort, and soon grew to be a stream of sick and starving people begging for food. Meat was so scarce that Back sent MacLeod and several men to start a fishery at the head of a deep bay on the south side of the lake. But that, too, produced much less food than they had hoped. They unsuccessfully tried growing cress, following Parry's example, to help prevent scurvy.

Famine soon became so serious that Back took several radical measures to curb it. He dispersed all the men to fish and hunt in other parts of the lake, reduced everyone's daily dried meat ration, and forbade feeding the dogs. He discharged the staunch De Charloit, along with two Iroquois paddlers and one voyageur, La Charité, because the expedition would no longer use canoes and their services were redundant. He also sent MacLeod with his family to the fishery, hoping he would have better luck there, and with hunting, since he was a first-class rifle shot. He stayed there nearly two months.

Akaitcho and some of his men suddenly appeared as if from nowhere. The old chief was wearing the silver medal presented to him at Fort Enterprise by Franklin and Richardson. He was evidently delighted when Back gave him some presents from his old friends, although he did not enquire directly about them. Back persuaded Akaitcho to take over responsibility for the host of starving Indians, whereupon he and his hunters took off to search for the elusive caribou. They found and killed some animals too far away to bring to the fort, so they cached the meat – with luck out of reach of ubiquitous wolverines – and planned to collect it later.

Despite having dispersed as many people as possible, the famine continued and a large group of men returned from the fisheries with doleful news of their failure. Dispirited lethargic Indians hung around the fort, glad of even a handful of mouldy dog meat. 'When I thought myself most safe,' Back – usually optimistic – wrote, 'I was, perhaps, in greatest danger. However, it was of no use to sit still and mope.'

To add to everyone's misery the temperature dropped to $-75°F$ ($-59°C$). The hall filled with apathetic Indian invalids who sat around the fire eating bits of caribou clothing. Dr King was kept busy attending to the legion of sick. He describes one particularly miserable pathetic family: 'The father torpid and despairing, the mother with a hollow and sepulchral wail vainly endeavouring to soothe the infant which with unceasing moan clung to her shrivelled and exhausted breast, the passive child gazing vacantly around.'

The two British officers tried to make a cheerful Christmas dinner of pemmican, over which they discussed their friends, imagining them at home having just eaten a feast of roast beef and plum pudding. Their pemmican stores were now down to less than half the amount they had set aside for next year's journey and for 'sea service'. The expedition's men, far from being moody or sullen were, encouraged by Back's example, cheerful and in good spirits, despite the cold and their scanty rations. Sitting near the fire Back tried to paint, but his ink and brush point froze on the paper and his hands had become dry and cracked with open sores. He wrote: 'Nothing but the passing wind broke the awful solitude of this barren and desolate spot.'

MacLeod returned on 9 February, followed by a party of men hauling toboggans laden with meat. He told of Indians starving all over the country because, although caribou seemed to be returning, they were skittish and hard to shoot. Sometimes Indians abandoned to their fate the sick and feeble who could not keep up with the tribe, constantly on the move following the caribou. Back empathized with their predicament, but he vociferously condemned some 'barbarous outrages . . . almost too revolting to be mentioned', referring to reported acts of infanticide, murder, and cannibalism to which Indians sometimes resorted during famines.

Akaitcho remained near Fort Reliance during much of the winter and encouraged his Indians to hunt. MacLeod and his family again took off to the fishery so as to reduce the number of hungry mouths at the fort, but again he had little luck. Maufelly turned up unexpectedly, having shot some caribou that he had cached only two days' march away.

Back sent King, Sinclair and the carpenters to find the clump of pines noticed by De Charloit in the fall, with orders to saw them into planks. That done they were to drag them, and all necessary ironwork, to a bay on the west shore of Artillery Lake (Timber Bay on modern charts) where he intended they should build the boats.

A messenger arrived from Fort Resolution with a package, and reported that another packet had been sent separately with Augustus and an Iroquois voyageur. On hearing that Back was in the country again, Augustus had walked from Hudson Bay to Great Slave Lake to offer his services. The three men had set out from Fort Resolution, heading for Fort Reliance, but lost their way in a storm crossing Great Slave Lake, and could not communicate with each other because they had no common language. The voyageur and the Iroquois turned round and found their way back to Fort Resolution, but Augustus pushed on to Fort Reliance alone with only ten pounds of pemmican, and no gun or bow and arrows. This loyal act does not jibe with an unkind remark Augustus reportedly (by Franklin) made to missionary West about Back. A search party from Fort Resolution returned after eighteen days with no news or sign of him, and presumed he had died in the storm.

At the same time, adding to Back's melancholy over the fate of Augustus, an Iroquois hunter shot two ravens which had become camp mascots. 'In any other situation such an event would perhaps have seemed too trifling to be noticed,' Back wrote, 'but in our case the ravens were the only link between us and the dreary solitude without, and their loss therefore was painfully felt. When they were gone I felt more lonely, and the moaning wind seemed as if complaining of the barbarity.'

On 26 April 1834 – anniversary of the expedition leaving Montreal – a messenger arrived with a packet from England that included extracts from *The Times* and *Morning Herald*.

'He is returned, sir!' the messenger shouted, thrusting the packet into Back's hand.

At first, Back thought the messenger meant that Augustus was safe, but sadly the man corrected him. It was Captain Ross who had returned.

A letter, dated 22 October 1833, from Sir Charles Ogle, Chairman of the Arctic Land Expedition, read: 'Captain Ross and the survivors of his party returned to England a few days ago in a whaler which picked them up in Barrow's Straits – and thus one object of your labours is happily attained. You are now directed to turn your attention to your second object, viz. the completing the coast line of the north-eastern extremity of America.'

Accompanying the letter was a copy of John Ross's chart, forwarded from the Hydrographer's Office, showing Boothia as a peninsula, and dispelling any ideas Back may have had of making a complete sea journey east along the Arctic coast to reach Repulse Bay. Richardson had already written of an Indian report that there was 'a Peninsula projecting far to the North', but no one had taken any notice.

Back was pleased with the news, partly because it justified his previously stated opinion that the Rosses were safely wintering at Fury Beach, partly because of the wisdom and sensitivity of his expedition's promoters, who had thereby 'rescued the British nation from an imputation of indifference which it was far indeed from meriting'.

Instead of his original plan to use two boats, Back decided to go to the Arctic coast in only one boat, and with the strongest possible crew. The second boat would go with MacLeod as far as Sandhill Bay to await the returning party in the fall. By this change of plan supplies of pemmican, much depleted after the disastrous winter, would stretch further.

Spring eventually arrived, and with it their fortunes turned around. On 13 May a solitary goose, harbinger of warmer weather, flew north over Fort Reliance. Snow began to melt, patches of earth and dead grass showed through, and catkins hung from willow branches. In the next few days new life returned – a fly, some butterflies, and several birds – gulls, grosbeaks, yellowlegs and robins. In a swamp behind the house King shot a duck, onto which a bald eagle promptly swooped, carrying it off in its talons.

On 3 June Akaitcho and thirty hunters arrived with the sad news that they had found the remains of Augustus not far from Rivière à Jean, an easy day's march from Fort Resolution. Back was desolate. 'It appeared the gallant little fellow was retracing his steps to the establishment when, either exhausted by suffering or privation, or caught in the midst of an open traverse in one of those terrible snow storms which . . . blow through the frame, he had sunk to rise no more.' One of the artillerymen, Williamson, who had been discharged because of ill health, was also lost without trace on Great Slave Lake.

On 7 June 1834, Back, King and their crew left Fort Reliance, having shuttered the houses, locked all their papers in trunks and stored them in the cellar. It was the start of the journey down a river that now bears the name of Back, and for which justly he will be most remembered.

CHAPTER 18

Descent of the Thlew-ee-choh

1834

Hawk Rapids, Back River, N.W.T., September 4, 1834.
Sketch by Back.

At the beginning of the greatest adventure of his life, George Back wrote: 'There is something exciting in the first start even upon an ordinary journey. The bustle of preparation, the act of departing, which seems like a decided step taken, the prospect of change, and consequent stretching out of the imagination, have at all times the effect of stirring the blood, and giving a quicker motion to the spirits. It may be conceived then with what sensations I set forth on my journey into the Arctic wilderness.' He was leaving behind a wretchedly sad, dreary, monotonous and inactive winter, during which he had been surrounded by starving and suffering Indians. He continues: 'Before me were novelty and enterprise; hope, curiosity, and love of adventure were my companions; and even the prospect of difficulties and dangers to be encountered, with the responsibility inseparable from command, instead of damping rather heightened the enjoyment of the moment.' This was, in fact, the first expedition he had led. 'In turning my back on the Fort,' Back confesses, 'I felt my breast lightened, and my spirit, as it were, set free again.' As they went on their way, King evidently felt the same.

As the men climbed the rocky outcrops on the north side of the Ah-hel-dessy River they could hear, not far away, the thundering of water – Parry's Falls. On reaching Timber Bay they found that the carpenters had nearly finished building two boats. Each was thirty feet long overall with a twenty-four-foot keel, a wide beam, and sharp bow and stern, similar in form to a York boat. There was plenty of space for cargo stowage in the well, which was coated with pitch. Carvel lower planks, laid flush, would be less likely to catch on rocks in rapids, and more easily repaired than a clinker-built hull in which upper boards overlapped each other, and were clinched with copper nails. Unfortunately, the planks they had sawn in the nearby forest were knotty; the timber was of poor quality, which is hardly surprising when cut so near the treeline where trees are mostly small and scrawny. The boats were too heavy to be carried by the small crew. This portended badly for portaging, so Back decided to go ahead with one boat only. As it turned out they did few major portages descending the river; however, the weight would be a disadvantage on their return.

On 10 June the men dragged the larger boat, set on sledges shoed with iron runners, across a swamp to the shore of Artillery Lake where it was ready to take to the ice. They launched the smaller boat into a pool to allow its timbers to swell and tighten the seams. It would remain there until needed by MacLeod in the autumn for going to meet the party on their return. MacLeod, Maufelly, and two other men, were several days ahead trying to hunt and cache meat, and to look for shortcuts. The boat crew comprised Back, King, Malley (Back's servant), three Scotsmen, three artillerymen, and two métis, together with six strong dogs. Back went forward on foot to scout the route and to look for cache markers placed by MacLeod, leaving King to bring up the rear with the boat. By following markers left by the advance party, they could cut a straight course from one headland to the next.

They were now well beyond treeline and rough ice soon ripped the runners off the sledges. Back summoned the carpenters – the Matthews brothers (who were not accompanying the party down-river because of lack of space) – to bring wood for repairs, and also to make spare runners by cutting an old whipsaw into strips.

The dogs wore leather booties to protect their feet from sharp spicules of ice. Back wore two pairs of moccasins and thick blanket socks with pieces of undressed hairy buffalo skin between. He decided to march at night and sleep by day so as to have firmer ice to walk on, and also to avoid travelling when glare off the ice was strong. One carpenter had already become temporarily snowblind, nevertheless Back still expected him to work: 'squeamishness is little heeded in such travelling as this, and shirking is quite out of the question . . . pity for temporary ailments might be felt but was not to be expressed, the restraint, however painful, being absolutely indispensable.' The Royal Navy boss's upper lip, stiffened by his youthful years in prison, must prevail.

As the days lengthened heat from the sun candled the shore ice, forming a lead of water through which the men could track the boat. They were at this point hauling upstream because, being south of the height of land, the rapids were still flowing against them. One boatman, Hugh Carron, slipped on shore ice, sank into water over his head, and was only saved by one of his mates grabbing his arm and hauling him out. While taking a shortcut, Peter Taylor, a métis, broke through some rotten ice. He had the presence of mind, however, to keep hold of his gun and by laying it across the hole was able to get some purchase and haul himself out onto firmer ice. In spring, when walking on dubious ice, a long pole is often carried to bridge such a hole, but the ice ahead may still break when trying to climb out. James Spence also fell through and got a ducking. Drying sodden clothes was difficult with only moss and a few scrubby bushes available for fuel. As a result, hypothermia was a constant hazard.

The weather was miserable with gales, snow squalls, and only occasional pale shafts of sunlight: 'Never was seen a more gloomy sky than which ushered in Midsummer's-day,' wrote Back. 'It was of a leaden grey colour with horizontal streaks of dirty brick-red clouds – except to the north, where, in strong contrast with the cold whiteness on which it rested, were accumulated, in one black mass, all the horrors of an hyperborean winter.' Hail, snow, and rain pelted them relentlessly, and it was more like a dreary day in December than midsummer. The men, clean-shaven despite all this miserable weather, attended divine service, held in the tent.

Navigating frozen lakes was utterly different from their autumn canoe journey. 'I had not thought it worth while,' Back confessed, 'to bring my last year's survey.' For one so meticulous, this was a dangerous and surprisingly foolish oversight, considering the shore-line's numerous bays and headlands. Heavy showers accelerated candling of the ice, and the heavy sledges repeatedly broke through the fragile surface.

When they were all ready to get going, Back ran into discipline problems with the 'mulish conduct' of one Indian hunter guide who was still lounging around camp wrapped in a blanket and smoking a pipe. The other guide went off hunting with some friends he had met along the way, presuming that his boss would be all right because he always had his 'little sun' – meaning his compass – which he only had to ask, and it would point him in any direction he wished. 'Experience had taught me the advantage of assuming and maintaining an air of superiority over the Indians,' Back rants. 'There is no need of unkindness or severity, all that is required is a steady firmness and never overlooking an attempt at deception, however plausible.'

Yet he concedes that Indians have many enviable qualities – humour and laughter, tolerance of cold and hunger, ability to live off the land, and lack of possessions – to name a few. He recounts how he struggled to keep up with Taylor, who refused to stop for a rest while following a hunter because the Indian put on a pro-longed burst of speed every time he thought Taylor was trying to overtake him. As on his previous expeditions, Back's relations with his own men, and the Indians, remained firm while he yet retained their respect and affection. This was perhaps his most endearing attribute, even though it meant that he related better to the 'lower orders' than to the higher ones – his fellow officers.

At last, on 27 June, the party reached Sandhill Bay where they saw the tents of MacLeod and his party of hunters. The nearby watershed meant that the expedition could soon paddle downstream towards their goal – the Arctic Ocean. The portage to the Thlew-ee-choh was only a quarter of a mile long, but the carpenters had warned Back that, because of the boat's soft and knotted timbers, it was not strong enough to be dragged that distance, or over any other portage for that matter. Back claims, laying rare blame on the carpenters, that: 'it was a contretemps for which I certainly was not prepared.' He says that, while building the boats, they should have reported this weakness, in which case he would have ordered better lumber from Fort Resolution. But he here contradicts himself, because avoiding transporting the timber the length of the lake was the very reason he decided to cut it close to Fort Reliance.

So the boat had to be carried, and Back was anxious lest the men drop and damage it when lifting it onto their shoulders. Carrying the heavy craft over rough ground taxed their strength and balance to the limit, and the prospect of having to shoulder a waterlogged boat was awesome. Next day they launched the boat into the Thlew-ee-choh, which was only partly free of ice, so they had to stop frequently to manhandle it over rapids too shallow to run.

At Muskox Lake, Back's turnaround point of ten months before, the men loaded enough food to last ten of them for the next three months. They had twenty-seven bags of pemmican weighing about ninety pounds each, two boxes of macaroni, some flour, a case of cocoa, and a two-gallon keg of rum. The total weight of the boat and its contents was nearly 5,000 pounds.

Among a group of Indians crowded round MacLeod's tent, Back noticed one in particular: 'my old acquaintance and Indian belle . . . Green Stockings' – more accurately the bedmate he had shared with fellow midshipman Robert Hood fourteen years before. He continues: 'I immediately recognised her, and called her by her name; at which she laughed, and said she was an old woman now . . . However, notwithstanding all this, she was still the beauty of her tribe.' When Back sketched her portrait, she was evidently pleased, 'with that consciousness which belongs to all belles, savage or polite'.

Back paints a word picture (his sketch has sadly not survived) of the scene around them in concise, poetic prose:

the sun shone out, and lighting up some parts cast others into deeper shade; the white ice reflected millions of dazzling rays; the rapid leapt and chafed in little ripples, which melted away into the unruffled surface of the slumbering lake; abrupt and craggy rocks frowned on the right; and, on the left, the brown landscape receded until it was lost in the distant blue mountains. The foreground was filled up with the ochre-coloured lodges of the Indians, contrasting with our own pale tents; and to the whole scene animation was given by the graceful motions of the unstartled deer, and the treacherous crawling of the wary hunters.

MacLeod and his party, including the carpenters, now turned round with orders to return to Sandhill Bay by mid-September. In the interval Macleod would go to Fort Resolution to collect extra stores, and later he would build a permanent fishing station somewhere near Fort Reliance.

After a heartfelt farewell to his trusted HBC friend, Back 'embarked for the ice' with his crew of ten men:

George Back	— commander
Richard King	— surgeon & naturalist
James McKay (Highlander)	— steersman
George Sinclair (métis)	— bowman & steersman
Charles McKenzie (Highlander)	— bowman
Peter Taylor (métis)	— middleman
James Spence (Orkneyman)	— middleman
Artilleryman John Ross (Highlander)	— middleman
Artilleryman William Malley (Lancashire)	— middleman
Artilleryman Hugh Carron (Irishman)	— middleman

The Great Fish River, or Thlew-ee-choh-dezeth to give it its full native title, is 530 miles (853 kilometres) long. In its course to the Arctic Ocean it has continuous stretches of rapids (eighty-three in all, some several kilometres long) and passes through seven large lakes. To the casual observer, bouncing over one whitewater rapid is just like another; to a boatman running them they are places of hidden hazard which require refined and practised skills in reading the water and guiding the boat down the safest path past rocks that loom like monsters waiting to upset and swallow the unwary.

Among Indians the Thlew-ee-choh had an evil reputation. On hearing that the expedition was about to depart, Akaitcho came over from his camp, pitched on a hill near the source of the river, in order to bid them farewell. He warned his former boss against treacherous Eskimos and of the dangers of being caught by winter. Back asked the chief to collect plenty of meat for their return and to look out for them beyond the mountains 'after two and a half moons'. Akaitcho agreed but stressed that no Indians would be around to help him if the onset of winter – or any other disaster – prevented their return upriver in the autumn.

A melancholy Akaitcho then watched the party prepare to push the boat out into midstream, and said, 'I have known the chief for a long time, and I am afraid I shall never see him again.' Within seconds of launching, steersman McKay misjudged the current and the boat slid up onto a shelving rock, twirled broadside, and almost capsized. After this scare Back ordered the crew in future to scout every rapid, and to portage regardless all guns, ammunition and scientific instruments, since one bad spill could be fatal to the expedition.

From Muskox Lake the river runs an almost straight course northeast towards a ninety-degree bend where it enters Beechey Lake. McKay and Sinclair had plenty of opportunity to show their skilful boatmanship on this first sixty-five-mile stretch, which has almost continuous rapids interspersed with small lakes. As the crew's experience and confidence grew, so they ran more and more rapids fully loaded. Back must have countermanded his original orders, with the exception that hunting gear and instruments had to be carried round whenever they ran a difficult rapid.

Back gives dramatic accounts of nearly every rapid they pass; however, the descriptions of King, and twenty years later of Anderson, are more restrained. King says the river was, 'by no means so formidable' as it was represented by his boss. Anderson writes: 'I do not find the Rapids nearly so bad as I was led to expect by Capt. Back's narrative,' and 'All the Rapids mentioned by Back were run without difficulty,' although he admits, 'The water must have been higher and the Rapids stronger when he passed.'

In 1977, David Pelly, an experienced canoeist, paddled the river in order to place a memorial to his forebear, John Henry Pelly, Governor of the HBC, on his eponymous lake. He comments: 'After close scouting, much discussion and careful consideration, we shot our canoes through most of the boiling rapids and swirling whitewater that were exciting, compelling and treacherous. There were more and wilder rapids than I had ever experienced in a single river.' One must remember that, according to the season, the changing volume of water dictates the difficulty of a river. Moreover, if David Pelly found the river challenging in a modern fibreglass canoe, consider what it would have been like for Back's crew in their awkward elephantine boat.

The expedition boatmen's concern was not so much whether their craft would make it down the rapids, as whether they could haul it back up the river on their return journey. Back tried to diminish their anxiety by reassuring them that the volume of water would have dropped greatly by then. After portaging round one particularly long rapid the crew noticed William Malley was missing. He eventually showed up having spent several hours lost, wandering across boulders and wading through swamps well away from the river. Soon after leaving Lake Superior he nearly drowned in Savannah Rapids so, following voyageur custom, this was named Malley's Rapids.

Despite many knocks the heavily loaded boat remained watertight and buoyant. The weather continued foul, with only two fine days in the month. Gales seldom lasted more than a day, however, and were generally followed by clear skies and warm weather.

At the head of Beechey Lake the toe of Bathurst Inlet lay only forty-five miles away across rough country. But the sudden southeast trending of the river suggested to Back that the Thlew-ee-choh was not going to enter the Arctic Ocean at that inlet as he had once supposed it might. In fact, he wondered if it wasn't leading him towards Chesterfield Inlet and Hudson Bay – where he certainly didn't want to go. At the end of Beechey Lake a further run of rapids culminated with a roar in 'an awful series of cascades, nearly two miles in length'. The boat had to be alternately lifted, launched, and lowered through the wildest water of the Cascades, which ran between some fantastic sandstone cliffs resembling, Back says, 'parts of old ruins or turrets rising out of low shelving prairies where deer ranged in thousands'.

After Baillie River, one of the main tributaries, the Thlew-ee-choh began trending northeast again in the direction they wanted, towards the Arctic Ocean. Of Hawk Rapids, Back writes: 'There was a deep and settled gloom in the abyss – the effect of which was heightened by the hollow roar of the rapid, still in deep shade, and by the screaming of three large hawks, which frightened from their aerie were hovering high above the middle of the pass, and gazing fixedly upon the first intruders on their solitude.'

Any encounter with unknown geography – be it climbing a mountain, crossing a desert or jungle, or running a wild river – is infinitely more difficult and impressive for the first pioneer than for the second and subsequent explorers. So we should excuse Back if he exaggerates his view of this wild and remote river, because fear of the unknown and a torrent of adrenaline are potent stimuli to describing our adventures with some license.

He now makes some pertinent observations about leadership:

It may perhaps appear to some persons that to persuade those whom I might have commanded was a gratuitous and unne-cessary trouble; but it should be borne in mind that, in services not purely military, the party is not, and cannot be, brought under strict habits of discipline. The success of such an expedition depends materially on the temper and disposi-tion of the leading men, who must sometimes be reasoned with, and at others kept in check, as circumstances may direct. It is necessary that they should feel a confidence in and attachment to their leader, not paying a mere sulky obedience to his orders; and what they do will thus be done heartily and with good will, not as the fulfillment of a contract.

On 19 July they entered Pelly Lake, the first of three large bodies of water comprising the lower part of the river; more perilous rapids separated the other two lakes, Garry and Macdougall. This confirmed the observation of the Indian who had told them that before arriving at the sea they would find an immense lake with many islands and deep bays in it. Much of Pelly Lake was still frozen so they had to cut a path through the ice with axes. This vindicated Back's decision not to start descending the river any earlier than he did. The current was often obscure and made navigating to the far end of the lake a difficult task.

Garry and Macdougall Lakes had the most convoluted outline so far. As their route trended generally southward, Back became concerned that they might yet end up in Hudson Bay. Soon, however, his mind was absorbed with other things when the river entered a gorge between 'two stupendous gneiss rocks, from five to eight hundred feet high, rising like islands on either side'. They could hear the roar of Rock Rapids before they saw them. Back writes: 'the rapid foamed, and boiled, and rushed with impetuous and deadly fury. At that part it was raised into an arch; while the sides were yawning and cavernous, swallowing huge masses of ice, and then again tossing the splintered fragments high into the air. A more terrific sight could not well be conceived.' Terror showed, too, on the men's faces. Even Anderson, generally contemptuous of Back's accounts, described Rock Rapids as 'strong and hazardous'.

The men tried to portage along the shore over scattered debris of rock, however steep cliffs soon barred the way, so they had no alternative but to run the falls. While the men controlled the boat from the shore with double safety lines tied to the bow and stern, McKay and Sinclair stood one at each end with poles to stave it off rocks. These cool and intrepid boatmen, communicating with each other by hand signals, guided the boat through the rapids only losing the keel plate which was stripped away by a boulder. Back rewarded the men with sincere words of praise and a generous glass of grog.

Rock Rapids was soon followed by Sinclair's Falls, Escape Rapid and Wolf Rapid (named after nine white wolves seen prowling round a herd of muskoxen). All these rapids required the utmost skill from both bowman and steersman. After making a zig-zag round the base of Mount Meadowbank – which reminded Back of Auld Reekie, Edinburgh's old town – the swollen river rolled straight on northeast between sandstone cliffs 'in sullen and deathlike silence . . . [It] raised such whirlpools and rapids as would have put the strength of a canoe in jeopardy.' Thereby Back justifies with reason his choice of boat over canoe.

After crossing Lake Franklin the expedition arrived at one final rapid before the river opened out into a wide reach. Upright stone markers – *inukshuks* – signs of an Eskimo meeting place, crowned the surrounding hills. Indeed, soon afterwards they saw a group of people congregated on shore waving their arms and shouting. Back took this for a show of welcome and ordered the boat to move towards shore where some Eskimos were brandishing spears, and yelling at them not to land. Nonetheless, Back stepped ashore alone and calmly walked toward them, calling out *'tima* (peace)', as he had done eight years before on the Arctic coast. He hoped this would persuade them he was not an enemy Indian, but a friendly European *kabloona* (foreigner). He adopted, as he says, 'the John Bull fashion of shaking each of them heartily by the hand'. How very English! 'Then patting their breasts, according to their own manner,' he continues, 'I conveyed to them, as well as I could, that white men and the Esquimaux were very good friends.'

The crew had great difficulty portaging round the last fall, so Back asked the Eskimos to help, which they willingly did. He then rewarded each Eskimo with two shiny new buttons, some fish-hooks, and various knick-knacks. He tried to exchange a few words with them, using a vocabulary one of the HBC men had written out for him. As a result the Eskimos were 'waggish enough to laugh at my patchwork discourse of mispronounced and misapplied words, and scarcely more intelligible signs'. Back then sauntered over to the tents of the Eskimos and began sketching them and writing down their names as they spoke them. This caused much mirth when he tried to read the names aloud.

Back asked an Eskimo to draw in the sand a map of the coast to the west. The man crudely marked out a large mass of land, rather than a shoreline, trending gently towards Point Turnagain (as Back had supposed). He led Back to the top of a nearby hill and showed him some mountains, the Adelaide Range, on a peninsula of the same name, which juts out to the west near the mouth of Chantrey Inlet. Yet again Back regretted that his faithful friend Augustus was not with him to translate accurately what the Eskimos were saying. They did not know of any ship – Parry's – having visited Prince Regent's Inlet (which was, unknown then to Back, separated by the foot of the Boothia Peninsula).

Threading their way through some sandbanks they saw to the

north a majestic headland, which Back named after Princess Victoria. It was now 29 July 1834. They had reached the Arctic Ocean at the mouth of the Thlew-ee-choh-dezeth, the Great Fish River, 'after a violent and tortuous course of five hundred and thirty geographical miles, running through an iron-ribbed country without a single tree on the whole line of its banks, expanding into fine lakes with clear horizons, most embarrassing to the navigator, and broken into falls, cascades, and rapids to the number of no less than eighty-three in the whole.' Those words cannot be bettered to summarize Back's remarkable achievement in descending the river that would eventually, and in his case deservedly, bear his name.

CHAPTER 19

The Unmapped Ocean

1834–35

Ripon Island, Cape Hay and Hutton Browne Bluff, Chantrey Inlet,
N.W.T., August 7, 1834. Sketch by Back.

George Back's drawing of Victoria Headland, like a whale surfacing
from the ocean, shows their tiny boat in the foreground. The vast
empty land emphasizes their accomplishment of having made one
of the longest and most spectacular descents of any North American wilderness river. Now that John Ross was safely ensconced at
home, Back could, in good conscience, turn his attention to his
second objective, to chart the unmapped Arctic coast west to Point
Turnagain.

Beyond Victoria Headland at Point Backhouse, Back climbed a
hill with an Eskimo who pointed out a substantial stretch of land
that lay between them and Point Turnagain. After rowing across
Irby and Mangles Bay (named after two insignificant Eastern
travellers) the expedition reached Cape Beaufort. To the north a
solid body of pack ice extended to the horizon blocking their way

forward. Nothing less than a mighty south wind would push that ice out of Chantrey Inlet and allow them to follow their planned route westwards. On 31 July a fresh breeze pressed the ice to the west and cleared an open lead off the eastern shore of the inlet. They sailed into the lee of King Island; then they crossed a short stretch of open sea to reach the shelter of Montreal Island, thereby reducing stress on their battered open boat.

On Montreal Island the men again became openly dispirited at the prospect of their impending return up the hazardous river which they had so recently descended. To divert attention from these melancholy thoughts, Back sent them to hunt a young cow muskox he had seen feeding among nearby rocks, which they did successfully. Older animals were generally inedible because of a strong taste and smell of musk, but when they cooked this one it provided two tasty meals. King shot a red-breasted phalarope, one of many birds that thrived on the island, along with plovers, ducks, tern, brown cranes, loons, and gulls.

From a hill in the middle of the island Back observed the ice moving according to the wind direction. A gale howled from the north, causing surf and ice to pound the beach where they were camped. When the storm subsided they launched the boat and drifted backwards with the tide to the mouth of Elliot Bay. They could not cook the three deer they had just shot because torrential rain had sodden their only fuel of moss and fern.

The naming of geographical points and headlands in this part of Chantrey Inlet is quite confusing when comparing Back's map with the modern one. Back's Cape Beaufort has become Cape Barclay; his Point Bowles is now Cape Hay; while what Back named Cape Hay is now Cape Britannia on the Kinngaak Peninsula. Such is the transience of eponymous fame. On the west side of Chantrey Inlet there are several inconsistencies. Montreal Island is much smaller than it appears on Back's map, and lies further north of Elliot Bay and Point Gage than he shows; and there is no island along the coast between it and Point Ogle.

The ultimate irony is Back's naming of Mount Barrow: 'a green hill about seventy or eighty feet high, being the most remarkable feature in that flat desert of sand'. Sir John Barrow, whose name is inseparably connected with polar discovery, was one of the few senior contemporaries whom Back did not alienate, and one might think that in the naming game Barrow deserved better than this insignificant hillock. He did, however, get his name appended later to an inlet between Points Ogle and Richardson, as well as a multitude of other points and bays all over the Arctic.

The weather cleared, as it will, given patience. A strong wind arose and, after a pleasant sail, they overtook the drift ice and reached Point Ogle, which became an island at high tide. However, rain returned and soaked them to the skin. Fresh water was scarce and they could find no fuel, so they had to eat their food cold. Everyone felt wretched. McKenzie became sick, swollen, and bloated; Sinclair was suffering from constant exposure to cold and wet. Colossal upright slabs of ice piled up on the beach like 'a magnificent Stonehenge'. The shallow sandy shore offered no channel for the boat, and it was futile trying to lift it round the ice or move blocks aside for its passage. On the eastern shore across Chantrey Inlet, Back could see a chain of hills that are part of the Canadian Shield extending into the Boothia Peninsula.

On an excursion searching for moss and fern, King picked up some whale vertebrae and pieces of an old kayak. The men returned with a log of pine driftwood nine feet long by nine inches in diameter which Back was certain came from the mouth of the Mackenzie. He considered, therefore, that it was, 'incontrovertible proof of the set of a current from the westward along the coast'.

A northwesterly wind pushed the ice eastwards, which convinced Back that it must be heading for a major sea, or at least a very deep opening. However, he missed the crucial point that the land they could see to the north was King William IV Island, and the ice he was watching flowed between it and the Boothia Peninsula towards the modern-named Rae Strait and Ross Strait. He postulated that this passage might be 'in favour of the existence of a southern channel to Regent's Inlet'. In this he wrongly presumed that the Boothia Peninsula was an island with a passage between it and the mainland – which it might have been but for a small neck of land at Spence Bay. In standing firm on this idea he disregarded Eskimo and Indian opinions confirming that a peninsula, which was also shown on John Ross's chart, projected far to the north – Boothia Felix.

Ten years later, if Franklin had understood that such an open passage – the straits of Ross and Rae – existed to the east of King William Island he might not have been tempted to follow its western coast into the trap of Victoria Strait, which is almost always, then and now, choked with heavy pack ice. He could thereby perhaps have avoided the loss of men who, once stuck in the ice, strayed off aimlessly in various directions trying to find a way out of their gelid predicament. In particular they sought, as a means of escape, the isolated mouth of Back's Great Fish River which, as we know, would not have helped them escape from their Arctic imprisonment, given the equipment available to them.

From Mount Barrow, King scanned with a telescope the coast to the north of Cape Hay, confirming his opinion that uninterrupted shore ran north and south with no sign of a passage leading eastwards. He proposed exploring that coast to prove his point. But it was now 11 August and Back's Official Instructions from Lord Goderich clearly stated: 'whatever may be its prospects or success, you are on no account to prolong it beyond such a period of the year (varying from the 12th to the 20th of August, according to the distance which you may have attained) as will insure your return to your winter quarters before the severe weather sets in.' So King's proposal got no support from his boss.

In order to keep the men occupied Back dispatched a party to Mount Barrow, 'furnished with a telescope and compass to get the bearings to the westward, and occupied myself during their absence in obtaining observations for the dip and intensity'. The exploring party, comprising McKay, Sinclair and Taylor, returned at 11 p.m., 'fagged and depressed', having not got far because the land was so swampy and the distant view was obscured by fog. During a break in the weather, however, they had a sight of some blue mountains (Adelaide Range) with a large body of water in between (Barrow Inlet).

On their return the men reported nothing untoward, though King claims to have noted that their 'evasive manner at the time gave indications of something unusual having occurred'. Back mentions nothing out of the ordinary in his account. An incident only came to light after the expedition had returned to England, and a report was later sent to HBC Governor George Simpson, who wrote: 'I scarcely know what to make of this report which I hope may turn out to be groundless.' But it wasn't.

In Scotland, on 17 December 1835, at Stornoway on the Isle of Lewis in the Hebrides, William Morrison, Justice of the Peace, held an inquiry based on the statement of a certain Malcolm Smith, made under oath and signed with an X. He reported a conversation with a Highland artilleryman member of the crew, John Ross, who heard the three men of the scouting party discussing the incident. He and one other had pledged to reveal nothing while in America, but back in London they reported the matter to Dr King, 'not having opportunity of giving the information to Captn Back' – why not, we are not told.

During their walkabout the three men had apparently shot some swans on a lake. This caused a crowd of curious Eskimos to congregate and fire off a few blunt arrows, which King notes was a token of peaceful intentions. However the encounter turned nasty, and developed into a full-blown affray during which the rattled white men shot three of the Eskimos dead. King comments – smugly and after the fact – that it should act as a warning to future travellers in unexplored country not to allow their subordinates to wander any distance without supervision of an officer.

The weather remained foul so the boat became locked ashore by surf and waves. Back writes: 'I had long observed a depression of spirits in my steersmen . . . but I could not account for the gloom which now spread itself as if by infection over the rest; except, indeed the artillerymen, whose steady conduct was such as to deserve the highest commendation.' King also noticed it. Could the melancholy faces of those involved in killing the Eskimos have been due to apprehension that they might have become sitting targets for retribution? In order to lighten the men's mood Back sent them off to hunt, and they returned with three hares and a brace of ducks.

With no reasonable way forward, Back became despondent: 'there was no expedient by which we could overcome the obstacles before us . . . the close-wedged ice, the constant fogs.' For some time he had been thinking of dividing the party and leaving four men to guard the boat while he, King, and four fit men would set out for Point Turnagain, hoping to fill in that blank on the map. But he abandoned this idea because the ground was so soggy for walking, drinking water and moss for fuel were scarce, and it was already 15 August. The Official Instructions gave no orders about exploring eastwards, only to the west. He assembled the men, they unfurled the British flag as a sign of sovereignty, and, as King says, 'Captain Back sounded a retreat.' It was a wise decision by Back, however King did not think so, and did not keep his thought to himself.

When the gale abated they sailed fast down Chantrey Inlet, but the wind rose again to a hurricane, forcing them to shelter under Victoria Headland. When they crossed the bar at the river's mouth, several crewmen tossed their caps in the air with joy at having left sea and ice behind. The river had dropped at least three feet since they were last there. At Whirlpool Rapid they had to make two long portages. This time, however, the Eskimos offered no help, but remained up on a hill, sitting in line watching them. They might well have heard news of the affray and so kept their distance. As a peace offering, Back left a stash of presents for them – iron hoops and brass rings, awls, fishhooks and beads. Next morning the Eskimos again watched the crew from behind some rocks high on a hill, but they made no attempt to come down for a meeting.

Back's *Narrative* now takes a strange turn. He has spent 434 pages getting to this point, often in meticulous detail. Then, almost as an afterthought, in a mere eight pages he disposes of the expedition's return journey upriver, arguably one of the most remarkable and arduous feats in the annals of river – or any other sort of – exploration. It is as if he was in as much of a hurry to get the awful journey over as he was to complete writing about it. So I have little choice but to do the same, since even King's account gives little more information.

At the end of a six-week trip on the Back River, after the descent of its eighty-three rapids in tough plastic boats, canoeists wearing weatherproof clothing and eating lightweight freeze-dried meals would likely heave a sigh of relief, pull out a satellite phone, and call up a turbo-prop Otter floatplane to fetch them back to

Yellowknife for a hot bath and a cold beer. Instead, Back and his men faced slithering along a slippery riverbank and across boulder-fields, while tracking their water-sodden boat against boisterous whitewater rapids, and portaging its dead weight round falls. All this, with the prospect of spending another uncomfortable and hungry winter at Fort Reliance before they could make a spring exit down several hundred miles of inland waterways to catch a ship home. He admits that it was 'exceedingly fatiguing from the uncertainty of the footing, the shingly surface generally sliding away under the pressure of each step, so that the people were constantly falling and hurting themselves'. The boat also took a hammering and needed frequent repair by caulking with oakum and grease.

At the narrows between Garry and Pelly Lakes, some sixty or seventy Eskimos were angrily waving spears, so Back's party stayed well away. In Hawk Rapids the boat almost got away from them when the hemp hauling line broke, but by quick thinking the crew managed to hold it from being swept away in the current. The men shot a fat caribou which provided respite from meals of old and mouldy pemmican, but they had great difficulty starting a fire because all the moss was rain-soaked. Snow fell three days later, at the Cascades below Beechey Lake.

On 4 September hundreds of geese flew south heralding fall and incipient winter. Back paints a beautiful word picture of fall in the Barrens: 'Not a deer was seen; the [Labrador] tea plant had evidently been frozen, the dwarf birch was almost leafless, the willow was bright yellow, and the whole country was clothed in a livery of sober brown. Five musk-oxen were the only living creatures about; all others having deserted a place which the year before was teeming with life.' All along the return route they picked up caches of meat laid down on their outward journey, but every carcass was spoiled either by wolverine and ground squirrels or by mould. The meat might have been more secure if they had made wooden cache boxes which they could have used later for firewood.

They reached Muskox Lake, passed Icy River (icebound as ever), and arrived at the topmost portage on the Thlew-ee-choh. Next day, 15 September, they had a joyful reunion with their loyal and reliable friend, MacLeod, who, together with four boatmen and two Indians, had been in camp at Sandhill Bay for several days. In their absence MacLeod had evidently been busy. He had set up two fisheries, and had crossed Great Slave Lake to collect from Fort Resolution forty bags of pemmican and other supplies forwarded from York Factory by the HBC. In the country north and east of Great Slave Lake the Indians could not remember a more wet and dismal summer; so things did not augur well for another winter at Fort Reliance.

It was late September when they crossed Aylmer, Clinton Colden, and Artillery Lakes. Water froze on the boat's gunwales and the oars, and one of the chronometers stopped because of the severe cold. They were in Yellow Knife country again. The river now flowed in their favour so they shot rapids instead of hauling their deadbeat boat against the current. At the start of the short but very rough Ah-hel-dessy (or Lockhart) River, which comprised a series of huge waterfalls, they pulled the boat ashore and hid it in some willows along with all its gear. It would safely stay there until the following spring when it could be recovered by sledge.

The crew, each carrying a seventy-five-pound load, set off through the hills and woods east of the river, which they could hear thundering through distant gorges. Not far away they could see spray from Parry's Falls boiling up from a defile about 500 feet deep. Back was impressed: 'The whole face of the rocks forming the chasm was entirely coated with blue, green, and white ice, in thousands of pendant icicles: and there were, moreover, caverns, fissures, and overhanging ledges in all imaginable varieties of form, so curious and beautiful as to surpass any thing of which I had ever heard or read. The immediate approaches were extremely hazardous . . . Niagara, Wilberforce's Falls in Hood's River, the falls of Kakabikka near Lake Superior, the Swiss or Italian falls . . . are not to be compared to this for splendour of effect. It was the most imposing spectacle I had ever witnessed.'

They reached Fort Reliance after four months absence, tired but healthy. Sadly the house was not in equally good shape. It tilted drunkenly out of kilter, and the mud plaster of the walls had been washed away leaving scabrous pockmarks. A lightning bolt had struck and demolished an upturned canoe.

Far from dreaming of the comforts of home – still eight months away – Back began contemplating a future possibility of walking from Beechey Lake to Bathurst Inlet in order to fill gaps in that tantalizingly uncharted span of geography. But he realized that such a venture might take another couple of seasons, and would require recruiting an entirely new crew. That he could even entertain the thought of such an extension to their recent strenuous journey says much about his tenacity. More ordinary people would have been happy to pack up and head home as fast as possible. Dr King, however, was less laudatory (typical of this prickly relationship), as he wrote: 'Captain Back had determined upon relinquishing any further attempts at discovery by land.' As King saw it, they had given up too early and returned south before completing their task of surveying a new section of the Arctic coast.

In his journal, Back summarizes the following winter as briefly as he did the return journey upstream on the Thlew-ee-choh. To reduce pressure on Fort Reliance he sent MacLeod away, first to the fisheries and then to Fort Resolution. At their fort the two officers continued to make regular scientific observations, wrote their journals, and touched up maps and drawings done in the field. Every other night they held classes for the men, and the Sunday routine of Divine Service and rest was unchanged. On New Year's Day 1835 everyone shared in a boozy feast to lighten the tedium of a long dark winter. By contrast with the previous year, they were not burdened with sick and starving Indians hanging around the fort. Nevertheless, judging from King's snide comments about his boss, their evenings together were probably not much fun.

The Yellow Knives were still in the vicinity, but Akaitcho was no longer the powerful chief of yore. This old friend of the previous land expeditions had grown 'peevish and fickle' in old age, and his once absolute authority was no more. However, he still turned up occasionally with meat. The Yellow Knives had fallen out mightily with neighbouring Slave Indians, which accounted for them roaming around this east end of Great Slave Lake rather than in the vicinity of the Yellowknife River. Fed up with constant rapine, enslavement, and humiliation, the Slaves had massacred their Yellow Knife tormentors and pushed them out of their own home territory. Adding to their misery, an epidemic – probably measles or smallpox – killed off many more.

At first the winter was severe but the weather turned mild after January, promising an early breakup. Back left Fort Reliance on the first day of spring, 21 March 1835, after taking leave of MacLeod, who had served the expedition so faithfully. At Fort Chipewyan he waited for the rivers to open so, in order to tidy up some expedition business, he could return 'by way of Canada'. He instructed King and the Scotsmen to take the shortest route home by heading to York Factory to catch the annual HBC ship to England. Meanwhile Back recruited a crew of Canadian voyageurs and Iroquois to paddle him to Montreal – a mere couple of thousand miles, give or take.

On 15 May flocks of swans, geese, and ducks flew overhead; catkins hung on the branch, willow shoots burst open, and anemones appeared on sunny eskers. Women around the fort began to tap trees for sugary sap, and to plant potatoes and barley.

Two months later Back reached Sault Ste Marie on Lake Superior. On 6 August 1835 he arrived at Lachine, near Montreal, 'having since I quitted it travelled over a distance of seven thousand five hundred miles, including twelve hundred of discovery'. But, as King would aver, with very little contribution to new mapping of the Arctic coastline.

Back also came in for a tongue-lashing from HBC factor William McTavish, with whom he had exchanged harsh words during his 1820 winter journey. McTavish wrote home to his family in 1834, while Back was on the river: 'They have been playing the same tune, they have starved again this winter . . . You'll hear what a fine story they'll make out of this bungle, they will you may be sure take none of the blame themselves . . . They will return next summer and like other Expeditions will do little and speak a great deal.' McTavish obviously felt Back was a snob who looked down on the factors because of their lack of formal manners. He goes on waspishly about 'the elegance of manner so peculiarly [Back's] . . . the capers and grimaces of a Frenchified fool'. It is hard to know what had so upset McTavish since he had previously, on the several expeditions with whom he had dealt, seemed friendly to Back.

On 17 August 1835, at New York, Back embarked on the packet *North America*. It docked three weeks later in Liverpool, on 8

September, after an absence of two years and nearly seven months. King and the Scotsmen, after a tough and tedious journey to York Factory without major incident, reached England in October 1835.

Back, never one for modesty or diffidence, yet fails to mention that he had not lost a single man under his command during his journey to the Arctic Ocean and back. (Williamson, alone, had died in a storm on Great Slave Lake heading for Fort Resolution after being discharged because of ill health; and Augustus had not yet joined them when he died.) In the days when most voyages of discovery entailed a high toll, Back's record is outstanding, especially when compared with that of Franklin.

Many bouquets showered Back on his return to England. The Royal Geographical Society, then in premises at 21 Regent Street, made him a Fellow, awarded him the Founder's Gold Medal and the Patron's Silver Medal. Subscribers to the Arctic Land Expedition lauded him as a hero and presented him with an inscribed silver plate dinner service. Sir John Barrow was unreservedly complimentary: 'He never shrunk from difficulties, never murmured, never desponded. Like true British seamen, the greater the danger the more firmly he stuck to the bark, determined to hold on, sink or swim. The praiseworthy object alone which he had in view took full possession of his mind.'

Back was promoted by Order in Council to the recently reinstated rank of post captain. This was an unusual advancement because he had not served the prescribed year at sea since being elevated to commander; the only other precedent for such promotion was William IV, the Sailor King. At a royal audience, Back presented copies of his *Narrative of the Arctic Land Expedition* to the king, who commanded him to stay for dinner. 'You and I, sir,' said His Majesty, 'are the only two Captains by Order in Council in the navy.' Back had yet to command a ship – but that was soon about to change.

PART SIX

HMS *TERROR* EXPEDITION

CHAPTER 20

Back's Last Blank on the Map

1836–37

Boats in swell among ice, by Back.

George Back barely had time to recover from the rigours of his two-year-long Great Fish River adventure before the government, nudged by the Royal Geographical Society, invited him to lead another expedition to fill in a last blank on the map of the Arctic – the coastline between Prince Regent's Inlet and Point Turnagain. In particular, his orders were threefold: to determine whether Boothia Felix was a peninsula or not; to complete the final route through the North West Passage; and to discover if it was 'navigable by ships of considerable burthen'.

On 13 May 1836 newly promoted Captain Back was appointed to command HMS *Terror*, then lying at Chatham alongside the hulk of *Hussar* (on which he had painted scenery for his theatricals while he was a midshipman serving in *Bulwark*). It was to be yet another large and expensive sea-mounted expedition similar to those of Parry and the Rosses. *Terror*'s crew of sixty were all volunteers, some of whom had spent their working lives on Greenland whalers. Back's second-in-command was Lieutenant William Smyth, a noted artist and traveller in South America, who had been with Beechey in *Blossom*. The two mates would later each make rival claims to be the first discoverer of the North West Passage: Graham Gore died on Franklin's fateful last expedition, and Robert McClure commanded one of the many searches for it. Also in the crew was an ice mate, who brought special knowledge of the quirks of frozen seas.

Back's orders from Their Lordships of the Admiralty, under the signature of Sir John Barrow, were to proceed either to Wager Bay (first choice), or to Repulse Bay, one of which would become his icebound winter anchorage and stepping-off point for an overland approach to Prince Regent's Inlet, thought to be the key to unravelling the secret of Boothia. This meant that Back would sail through Hudson Strait towards Southampton Island, which effectively guards the mouth of both Wager and Repulse Bays. He could then decide whether to sail north of Southampton Island through Frozen Strait, or by Welcome Sound to the south. As it happens, he chose wrongly – Frozen Strait to the north – whereas in almost any year Welcome Sound would have been passable and more protected.

One party was instructed to follow the Melville Peninsula north to the western end of Fury and Hecla Strait, while the main party was to head westwards towards Chantrey Inlet and the mouth of the Back River, and thence along the coast to Point Turnagain. Wager Bay would, in fact, be closer to the Arctic Ocean at Chantrey Inlet but would involve a long hike cross-country. Repulse Bay lies south of an isthmus (later named after Rae) separating it from the lowest point of the Gulf of Boothia (and, had they known it for sure, on the wrong side of the Boothia Peninsula).

This exploration was to be completed in one season in order that 'this Arctic Expedition may be distinguished from all others by the promptitude of its execution, and by escaping from the gloomy and unprofitable waste of eight months' detention'. They should then return to England in the fall of the same year. A quick look at a map will show how misinformed and misguided these instructions were, because they completely missed the fact that Boothia is a peninsula (albeit with a very narrow neck – at Spence Bay) and there was no easy way across it to link Prince Regent's Inlet with the North West Passage.

This sea-borne venture opposed diametrically the philosophy of Richard King, Back's recent colleague, who railed at the failures of the Great Fish River Expedition. He claimed that on launching their wooden locally-built boat, 'not a single individual composing our party ever expected to reach the sea at all . . . the river was fortunately, however, by no means so formidable as it had been represented.' This dig at his boss refers to the impossibility – if horrific accounts of the rapids by local Indians were true – of ever being able to portage the heavy boat.

The splenetic and contrary Dr King proposed to the government a strong case for him to lead an overland expedition to Chantrey Inlet. It would consist of a party of only six men, living off the land and travelling on foot and by dog team; the cost would be less than £1,000 – a fraction of the budget of Back's previous and present expeditions. King had even cached – when stormbound with Back on Montreal Island in Chantrey Inlet two years previously – supplies that would be available should he lead the overland journey he was proposing.

King stressed the importance of heeding the description of the country and the counsel of local Indians and Eskimos rather than listening to fur traders. As an example, he mentioned the reliance of Back and Richardson, in planning an approach to the Arctic Ocean, on Blackmeat's information and the accuracy of his drawings. Sadly for King, his acerbic personality had so alienated him from the authorities that no one took his proposal seriously. Many (including Franklin) derisively opposed it, and it died on the drawing board. King's emphasis on relying on natives, and imitating their mode of travel, was yet to be vindicated by Dr John Rae, doyen of Arctic explorers of a later decade, and reinforced much later by Vilhjalmur Stefansson.

King took a final dig at his former commander, and at the

264 THE MAN WHO MAPPED THE ARCTIC

government, noting that: 'the officer undertaking the enterprise generally dictates his own orders; – at least, such was the case with Captain Back.' In other words, he considered that if Back had followed 'discretionary orders' when they were at the mouth of Chantrey Inlet, he could easily have countermanded his Official Instructions and journeyed no more than 116 miles east to determine whether or not Boothia was a peninsula.

King summarized his request to the government thus: 'The question has been asked, how I can anticipate success in an undertaking which has baffled a Parry, a Franklin, and a Back? I will state in reply, that if I were to pursue the plan adopted by the latter officers, of fixing upon a wintering ground so situated as to oblige me to drag boat and baggage over some two hundred miles of ice, to reach that stream which is to carry me to the scene of discovery, and, when there, to embark in a vessel that I knew my whole force to be incapable of carrying, very far from expecting to achieve more than those officers have done, I very much question if I could effect so much.' History would show that King was right, but his pleas fell on too many already hostile and deaf ears.

HMS *Terror*, a 340-ton bomb vessel, had been strengthened with massive iron and copper fastenings and rivets. Carpenters had repaired a leak discovered on a preliminary trial run to Hull. She was fitted with a newfangled warming device consisting of a 240-foot wrought iron bore pipe, five-eighths of an inch in diameter, running round nearly the whole ship. The pipe was filled with a strong solution of brine, heated by a coal furnace and circulated by a forcing pump. Expansion tubes, fitted abaft the first bend, aimed to prevent excessive pressure bursting the pipes. For insulation the men would build a housing over the ship and bank the decks with snow.

The apparatus failed totally. Furnaces sent a current of warm air down the centre of the ship, while its cold sides encouraged condensation, which streamed down the cabin walls until they were iced solid and deck gratings were awash, while open coal stoves, intended to dry any vapour, gave off suffocating sulphurous fumes. To disperse some of these noxious gases, Back devised a canvas funnel which immediately reduced both humidity and temperature between decks. However, this was not enough to salvage the poor design.

Three large, comparatively light, whalers were built to fit on sledges, shoed with iron runners so they could be hauled overland. From previous experience, Back had 3,000 pounds of spicy pemmican specially prepared, and he took a large supply of preserved meat. The crew's clothing included fur and felt caps with flaps (known as Welsh wigs), swanskin underwear, carpet or duffle boots insulated with cork insoles and bearskin blankets.

Before sailing Back was summoned to Brighton for a royal audience with King William IV in order to explain the expedition's objectives. At dinner the king introduced Back to Queen Adelaide. 'My dear,' he reportedly quipped, 'this is the gentleman who made his dinner off a pair of leather trowsers!'

Because of contrary winds a steamboat towed *Terror* to the Orkneys where, for easier handling, the rear mast was fore-and-aft rigged like a barque. The other two masts remained square-rigged. After an uneventful Atlantic crossing – if such can ever be imagined in the cumbersome ships of those days – *Terror* reached Davis Strait where the men saw their first icebergs, one at least 300 feet high. Then she entered the pack ice. Light winds caused the crew to set studding sails (extensions of the square mainsails), and also a boom foresail, which could be moved quickly to alter course in narrow ice leads. Back described the scene: 'The tall ship with all her sails set thread[ed] her graceful way through the masses of ice, upon a sea as smooth as an inland lake. What a contrast from the mountainous waves over which we had been tossing and tumbling for weeks past!'

On 30 July *Terror* passed Cape Chidley, the northernmost tip of Labrador, and entered Hudson Strait. Off Savage Islands, Eskimos paddling thirty kayaks and three umiaks surrounded the ship, urging the crew to trade. One woman offered her child in exchange for some needles and old clothes; another told a balding officer she would trade her hair in exchange for a curtain ring. Eskimos also cut several lengths of rope from the ship's side – such pilfering habits with which Back was familiar.

The calm did not last long. Soon a gale forced Back to order his ship into the lee of a huge iceberg. Rowing the ship's boats, sailors set two ice anchors into the iceberg and warped her tight with hawsers. Snugly nestled out of the gale, Back was aware that any moment the unstable iceberg could topple and capsize *Terror*. Newcomers to pack ice thought they were stuck forever, and even the hardened Greenland seamen said they had never seen such heavy ice. Experienced sailors, however, looked forward to sudden, inexplicable changes that can occur with, as Back puts it, 'the change of wind, the tide or current, or some of those unaccountable circumstances which, in a few hours even of entire calm, create so sudden and marvellous a change of scene'.

Terror crept forward laboriously through Hudson Strait until, on 23 August, she lay abeam Southampton Island. The pack ice had given way to huge ragged floes. Often twenty feet high, they tilted so it was impossible to walk on them. 'Cheerless indeed was the prospect,' Back dolefully remarks, 'for, excepting within a few feet of the ship where the black streaks of water looked like inky lines on a fair sheet of paper, far as the eye could reach all was ice.' This constant, unpredictable ebb and flow of the pack posed a steady threat to the ship, so Back ordered the rudder to be removed and slung astern to prevent it being damaged by a floe coming from behind. He must have wondered if he would not have been better approaching Welcome Sound via the southern coast of South-ampton Island because of its ice-free reputation.

The ship was stuck near the mouth of Frozen Strait, somewhere between Cape Comfort and Cape Bylot. Tantalized by being so close to shore, yet unable to land, Back ordered all officers and men onto the ice and, under Lieutenant Smyth's direction, to clear a space through the sludge with ice saws, axes, ice chisels, hand-spikes, and long poles. This they did with the 'merriment of schoolboys'. On a similar date in 1822, at this very place, Parry described finding open, ice-free water.

One evening when the men were outside chasing each other in a game of tag – called 'baiting the bear' – the ice mate on watch at the masthead spied a large polar bear approaching. Everyone, including the marine sergeant's bulldog, raced for the ship. The bear stood tall about fifty yards off, sniffing the air for a scent. Whereupon the men shot the majestic beast, hauled the carcass on board, and hung it from the mainstay. Later an Arctic fox, catching a whiff of bear, came close to the ship and Mate Gore shot the harmless creature. Fortunately, a raven wheeling round the ship avoided the bored sailors' musket practice. 'What must be the wearisome uniformity of life,' Back wrote disparagingly, 'in which incidents such as these became memorable.' He had earlier complained that: 'Not an incident occurred to relieve for a moment the dull monotony of our unprofitable detention . . . no occupation, no amusement, however ordinarily gratifying, had power to please or even distract the thoughts.' It was not a jolly prospect for a long dark winter ahead.

During a gale on 20 September a floe split in two. Pressure curled and crumbled the windward ice forcing it eighteen feet up against *Terror*'s side, which, Back reports, 'creaked as if it were in agony'. Strong as she was, if smaller plates of ice had not been forced under the bottom of the ship and lifted her bow two feet out of the water, she would almost certainly have been crushed and her timbers stove in. Back summoned the crew on deck and spelled out emergency orders in event of the ship foundering under 'the impact of an icy continent driven onward by a furious storm'. All provisions and essentials for survival after shipwreck were brought from the holds and stored on deck. In emergency, the sailors could throw the stores over the side onto a floe, and with luck still retrieve them.

With approaching winter the days shortened and the temperature dropped. After thirty-four days the ship was still icebound and virtually helpless, so Back asked each officer for a written opinion as to what they should do now. They were unanimous about the need to prepare to abandon ship should a sudden crisis arise. She was now tilted askew by floes, and stuck only three miles from shore where the crew could see bays with suitable harbours and anchorages. So near, yet so far. Three whale boats and two cutters – fully provisioned and outfitted with guns, ammunition, and other essential survival gear – were slung alongside ready to be lowered at a moment's notice.

Back comments on how unsociable, undisciplined, and sloppy about their personal comfort were the crew who, he admits, had been 'hastily gathered together, and for the most part composed of people who had never before been out of a collier'. Although some had sailed in Greenland whalers, he notes, with naval immodesty, the few sailors on board who had served on men-of-war were worth all the rest put together.

This is harsh unspoken self-censure on Back's selection of a crew for what was to be a serious and expensive voyage of Arctic exploration. Again Back reflects how preferable regular servicemen are for all hazardous or difficult enterprises, and he notes how many of the random crew secreted their food allowance along with other 'unmanly and unsailorlike practices'. His ultimate wail is: 'give me the old Jack Tar who would stand up for. his ship and give his life for his messmate.' Why, if all this was true, did the Admiralty, and Back himself as captain-elect, not ensure in the first place that the entire crew was composed of regular Royal Navy seamen? In England there were still plenty of willing hands around, despite the downsizing of the navy after the Napoleonic wars.

In order to keep his apparently slovenly men busy, each day Back had them exercising and playing football out on the ice. Nonetheless, many of them began to complain of joint pains, widespread skin bruising, numb legs, bleeding gums and loose teeth – all signs of scurvy. This happened despite large amounts of antiscorbutics (fresh preserved meat, pickles and lime juice) in the original ship's manifest. Back ordered the purser to increase dispensing lime juice from two to three times a week, together with extra preserved soup, spruce beer, cranberries, and other fruit. Unfortunately the cargo of carrots had rotted in their casks because the sand they were stored in had become wet; they were not even appreciated by the pigs carried on board as bacon-on-the-trotter. Again there is no mention of fresh seal meat, which could have been their most powerful weapon against scurvy.

A near-hurricane raged just before Christmas with the temperature at −20°F (−30°C). It had been −63°F (−53°C) a few days before. Nevertheless, when the gale abated the officers dined together, finishing the meal with plum pudding; the men put on a Christmas farce. By now a sixth of the crew were sick, together with five or six officers. This demonstrated that the cause of the illness was not a difference between the diet of officers and men. Back ordered the officers to supervise the men in removing all their clothes and hanging them to dry on returning to the ship after exercising outside.

By 12 January 1837 *Terror* was still icebound in a floe three miles offshore of Southampton Island. Her drift steadily increased until the beginning of February, when the distance was ten miles. With continuing sickness on board, despite every precaution they could devise, Back writes: 'the time since we left England, though but eight months, seemed longer than any three years of my former not unadventurous life. Days were weeks, weeks months, months almost years. There were no marks to separate one day from another, no rule whereby to measure time; all was one dull and cheerless uniformity of dark and cold.' These were grim words from a man who had undergone the hardships of three previous expeditions, each lasting several years. Moreover, by now he was no longer a youngster.

With the advent of spring, as ice began to break up, danger became more acute because the ship was no longer securely frozen into a floe. Back was awakened by a hoarse, rushing sound, followed by severe shocks against the hull. The officer of the watch reported that the floe alongside was breaking up. On deck, Back saw a rent in the ice and heard a crashing, grinding noise from below. As more cracks opened up, a thirty-foot-high wall of ice bore down on them with the pandemonium of an earthquake. Several men were thrown down on deck by shocks to the ship's frame. Then quite suddenly the whole chaotic tumult ceased and was replaced by an eerie calm.

A few months before, they would have relished suddenly being freed from the grip of ice and able to move again, but now it presaged imminent disaster. The poor ship was lifted and tossed about like a cork; one moment threatened with being crushed by violent pressure of ice nipping at the hull, the next heeling over at an absurdly drunken angle until the leeward boats touched water. The carpenter was busy below decks inspecting beams and stanchions for stresses and strains. The sailors were kept constantly busy at the pumps. Back writes of 'the awful grandeur of these gigantic piles . . . the terrible sublimity of which lay in the rolling onward of these mighty engines of destruction . . . she trembled on the brink of eternity'.

For the next month *Terror* was continually buffeted and thrown about by fickle ice. The captain gave new orders for abandoning ship: boats were to be lowered and rowed to the largest nearby ice pan, and crewmen were to protect invalids from the weather and care for them 'as Christians and British seamen'.

Three miles off Point Terror the ship was again lifted up by ice. A rolling wave thirty feet high, crowned by a square mass of blue ice the size of a house and weighing many tons, hung on its crest before crashing into the hollow where the ship was embedded. Yet again the crew thought their final moment had come. They crowded on deck, terrified invalids tottering behind them, knowing that if the ship went down they would likely all perish. In fact, the pages of Back's account of these terrible months gets tedious with breathless repetition of the unimaginable horrors of being on a floundering ship totally out of control, and with the ever-present prospect of an icy grave for all aboard. A surfeit of too much horror can dull the mind and spirit.

Again Back consulted the officers, the ice mate, and some of the more experienced leading seamen. They all agreed that a fully provisioned cutter should be kept ready on a nearby floe so that, if the ship sank, any surviving crewmen could head for Hudson Bay to report *Terror*'s plight. The question was just how long the ship could withstand a constant attack by rogue ice which appeared bound to send it to the bottom eventually.

During this nightmare passage a Royal Marine, Alexander Young, died and was 'committed to the deep' through a hole in the ice – the third shipmate to perish from scurvy. A snow bunting hovered for a few seconds over the hole, and then flew away. Its symbolism was not lost on the crew, several of whom remained sick, lethargic and unable to work. Most were lame from scorbutic, stiff, swollen knees and ankles. Back wrote an official letter for the record to Dr Donovan, the ship's doctor, asking his opinion of the probable consequences should the ship remain ice-locked for another winter. The doctor replied gloomily that it would be fatal to many officers and men, especially since he had no more antiscorbutics or medicines.

Again Back had failed to heed the experience of his predecessors – and his own from previous expeditions – in understanding the need of fresh food to fend off scurvy. James Lind, in his 1753 *Treatise on the Scurvy*, had spelled out the requisites for its prevention – all confirmed by Cook and other contemporary navigators. Parry, during his 1820s expeditions, grew mustard and cress on board, and whenever possible ate fish, seal, and walrus; he lost only one man of a hundred-strong crew. John Ross's achievement during four long Arctic winters is even more remarkable. Because he understood the importance of fresh meat, and of using local natives to hunt for it, only one man of his crew of twenty-two died of scurvy. Back's crew on *Terror* included no Eskimos with hunting expertise, and consequently they had no fresh seals or walruses to eat once those live pigs aboard had been slaughtered. The Royal Navy took a long time to learn its lessons. Captain Robert Falcon Scott RN repeated exactly the same mistakes in the Antarctic a couple of generations later.

On 11 July cheers erupted from the crew as loud rumblings announced that *Terror*, until then encased in a protective ice floe, had broken free of her stranglehold. Back looked over the stern and saw 'the dark bubbling water below and enormous masses of ice gently vibrating and springing to the surface'. As the ship turned on her beam ends with the leeward boats hanging into the water, flying objects bombarded any men still between decks. They rushed for the companionway and clambered on deck, fearing 'that a few moments only trembled between them and eternity'.

After losing sight of Southampton Island for the next six weeks *Terror* drifted southeast along Hudson Strait, still choked with ice. She passed south of Nottingham and Salisbury Islands, north of Charles Island, and across the wide mouth of Ungava Bay. She reached an exit to open ocean between Resolution Island and Button Islands off Labrador's most northern point, Cape Chidley. There Back noted the 'frowning grandeur' of the cliffs of that fjord-riven tip of northern Labrador.

It seemed that at last they were free, yet Back was still considering whether he could accomplish the original purpose of his expedition – even with a scurvy-depleted exhausted crew and a severely damaged leaking ship. Again he asked for written opinions from the three lieutenants, and the ice mate, who each separately but unanimously decided there was no option other than to make for England without delay. 'My own sense of duty finally concurring in this opinion,' Back writes, 'the resolution was most reluctantly adopted.' The crew assembled on the quarterdeck to be told they were going home. At this they erupted – as British sailors apparently did on all such occasions – with three hearty cheers. Can one blame them?

The carpenters inspected *Terror* closely. They reported that pressure on the keel had sprung the deck amidships, and might also have broken her back. To plug some of the leaks they shored her up below decks, caulked and tarred the deck seams, and wrapped chains round the hull and tightened them with the capstan. They also inserted new stay bolts in the broken tiller. Lieutenant Smyth devised a method of hanging the spare rudder upside down as an alternative to using the fractured sternpost. However, the prospect of setting off across the Atlantic in such a sieve was unappealing.

A fair wind blew them past Cape Farewell, the southern tip of Greenland. But the leaks increased and, despite continuous pumping by the crew, *Terror* became daily more waterlogged. Her average speed dropped to two or three knots, she heeled constantly to starboard and was barely steerable, especially when the wind rose to gale force. On 1 September, Lieutenant Smyth reported to his captain that the crew could no longer keep up with the pumping necessary to keep the ship afloat. In short, *Terror* was sinking.

Until then they had been aiming for Stromness in the Orkneys, but Back decided to alter course for the nearest land – Lough Swilly, just south of Malin Head on the north coast of Ireland. The masthead lookout spied a sail in the distance, and shortly afterwards cried, 'Land ahoy!' The sailors fired rockets and guns to summon a pilot. Under his direction *Terror* glided silently past the lights of a fisherman's cottage, and near midnight anchored safely in Lough Swilly. As the chains rattled, Back remarks succinctly: 'Fifteen long months had elapsed since that pleasing sound of a falling anchor had greeted us.'

Because *Terror* was sinking slowly by the head, Back decided to run her ashore on a carefully chosen sandy beach nearby. At low tide the officers and carpenters inspected the ship's bottom and found a gaping hole between the broken keel and the sternpost through which water poured, the forefoot had disappeared, and numerous bolts were loose or broken. Considering the strained and twisted frame, the seamen marvelled that *Terror* had stayed afloat during the gales on her Atlantic crossing.

Back reported the state of *Terror* and her crew to the government, which immediately sent a ship to carry invalids to Devonport. A party of Chatham shipwrights arrived on the steamer *Columbia*, and in six weeks had *Terror* seaworthy again. During this wait many families in Lough Swilly took sailors into their homes, and fed and nursed them back to health. Eventually, on 18 October 1837, *Terror* sailed round the coast to Devonport, and then to Chatham where she was put out of commission and taken into dry dock for repair and refit. This was so well done that she soon put to sea again, and sailed south to the Antarctic, captained by Francis Crozier, under overall command of James Ross on *Erebus*. Finally she went north yet again with Franklin on a one way ticket to his, and her, grave in the North West Passage.

So ended an expedition of meagre achievement, considering its overambitious goals. Pierre Berton casts it as 'an unmitigated disaster', which is unduly harsh considering the dreadful ice conditions that prevented Back even reaching the land he intended to survey. In fact, it was a triumph of coping with overwhelming odds. Sir John Barrow wrote: 'The whole voyage was of a nature so extraordinary and unparalleled in the history of voyages, ancient and modern, as not to be forgotten.'

The quality of Back's leadership was never in question. His entry in the *Dictionary of National Biography* reads: 'It may be safely said that few sailors ever survived more terrible perils and hardships than Back did in the two expeditions under Franklin, and the two which he commanded himself.' And the *Geographical Magazine* eulogizes: 'During this service, Captain Back displayed all the qualities of a great commander, and to his constant good-humour and cheerfulness, firmness, and presence of mind in moments of peril, and seaman-like skill, were due the preservation of the crew and of the good ship, which was destined to see much more service.'

In spite of the *Terror* crew's success in overcoming great odds, and Back's excellent leadership, nevertheless, given its grand goals, the expedition was a failure.

CHAPTER 21

Arctic Councillor

1837–87

Young male deer, by Back.

It is sad that anticlimax was the note on which George Back's fifth, and final, major expedition and his adventurous career had to end. The Great Fish River was Back's zenith; from then on things slid steadily downward. Partly this was because he was ageing naturally, when wisdom overrode the drive and rashness of his ambitious youth; partly because he had no firm job to keep him occupied, despite his steady rise through the ranks to admiral; partly because poor health drained his vigour, the probable reason why he did not accompany Franklin on his fatal final expedition.

The years were not wanting in boosts to his ego – as if that was ever necessary – and were filled with an avalanche of honours and awards. In February 1836 the Royal Geographical Society made him a Fellow, awarded him the Founder's Gold Medal and the Patron's

Silver Medal. The *Société de Géographie de Paris* also gave him a gold medal for Arctic discoveries.

After his return in *Terror* from Southampton Island, he was busy penning his *Narrative* of the *Terror* débâcle, a copy of which he sent to Queen Victoria, possibly as a nudge to remind her to knight him. Anyway, on 18 March 1839 Sir George he deservedly became. Had he died on *Terror* he might – since the public have an insatiable appetite for high drama – have been beatified and passed into Arctic mythology, as his former boss, John Franklin, was to be. Explorers who return safely, however awful the experiences they survive, take second place to those who die tragically.

Even though Back was only forty-two years old it is certain that his health had been severely undermined by the stresses of almost continuous expeditioning since the age of eighteen, and with five years imprisonment before that. He suffered constant headaches, insomnia and general 'emaciation', for which he went to take the waters at Marianske Lazne, in Czechoslovakia (known also as Marienbad). But this did not seem to help, so he went south to Italy again, his favourite haunt, as one might expect of an artist.

In Florence, Back met Francis Crozier, destined to be second-in-command of Franklin's final expedition and to die on it. Crozier wrote to James Ross that Back had left the impression of being vain and narcissistic; and one acquaintance in Italy remarked: 'if he was in love with himself he had no right to suppose every lady he met was the same.' Despite the corns on Back's feet being 'queer' (his piles seem to have settled) he managed to attend an audience in the Vatican with Pope Gregory XVI whose ring hand he kissed. The pope asked if Back had been to the North Pole and said how 'florid and healthy' he looked – doubtless he thought from the cold.

Back returned to England because, being still on the active list, he was keen to see how job prospects were shaping. But they weren't, because a backlog of senior officers was still awaiting dead men's shoes. One highlight was an invitation from Franklin, who had just returned from a vexatious spell as governor of the penal colony of Van Diemen's Land (later Tasmania), to join a trio of himself, Hepburn and Richardson for dinner. This invitation was a surprisingly magnanimous and conciliatory gesture on the part of Back's old boss, considering how antipathetic each of these three expressly felt about him. However, this did not stop Back from trying to discourage the Admiralty from selecting Franklin to lead the 1845 expedition. Back said Franklin was too old – nearly fifty-nine – and was in poor physical shape should he have to walk anywhere. Back's sound views, however, were ignored.

During three years downtime in London, from 1843 onwards, Back did some serious courting of the recently widowed Theodosia Elizabeth Hammond, then living at 109 Gloucester Place, Portman Square. They were married in a quiet wedding at St Mary's Church on the morning of 13 October 1846. His brother, Charles, was best man. Immediately after lunch the couple set off on their honeymoon in a carriage, accompanied by a maid and courier, to Folkestone where they passed 'a happy night'. During their long post-nuptial holiday Theo (as Back refers to her) kept a journal cataloguing her many travel miseries, with details of the myriad museums, galleries, churches and cathedrals they visited. She refers to her husband repeatedly as 'Sir George'. One wonders if their pillow talk was as knightly formal.

For ten months Back proved to be the perfect tour guide while he and Theo meandered the length of Europe from Paris to Avignon, Cannes, Genoa, Florence, Rome and Naples. They climbed Vesuvius – a second time for Back – and Theo was wimpish throughout, leaning heavily on her chevalier of whom she wrote: 'but for the kindness and help of Sir George, I do not believe I ever would have conquered it . . . I fell at every yard, and generally slid back, making a dozen yards to gain one.' She was scared of horses and mountain roads, she disliked the effluvia of towns, and admits she had become 'a sad coward'. With terror as her constant companion she cannot have been a very lively mate on such a long peripatetic journey. One has to give her credit for hanging on in the wake of her gallant tough explorer husband, never a man to give in to trifles. Their return was by way of Bologna, Venice, Milan, Lucerne, Cologne and Boulogne. In London again, Back moved into Theo's comfortable home in Gloucester Place.

While the Backs had been away in Europe the nation became anxious about Franklin and his crew, of whom little had been heard since they set off on 19 May 1845 in his ship *Erebus*, along with Back's *Terror* under the command of Francis Crozier. It was to be a grandiose expedition, intended to lay to rest the mystery of the North West Passage. Five invalids were dropped in Greenland on the way out, leaving the total complement of both ships at 129 souls. The last sight and sound of them was when a whaler captain, Mr Martin, spoke to Franklin while the two expedition ships were moored to an iceberg in Lancaster Sound. All appeared then to be going swimmingly.

On return from their honeymoon Back was invited to join the Arctic Council, a committee formed in the 1830s to advise the Admiralty, and especially its vibrant second secretary, John Barrow, on North West Passage matters. It comprised such other luminaries as Parry, Bird, James Ross (noticeably absent was his Uncle John), Beaufort, Sabine, Hamilton, Richardson, Beechey – the order, from left to right, in which they appear in the famous Arctic Council group portrait.

It was now 1847, and the Franklin expedition had been absent two years without a jot more news. The unpopular John Ross expressed gloomy views about them, but no one listened to the old blowhard, preferring to savour the anticipated glory of Britain being the first to traverse the North West Passage. Waspish Dr King jumped in with his unsolicited, and resented, advice that the best way to search would be an overland expedition down the Great Fish (Back) River. He suspected – rightly, as he so often was – that Franklin might have got stuck in pack ice to the west of King William Island.

By the next year mild anxiety had turned to deep concern. Lady Jane Franklin let her guard down for the first time and admitted that her glorious husband might be in trouble. She began to mobilize the government and the Arctic Council to send a search party. In fact, Franklin was already two years dead. John Barrow had now died, and his place at the Admiralty had been taken by his energetic nephew, John Barrow junior.

Over the next dozen or so years more than fifty parties were sent out to search for Franklin at the (present day) cost of several million pounds sterling – certainly Lady Jane's contribution was large enough to seriously diminish her fortune, to the disgust of her stepdaughter, Eleanor. The first major rescue attempt, in 1842–50, was three-pronged: James Ross would approach from the west by sea, Richardson and Rae by land via the Mackenzie River, and two ships under overall command of Henry Kellet would sail round Cape Horn and pass through the Bering Strait. Thereafter many searches followed, led by a galaxy of Arctic names at great cost but to no avail. Back however, was not among the searchers. Though a whole decade younger than Franklin, the toll taken on Back by the Arctic was now ruling out further travel in that challenging environment.

Of Franklin's fate little hard fact emerged until F. Leopold McClintock's party reported in 1857. Leaving his yacht *Fox* anchored at the eastern end of the Bellot Strait, then completely jammed with pack ice, he and his officers set off with dog teams and sledges, each travelling in different directions to scour the western side of Boothia Peninsula. Lieutenant William Hobson would search King William Island, and Lieutenant Allen Young would go north to Prince of Wales Island, while McClintock would head for the mouth of the Great Fish River. Incidentally he would discover Rae Strait, which was crucial to finding a sea route through the North West Passage.

During these southern forays McClintock met several groups of Eskimos, heard conflicting stories about sightings of white men some years before, and collected a variety of relics that undoubtedly came from the Franklin expedition – notably one brass Royal Navy button. McClintock then found a skeleton, undoubtedly a sailor, judging from his clothing remnants. But the prize went to Hobson, sledging counterclockwise round King William Island just a week ahead of his boss. He left a note for McClintock in a cairn near Point Victory on the north west coast saying that he had found a written record of the Franklin expedition.

That record itself tells simply, succinctly if tersely, as much of the sad tale as anyone needed to know. In a tin case was one of the printed forms supplied to explorer ships, intended to be thrown overboard in a bottle asking, in six languages, whoever found it to forward it to the Admiralty. The record was written in two different hands dated a year apart. The first, of 28 May 1847, had the standard blank spaces filled in and signed by Lieutenant Gore and Mate Des Voeux. It told laconically of *Erebus* and *Terror* wintering at Beechey Island (in fact, he wrote both year and longitude wrongly) and of their exploration of Wellington Channel and Cornwallis Island. It concluded with the ironic summary: 'All well.' Evidently during that first season they had achieved an incomparable programme of exploration.

The second part of the record, dated 25 April 1848, was written in Victorian style round the margin of the report form in neat handwriting, mainly that of Lieutenant Fitzjames. It tells how *Erebus* and *Terror* were deserted three days before, 'having been beset since 12th September, 1846', when the officers and crews, consisting of 105 men, had landed there. The last words of Fitzjames – by then Captain of *Erebus* – were: 'Sir John Franklin died on the 11th. June 1847 and the total loss by deaths in the expedition has been to this date 9 officers & 15 men.' Written under the signature 'F.R.M. Crozier, Captain and Senior Officer' was the addendum, 'and start on tomorrow 26th for Back's Fish River'.

McClintock and his men, pushing on to within fifty miles of Point Victory, found a loaded sledge that told much of Crozier's fate and the foolishness of it all. A boat (700–800 pounds) was mounted on top of a sledge built of oak and iron (650 pounds). In the boat were the skeletons of two men; it was loaded with sundry items, including two loaded and cocked double-barrelled guns, knives, cut-down bayonet scabbards, two rolls of sheet lead, twenty-six pieces of silver cutlery, delftware teacups, a bible, and several religious books, plus *The Vicar of Wakefield*, seven or eight pairs of boots, toiletries, five pocket watches, and a cigar case – overall weight about 1,500 pounds. Of these articles McClintock benignly says they were 'truly astonishing in variety, and such as, for the most part, modern sledge-travellers in these regions would consider a mere accumulation of dead weight, but slightly useful, and very likely to break down the strength of the sledge-crews'. He omitted saying that his own men were starved, scorbutic and dying.

Nearby they also found a four-foot-high pile of woollen clothing, four iron cookstoves, several brass curtain rods, a library of religious books, a lightning conductor and brass button polish – weight about ten tons. All this had not got far from where they abandoned ship, but evidently the other sledge was intended to be hauled overland to the mouth of the Great Fish River – and then what? Up the river as Back had done with such difficulty, and then halfway across Canada? This imbecility is included in such detail because it helps to understand the mindset of the Royal Navy of the time, one which we know persisted in the explorers of the next century. It also casts light on Back himself and the influences that shaped his character.

Franklin's first winter quarters had been found on Beechey Island, together with the graves of three seamen. Then, in October 1854, Rae – travelling native as he had proved conclusively could be done successfully – met some Eskimos who reported having seen, some years before, a party of white men hauling boats towards the mouth of the Great Fish River. Near Chantrey Inlet, Rae found the remains of thirty men surrounded by guns, crested silver spoons and forks, and kettles which contained human bones – proof that the starving men had resorted to cannibalism. Dr Rae, being familiar with human anatomy, wrote that it was 'as terrible as imagination can conceive'. This revelation caused an uproar in Britain's prudish Victorian press. It was nearly the final chapter of that sad expedition; the final chapter has yet to be written – if it ever will be, since the public appetite for the Franklin story seems insatiable.

While Back was serving on the Arctic Council the Admiralty gave him a desk job to advise on the most suitable harbour for a packet steamer service to Ireland. He recommended Holyhead.

More honours followed: a prestigious Fellowship of the Royal Society, the Arctic Medal, and the Polar Star (which he himself designed to hang from a snow white ribbon) of which he was one of the first recipients; an honorary doctorate of civil law (DCL) from Oxford University; and a Captain's Good Service Pension.

In 1856 the Admiralty finally decided to abandon further searches for Franklin and his crew, who were all officially recorded as dead. The Crimean War, 1853–56, understandably diverted attention from the Arctic. Sabine and Back concurred, to the ire of Sophia Cracroft (Franklin's niece and Lady Jane's confidante) who wrote, concerning abandoning the search: 'That miserable Sir G. Back will say anything that a Lord of the Admiralty tells him, & is held in contempt or something worse by all who have served with him.' This is patently untrue, since many people admired Back, even given the number he upset along the way. She followed her fusillade with a venomous letter to Henry Grinnell, an American benefactor and sponsor of several search expeditions: 'He [Back] is never the man to originate a handsome act, but if he finds it popular, & that it will be successful, he steps in to take as much of the credit as he can secure. You must not think it is a harshness or severity when I describe him as intensely selfish, sly, & sycophantic.'

Perhaps these were the very qualities which assisted Back's steady rise through the top echelons of the Royal Navy's promotion ladder — rear-admiral on the reserve list in 1857, vice-admiral in 1863, admiral in 1867. The gilt of these promotions was tarnished by Theodosia's death in 1861. She was buried in her father's vault in Kensal Green cemetery — not in the tomb of her first husband where, ironically, Back himself was destined to lie without other monument of his own.

During his widowed years Back was deeply involved with affairs of the Royal Geographical Society, serving as a member of the council for seven years, and vice-president, when many great explorers of the middle nineteenth century reported to him. David Livingstone wrote a detailed description, with a diagram, of his discovery of the Zambezi's Victoria Falls, incidentally commenting: 'the men go stark naked — the women have more sense and go decently covered.' Speke writes to him about the discovery of Lake Tanganyika: 'What Burton told me was this — he was kicking his legs about on the sofa one day not knowing what to do with his leave from India drawing well nigh to an end when you went up to him and asked him if he would like to go and determine what the Lake in Beckman's map really was.'

The RGS archives contain files of Back's correspondence with all and sundry, and many dinner invitations from the rich and famous. Typical is a note he wrote on a programme for a selection of vocal music held at the anniversary banquet of the Royal Academy of Arts on 5 May 1860:

I dined at the R Academy – Best dressed at 4.30. Looked at the Paintings – my old ship HMS 'Terror' among the ice of Frozen Strait (1837 March) – printed by Mr E. Cooke ARA from an original sketch of mine. It was much admired. Lord Palmerston, Russell, Duke of Somerset, Mr Gladstone, Mr Sidney Herbert etc etc (the Ministers) sat on the right of the President Sir C. Eastlake and the Duke of Rutland, Earls of Derby & Normandy, Mr Disraeli, Sir John Pakington, Lord Stanhope etc etc on the left. Bishops of London & Oxford, Presidents of Royal Society etc etc etc & Mr S.L.Mosley of the US of America etc etc were there – about 170 persons. I sat next to Professor Faraday. The burst of lights when the Queens health was drunk was very effective. Geo Back R. Admiral.

Charles Dickens, in 1856, wrote an adaptation of Wilkie Collins's play *The Frozen Deep* about two Arctic explorers who fell in love with the same girl. (Could he have read about Greenstockings in Franklin's *Narrative* of the first land expedition?) It was performed at Manchester Free Trade Hall, and later in front of Queen Victoria, with Back present. Dickens wrote to thank him for attending, and to apologize for calling him only *Captain* Back, saying that he had 'so long known and sympathised with Sir George Back in the earlier endurances and glories of his great career that he trusts his best excuse may lie in the fidelity with which he followed Sir George in print long ago'.

Sophia Cracroft, surprisingly, asked Back to unveil a monument to her Uncle John Franklin in Westminster Abbey on 31 July 1875; her invitation read: 'Surely, the hand of my dear Uncle's Companion and Friend is the fittest that could be selected.' Peculiar and inexplicable are such words from someone who had previously been so vitriolic in her dislike of Back. Lady Jane Franklin, Sophia's bosom friend, planned the epitaph but she died two weeks before the ceremony. Lord Tennyson, Franklin's nephew by marriage, eventually wrote the words:

Not here! the white North has thy bones; and thou,
    Heroic sailor-soul

> Art passing on thine happier voyage now
> Toward no earthly pole.

Back kept up a busy social schedule for another year, walking and dining out. Then, on 23 June 1878, aged eighty-two, he died peacefully at 109 Gloucester Place, Portman Square. His meticulously detailed will left £5,000 to his brother Charles, and many lesser legacies to a host of relatives. He remembered each of his servants separately with legacies ranging from £110 to £6 in cash, to three months' wages. In a codicil to his will he left to the Royal Geographical Society £600 to be invested and the interest used 'for the benefit of such Scientific Geographer or Discover [sic] or person who may be engaged in discovery or exploration'. The money is now presented by the Royal Geographical Society, as the Back Award, for 'applied or scientific geographical studies which make an outstanding contribution to the development of national or international public policy'. He also gifted to the RGS his portrait by Brockendon which today hangs in the president's lobby.

As Back had shown throughout his life, he mixed well with the 'lower orders', albeit on a higher social plane. He was awarded the Freedom of the Master Pilots of Newcastle, and he gave several annual dinners to the crew of the Ramsgate lifeboat. He also showed interest in, and left bequests to, the Royal National Lifeboat Institution, the Shipwrecked Fishermen and Mariners' Royal Benevolent Society, and the Royal Naval Schools, both male and female.

To live for eighty years in the nineteenth century was rare; it spoke of George Back's unusually strong constitution. Over eight decades we have watched him develop from a bumptious, ambitious young Royal Navy volunteer, through the tribulations of a teenage prisoner of war, via midshipman and expedition artist and surveyor, to become one of the toughest Arctic explorers of his time – which was notable for tough naval explorers. He also established himself as a noteworthy artist whose drawings and paintings, often done under terrible conditions, add greatly to our appreciation of scenes he describes so aptly in words.

During Back's youthful years he had the knack on the one hand of gaining people's affection, respect and admiration, on the other of driving them to distraction with his vanity and arrogance. With age he mellowed but he was still able to engender odium among those he crossed. Nevertheless his generosity shows through in the thought he put into composing his will – no servant was forgotten.

Back's physical toughness and mental stamina were never in doubt, and his dedication to the Arctic unassailable. He was a man of his time, with all the faults conferred by being trained in the Royal Navy and nurtured in class-conscious, hierarchical Britain. It is strange that it has taken so long for him to be recognized as one the great Arctic explorers.

Select Bibliography

GENERAL

Barrow, Sir John, *A Chronological History of Voyages into the Arctic Regions (1818)*. London: John Murray, 1818.

Berton, Pierre, *The Arctic Grail: The Quest for the North West Passage and to the North Pole, 1818–1909*. Toronto: McClelland & Stewart, 1988.

Cooke, A. and Holland, C., *The Exploration of Northern Canada, 500 to 1920: A Chronology*. Toronto: The Arctic History Press, 1978.

Fleming, Fergus, *Barrow's Boys*. London: Granta Books, 1998.

Holland, Clive (ed.), *Farthest North: A History of North Polar Exploration in Eye-Witness Accounts*. London: Robinson, 1994.

Holland, Clive (ed.), *Arctic Exploration and Development c.500 B.C. to 1915: an encyclopaedia*. New York: Garland, 1994.

Hopwood, Victor G. (ed.), *Explorers by Land to 1867*. Literary History of Canada. Toronto: University of Toronto Press, 1976. Vol. 1.

Kirwan, L.P., *A History of Polar Exploration*. Harmondsworth, England: Penguin, 1959.

Lloyd, Christopher, *Mr. Barrow of the Admiralty: A life of Sir John Barrow 1764–1848*. London: Collins, 1970.

Lopez, Barry, *Arctic Dreams*. Toronto: Bantam Books, 1987.

Mackenzie, Alexander, *Voyages from Montreal on the River St. Laurence, through the Continent of North America to the Frozen and Pacific Oceans in the Years 1789 and 1793*. London: Cadell, 1801.

Markham, Sir Clements R., *The Arctic Navy List*. London: 1875.

Mirsky, Jeannette, *To the Arctic: The Story of Northern Exploration from Earliest Times to the Present*. Chicago: University of Chicago Press, 1970.

Morris, James (Jan), *Heaven's Command*. London: Faber & Faber, 1973.

Nanton, Paul, *Arctic Breakthrough: Franklin's Expeditions, 1819–1847*. Toronto: Clarke, Irwin, 1970.

Savours, Ann, *Search for the North West Passage*. New York: St Martin's Press, 1999; London: Chatham Publishing, 1999.

Smucker, Samuel, *Arctic Exploration and Discoveries during the Nineteenth Century*. New York: Miller, Orton, 1857.

Sobel, Dava, *Longitude*. London: Fourth Estate, 1998.

Stefansson, Vilhjalmur, *The Friendly Arctic*. New York: Macmillan, 1921.

Stefansson, Vilhjalmur, *Unsolved Mysteries of the Arctic*. New York: Macmillan, 1938.

Struzik, E., 'North West Passage: The Quest for an Arctic Route to the East'. *Canadian Geographic*. Toronto: Key Porter, 1991.

BIOGRAPHICAL SKETCHES OF GEORGE BACK

A.H. B-y., 'Back, Sir George (1796–1878)', *Dictionary of National Biography*.

Chalmers, John W., 'Back and the Arctic', *North* (1972) 19 (3): 6–10.

Finden, William & Edward (engravers of Back's sketches), *Dict. Nat. Biog.* vii: 21–22.

Higginbotham, H., *Stockport: Ancient and Modern* vol. 2. London: Sampson Low, Marston, 1892.

Holland, Clive, 'Sir George Back', *Dictionary of Canadian Biography*, vol. 10, 1871–1880. Toronto: University of Toronto Press, (1972): 26.

MacLaren, I.S., 'George Back', *Profiles in Canadian Literature*, (ed.) Heath & Jeffrey. Dudurn Press, (1991): 25–51.

Neatby, L.H., 'George Back', *Arctic* (1983) 36 (1): 104–5.

Neatby, L.H., 'Mr Back of the Expedition', *Beaver* (1963) 294: 13–21.

Pares, Ann, *The Man Who Ate His Trousers: A Narrative of the Life of Admiral Sir George Back RN. 1796–1878*. Salisbury Printing Co., (privately printed) 2001.

Pelly, David F., 'Treasures of an Arctic Artist', *Canadian Geographical Journal* (1995), 115: 56–62.

Royal Geographical Society, George Back obituary. *RGS Proceedings*. 1879. I (I): 70–71.

Stockport Advertiser, Obituary of Admiral Sir George Back. 28 June 1878: Leading Article.

CANOES, CANOEING AND YORK BOATS

Adney and Chapell, *The Bark Canoes and Skin boats of America*. Washington: Smithsonian Institute, 1964 & 1983.

Adney, E.T., 'How an Indian birch-bark canoe is made', *Harper's Young People Magazine*, 29 July 1890, and *Outing*, Magazine, May 1900.

Barbeau, Marius, 'Voyageur Songs', *The Beaver*, June 1942: 15–19.

Glazebrook, G. de T, 'On the eclipse of the birchbark canoe', *History of Transportation in Canada* II: 27–29. Toronto: 1938.

Glover, Richard, 'York Boats', *The Beaver* 279 (March 1949): 19–23.

Gosselin, Bernard, *César's Bark Canoe*. (video) National Film Board of Canada, 1971.

Hodgkins and Hoyle, *Canoeing North into the Unknown: a record of River Travel 1874–1974*. Toronto: Natural Heritage/Natural History, 1994.

Howay, F.W., 'Building the Big Canoes', *The Beaver* 270 [1940]: 38–42.

Jennings, John, *The Canoe in Canadian Cultures*. Toronto: Natural Heritage/Natural History, 1999.

Kent, Timothy, *Birchbark Canoes of the Fur Trade*. Ossineke, Michigan: Silver Fox, 1997.

Lentz, John, 'Through the Barrens by Canoe', *Explorers' Journal*. vol. XLIII, no. 1, Mar. 1965.

MacLennan, Hugh, *The Rivers of Canada*. Toronto: Macmillan, 1974.

McPhee, John, *The Survival of the Bark Canoe*. New York: Farrar, Strauss, Giroux. 1975.

Morse, Eric, 'Canoe Routes of the Voyageurs', *Canadian Geographical Journal*, May 1961.

Morse, Eric, *Fur Trade Routes of Canada – Then and Now*. Toronto: Toronto University Press, 1979.

Nute, Grace, *The Voyageurs*. New York: Appleton, 1931.

Nute, Grace, *The Voyageurs' Highway*. St. Paul, 1941.

Nute, Grace, 'Jehu of the Waterways', *The Beaver*, Summer 1960: 15–19.

Raffan, James, *Bark, Skin and Cedar*. Toronto: Harper Collins, 1999.

Saunders, Richard M., 'The emergence of the *coureur de bois* as a social type', *Canadian Historical Assn Report*. Toronto: 1939. 22–33.

White, Bruce M., 'Montreal Canoes and their Cargoes', Paper to Fifth North American Fur Trade Conference, Montreal, 1985.

1 KING'S LETTER BOY, 1796–1809

Back, George, *A Long Yarn*. Unpublished memoir (up to 1819).

Back, George, Chapter notes for the above. SPRI MS 395/20.

George, M. Dorothy, *London Life in the Eighteenth Century*. London: Kegan Paul, 1925.

2 PRISONER OF NAPOLEON, 1809–14

Forester, C.S. (ed.), *The Adventures of John Wetherell – the authentic diary of a 19th Century British Seaman impressed into His Majesty's Service to fight Bonaparte*. London: Michael Joseph, 1954.

Fraser, Edward, *Napoleon the Gaoler. Personal experiences of British sailors & soldiers during the great Captivity.* London: Methuen, 1914.

Horne, Alistair, *Napoleon, Master of Europe: 1805–1807.* London: Weidenfield & Nicolson, 1979.

Lewis, Michael, *Napoleon and his British Captives.* London: Allen & Unwin, 1962.

Wolfe, R.B., *English Prisoners in France; containing Observations on their Manners and Habits, principally with reference to their Religious State, during nine years' residence in the Depots of Fontainbleu, Verdun, Givet, and Valenciennes.* London: Hatchards, 1830.

3 FRANKLIN'S MIDSHIPMAN, 1815–18

Dickens, G., *The Dress of the British Sailor.* National Maritime Museum publication. 355.14 (42)

Dundonald, Thomas, Tenth Earl, *The Autobiography of a Seaman.* London: Bentley, 1861.

Fisher, Lord, *Records.* London: Hodder & Stoughton, 1919.

Forester, C.S., *Mr Midshipman Hornblower.* London: Michael Joseph, 1950.

Gilbert, A.N., 'Buggery and the British Navy, 1700–1861', *Journal of Social History,* Denver: 1970, vol. 1.

Gilbert, A.N., 'Crime and Disorder: Criminality and the Symbolic Universe of the 18th Century British Naval Officer', in R.W. Love (ed.), *Changing interpretations and New Sources in Naval History.* New York: 1980.

Glover, Richard, 'The French fleet 1807–1814 Britain's Problem; and Madison's opportunity', *Journal of Modern History* 39 No. 3 (Sept 1967) 233–52.

Harvey, A.D., 'Prosecutions for Sodomy in England at the beginning of the Nineteenth Century', *Historical Journal,* 21: 1978. 939.

Kemp, Peter (ed.), *The Oxford Companion to Ships and the Sea.* Oxford: OUP, 1988.

King & Hattendorf (ed.), *Every Man Will Do His Duty.* New York: Henry Holt, 1997.

Lewis, Michael, *The Navy in Transition, 1814–1864: A Social History.* London: Hodder & Stoughton, 1965.

Lewis, Michael, *The Navy of Britain.* London: Allen & Unwin, 1948.

Lloyd C.C. & Coulter J.L.S., *Medicine and the Navy.* London: Livingstone, 1963.

Mackinnon, C.S., 'The Wintering Over of Royal Navy ships in the Canadian Arctic, 1819–1876', *Beaver,* Outfit 315, No. 3, 1984/85.

Macpherson, Charles, *Life on board a Man-of-War, by A British Seaman*. Glasgow: 1829.

Marryat, Frederick, *Mr Midshipman Easy*. (1792–1848). London: [s.n.], 1836.

Marshall, John, *A Royal Naval Biography*. London: Longman, 1825.

Markham, Sir Clements R., Log by CRM as midshipman on H.M.S. *Collingwood & Superb*. RGS archives.

May, W.H., *The Life of a Sailor*. London: Clowes, [n.d.]

Montagu, Victor, *A Middy's Recollections*. London: A & C Black, 1898.

O'Brien, Patrick, *Master and Commander*. Glasgow: Fontana/Collins, 1970.

Penn, Geoffrey, *Snotty: The Story of the Midshipman*. London: Hollis & Carter, 1957.

Rodger, N.A.M., *The Wooden World: an Anatomy of the Georgian Navy*. London: Collins, 1986.

Spavens, W., *The Narrative of William Spavens, a Chatham Pensioner by Himself*. Louth: 1796.

Beechey, Capt. F.W., *Voyage of Discovery towards the North Pole in the Dorothea and Trent under Captain David Buchan 1818*. London: Bentley, 1843.

Petermann, A., 'Sir John Franklin, the Sea of Spitzbergen, & whale-fisheries in the Arctic region', *Journal of the RGS*. vol. 23. London: John Murray, 1853.

4 TO HUDSON BAY, 1819

5 A YORK BOAT WEST, 1819–20

6 TO FORT CHIPEWYAN, 1820

7 FORT ENTERPRISE, 1820

8 BACK'S WINTER JOURNEY, 1820–21

9 THE HYPERBOREAN SEA, 1821

10 DEATHLY RETREAT SOUTH, 1821

11 THINGS WHICH MUST NOT BE KNOWN, 1821–22

Anon, 'Pemmican and How To Make It', *Beaver* 295. (Summer 1964): 53–54.

Arnason, T., Hebda, R. & Johns, T., 'Use of Plants for Food and Medicine by Native Peoples of Eastern Canada', *Canadian Journal of Botany* 59 (1981): 22–40.

Back, George, *Arctic Artist: The Journal and Paintings of George Back, Midshipman with Franklin, 1819–1822*, (ed.) C. Stuart Houston. Montreal: McGill-Queen's University Press, 1994.

Back, George, *Canadian Airs collected by Lt. Back R.N. during the late Arctic Expedition under Captain Franklin, with Symphonies and Accompaniments by*

Edward Knight, Junior: Words by George Soane Esq. A.B. London: J. Power. 1823.

Ballantyne, J.B., *Hudson Bay or Everyday life in the Wilds of North America; being six year's residence in the terrritories of Honourable Hudson's Bay Company. 1879.* Edmonton: Hurtig, 1972.

Bellot, J., *Memoirs, and his Journal of a Voyage in the Polar Seas in Search of Sir John Franklin.* London: Hurst & Blackett, 1855. 1: 252.

Brown, Jennifer, *Strangers in Blood: Fur Trade Company Families in Indian Country.* Vancouver: University of British Columbia Press, 1980.

Brown, Jennifer, 'Two companies in search of traders: Personnel and promotion patterns in Canada's early British fur trade', *Proceedings of the 2nd Congress, Canadian Ethnology Society.* vol. 2. National Museum of Man, Mercury Series, Ottawa. paper no. 28, 632–45.

Carpenter, Kenneth, *The History of Scurvy and Vitamin C.* Cambridge: Cambridge University Press, 1986.

Clouston, J.S., 'Orkney and the Hudson's Bay Company', *Beaver*, Dec. 1936: 4–8.

Cooke, A. and Holland, C., *The Exploration of Northern Canada, 500 to 1920: A Chronology.* Toronto: Arctic History Press, 1978.

Crowe, K.J., *A History of the Original Peoples of Canada.* Montreal: McGill-Queen's University Press, 1974.

Cyriax, Richard, 'Arctic Sledge Travelling by Officers of the Royal Navy, 1819–1849', *Mariner's Mirror* 49, no. 2, 1963.

Davis, Richard C. (ed.), *Rupert's Land: A Cultural Tapestry.* Waterloo: Wilfred Laurier University Press, 1988.

Davis, Richard C. (ed.), *Sir John Franklin's Journals and Correspondence: The First Arctic Land Expedition, 1819–1822.* Toronto: Champlain Society, 1995.

Dickason, Olive P., *Canada's First Nations: A History of Founding Peoples from Earliest Times.* Toronto: McClelland & Stewart, 1992.

Duckworth, Harry W., 'The Last Coureurs de Bois', *Beaver*, Spring 1984: 4–12.

Franklin, John, *Narrative of a Journey to the Shores of the Polar Sea, in the Years 1819, 20, 21, and 22.* London: John Murray, 1823.

Feeney, Robert, *Polar Journeys: the Role of Food and Nutrition in Early Exploration.* Fairbanks: University of Alaska Press, 1997.

Fuller, W.A., 'Samuel Hearne's Track: some obscurities clarified', *Arctic* 52, No. 3, Sept. 1999.

Gall, E.J. (Scotty), 'Travelling in the Old Days', *Moccasin Telegraph*, Commemorative Issue, 30, No. 1 (Winter 1970): 40–41.

Glazebrook, G. de T. (ed.), *The Hargrave Correspondence, 1821–43*. Toronto: Champlain Society, 1938 (Publications of the Champlain Society, Vol. 24).

Hanbury, David T., *Sport and Travel in the Northland of Canada*. London: Arnold, 1904.

Hearne, Samuel, *A Journey from Prince of Wales's Fort in Hudson's Bay to the Northern Ocean in the years 1769, 70, 71 & 72*. London: A. Strahan & T. Cadell, 1795 and (ed.) Glover, R. Toronto: Macmillan, 1958.

Holland, Clive, *John Franklin and the Fur Trade 1819–22*. pp. 97–III.

Holland, Clive, 'Captain Ross's welcome back: text of a humorous poem (1833)', *Polar Record* (1974), 17 (106): 47–48.

Hood, Robert, *To the Arctic by Canoe, 1819–1821: The Journal and Paintings of Robert Hood*, (ed.) C. Stuart Houston. Montreal: McGill-Queen's University Press, 1974.

Innis, H.A., *The Fur Trade in Canada*. New Haven: Yale University Press, 1930.

Johnson, Robert E., *Sir John Richardson: Arctic Explorer, Natural Historian, Naval Surgeon*. London: Taylor & Francis, 1976.

Lind, James, *A Treatise on the Scurvy*. Edinburgh: Millar, 1753. [and (ed.) Stewart & Guthrie, 1953].

Losey and Losey, 'Fort Enterprise, NWT', Occasional publication No. 9 *Boreal Institute for Northern Studies*. University of Alberta: 1970.

McIlraith, J., *Life of John Richardson*. London: Longmans Green, 1868.

Mackinnon, C.S., 'Some Logistics of Portage La Loche (Methye)', *Prarie Forum*, 5, no.II (1980). 51–65.

MacLaren, I.S., 'Retaining Captaincy of the Soul: Response to Nature in the First Franklin Expedition', *Essays In Canadian Writing* 28 (1984): 57–92.

MacLaren, I.S., 'Ariel: Samuel Hearne's accounts of the Massacre of Bloody Fall, 17 July 1771', *A review of International English Literature* 22 (1991) 7: 9–17.

Macleod, M.A. and Glover, R., 'Franklin's First Expedition as Seen by the Fur Traders', *Polar Record* 15, No. 98, 1971.

Masson, L.R. (ed.), *Les bourgeois de la Compagnie du Nord-Ouest*. 1889 Vol. I Quebec. (Reprinted by Antiquarian Press, New York, 1960: 146–150).

Morton, A.S., *Sir George Simpson, Overseas Governor of the Hudson's Bay Company*. Toronto: Dent, 1944.

Mowat, Farley, *Tundra: Selections from the great accounts of Arctic land Voyages*. Toronto: McClelland & Stewart, 1958.

Ray, A.J., *Indians and the Fur Trade: their role as Trappers, Hunters and*

Middlemen in the Lands Southwest of Hudson's Bay 1670–1870. Toronto: University of Toronto Press, 1974.

Rich, E.E. (ed.), *Colin Robertson's Correspondence Book.* Toronto: Champlain Society, 1939.

Rich, E.E., *Montreal and the Fur Trade.* Montreal: McGill University Press, 1966.

Richardson, John, *Arctic Ordeal: The Journal of John Richardson, Surgeon-Naturalist with Franklin, 1820–1822,* (ed.) C. Stuart Houston. Montreal: McGill-Queen's University Press, 1984.

Schoenherr and Wilson, 'With John Franklin to the Top of the World', (extracts from George Back's unpublished journal). Ottawa: PAC & NFBC, 1979.

Simpson, George, *Journal of occurrences in the Athabasca Department: 1820 and 1821, and report.* (ed.) Rich, E.E. Toronto: Champlain Society for the Hudson's Bay Record Society, 1938.

Stefansson, Vilhjalmur, 'Original Observations on Scurvy and My Opinion of the Medical Profession', *Medical Review of Reviews* 24 (1918): 257–64.

Van Kirk, Sylvia, *Many Tender Ties – Women in Fur-Trade Society in Western Canada, 1670–1870.* Winnipeg: Watson & Dwyer, 1980.

Voorhis, Ernest, 'Historical Forts and Trading Posts of the French Regime and on the English Fur Trading Companies'. Ottawa: Department of the Interior, 1930.

Weekes, Mary, 'Akaitcho, a Link with Franklin', *Beaver*, outfit 270, No. 1. 1939.

Wiebe, Rudy, *A Discovery of Strangers.* Toronto: Knopf, 1994.

Wiebe, Rudy, *Playing Dead: A Contemplation Concerning the Arctic.* Edmonton: NeWest Press, 1992.

Wonders and McClure, 'Barren Land Bugs', *The Beaver* 267 (Mar 1937).

12 TO THE NORTH COAST OF AMERICA, 1823–25

13 DOWN THE MACKENZIE, 1825–26

14 ESKIMO AFFRAYS, 1826–27

Davis, Richard C., *Sir John Franklin's Journals and Correspondence: The Second Arctic Land Expedition, 1825–1827.* Toronto: Champlain Society, 1998.

Franklin, John, *Narrative of a Second Expedition to the Shores of the Polar Sea, in the Years 1825, 1826, and 1827.* London: John Murray, 1828.

Harper, J. Russell, Transcription of *A Journal of the proceedings of the land Arctic Expedition under the command of John Franklin Esquire Captain R.N.*

F.R.S. etc. etc. by Lieut. G. Back R.N. SPRI 395/6 MG 30 D352 Vol. 63. files 2–6.

Schoenherr and Wilson, microfiches of GB's sketches of Franklin's Second Arctic Land Expedition. *Public Archives of Canada, Ottawa.* Picture Division, 1981.

Wallace, H.N., *The Navy, the Company, and Richard King.* Montreal: McGill-Queen's University Press, 1980.

15 TOUR OF THE CONTINENT, 1830–32

Back, George, 'Journal kept during a Tour of the Continent, August 1830–April 1832', 2 vols. SPRI MS 395/10/1–2; BJ.

Littlewood, Ian, *Sultry Climates: Travel and Sex since the Grand Tour.* London: John Murray, 2001.

16 RETURN TO THE BARRENS, 1833

17 HUNGER AT FORT RELIANCE, 1833–34

18 DESCENT OF THE THLEW-EE-CHOH, 1834

19 THE UNMAPPED OCEAN, 1834–35

Anderson, James, 'Chief Factor James Anderson's Back River Journal of 1855', *The Canadian Field-Naturalist.* Ottawa: Vol. 54, No 5, May–Dec. 1940. 63–67, 84–89, 107–109, 125–26; Jan.–Mar. 1941. 9–11, 21–26, 38–44.

Back, George, *The Arctic Land Expedition to the Mouth of the Great Fish River 1833–5.* London: John Murray, 1836.

Barrow, Sir John, 'Back's Arctic Expedition', *Quarterly Review* 56: 278; *Edinburgh Review* 63: 287.

Bertulli, Margaret, 'Fort Reliance: Gateway to the Arctic', *The Beaver* (1990/91) 70 (6): 48–54.

Christian, Edgar, Diary on the Thelon River – 1920s.

King, Richard, *Narrative of a Journey to the Shores of the Arctic Ocean in 1833, 4 & 5 under the command of Captain Back.* London: Bentley, 1836.

MacLaren, I.S., 'The Grandest Tour: the Aesthetics of Landscape in Sir George Back's Exploration's of the Eastern Arctic 1833–1837', *English Studies in Canada* (1984) 10 (4): 436–456.

Pelly, David F., *Expedition: An Arctic Journey through History on George Back's River.* Toronto: Betelgeuse Books, 1981.

Pelly, David F., 'Back River/Pelly Lake Expedition', *Explorers' Journal* (1978), 56 (2): 66–69.

Perkins, Robert, *Into the Great Solitude.* New York: Holt, 1991.

Templeman, William, 'Canoeing the Formidable Back River', *Canadian Geographic* (1987), 107: (2)

20 BACK'S LAST BLANK ON THE MAP, 1836–37

Back, George, *Narrative of an Expedition in H.M.S. Terror Undertaken with a View to Geographical Discovery on The Arctic Shores in the Years 1836–7*. London: John Murray, 1838.

MacLaren, I.S., 'From Exploration to Publication: The Evolution of a 19th-Century Arctic Narrative', *Arctic* 47.1 (1994): 43–53.

21 ARCTIC COUNCILLOR, 1837–87

Atwood, Margaret, 'Concerning Franklin and His Gallant Crew', *Books in Canada* 20, no. 4 (1991).

Beattie, Owen, 'Elevated Bone Lead Levels in a Crewman from the Last Arctic Expedition of Sir John Franklin', *The Franklin Era in Canadian Arctic History*. Patricia D. Sutherland, (ed.). Ottawa: National Museum of Man, 1985. 141–48.

Beattie, Owen and Geiger, John, *Frozen in Time: Unlocking the Secrets of the Doomed 1845 Arctic Expedition*. New York: Penguin, 1990.

Berton, Pierre, *Jane Franklin's Obsession*. Toronto: McClelland and Stewart, 1992.

Cyriax, Richard, *Sir John Franklin's Last Expedition: a chapter in the history of the Royal Navy*. London: Methuen, 1939.

Houston, C. Stuart, 'Dr. John Rae, the Most Efficient Arctic Explorer', *Annals of the Royal College of Physicians & Surgeons*. 20 (1987), 225–8.

King, Richard, *The Franklin Expedition from First to Last*. London: Churchill, 1855.

Klutschak, Heinrich, *Overland to Starvation Cove: With the Inuit in Search of Franklin, 1878–1880*. Toronto: University of Toronto Press, 1987.

Lamb, G.F., *Franklin – Happy Voyager*. London: Ernest Benn, 1956.

McClintock, F., *The Voyage of the 'Fox' in the Arctic Seas. A Narrative of the Discovery of the Fate of Sir John Franklin and his Companions*. Edmonton: Hurtig, 1972.

McGoogan, K., *Fatal Passage: the Untold Story of John Rae*. Toronto: HarperCollins, 2001.

Neatby, L.H., *In Quest of the Northwest Passage*. New York: Crowell, 1958.

Neatby, L.H., *The Search for Franklin*. Edmonton: Hurtig, 1970.

Owen, Roderic, *The Fate of Franklin*. London: Hutchinson, 1978.

Richards, R.L., *Doctor John Rae*. Whitby: Caedmon, 1985.

Stewart, D.A., 'Sir John Rae: Surgeon, Physician, Sailor, Explorer, Naturalist, Scholar', *British Medical Journal*. 1 (1931): 110–12.

Thomson, G.M., *The North-West Passage*. London: Secker & Warburg, 1975.

Traill, Henry Duff, *The Life of Sir John Franklin R.N.* London: John Murray, 1896.

Woodman, David C., *Strangers Among Us.* Montreal: McGill-Queen's University Press, 1992.

Woodman, David C., *Unravelling the Franklin Mystery: Inuit Testimony.* Montreal: McGill-Queens University Press, 1991.

MSS

PUBLIC RECORDS OFFICE (PRO)

i) Admiralty. Adm 1/582. Correspondence relating to the Back Expedition, 1833–35 vol. CO.6/15 – Colonial Office correspondence

pp. 11–12 & 28–31 & 34–38 & 52–55– JF to Henry Goulburn (Colonial Office)

pp. 39–40 – W.F.Wentzel to Edward Smith 2 May 1820

pp. 99–101 – Simon McGillivray to NWC agents 21 May 1819

pp. 113–14 – John Barrow to Lord Melville

pp. 149–51 – JF to W.F.Wentzel

HUDSON'S BAY COMPANY (HBC) ARCHIVES

E 15/1 – Franklin's second arctic expedition: Accounts and miscellaneous

E 15/2 – Back's first expedition: Accounts, correspondence and contracts 1832–35

ROYAL GEOGRAPHICAL SOCIETY (RGS) ARCHIVES

Correspondence block for Sir George Back for the years 1831–40, 1841–50, 1851–60

Obituary of George Back. *RGS Proceedings*, 1879. 1 (1): 70–71

NATIONAL MARITIME MUSEUM (NMM)

Various pictures and references of naval uniforms.

SCOTT POLAR RESEARCH INSTITUTE (SPRI)

MS 248. – Folder on Back in *Terror* in 1836, including Back, Watch Exercise Book, 21 Sept. 1836 to 2 Sept. 1837

MS 248/276 – JF's personal letter book of the expedition 17 Apr.–21 May 1819

pp. 29–33 – John Pritchard and Sir Alexander Mackenzie to JF

pp. 183–84 – JF to Edward Smith

pp. 192–94 – Partners of NWC, Ft. Chip to JF, Feb. 1821

pp. 198–99 – GB to JF, 8 Nov. 1820

MS 395. Back, 'Sir George Back Diaries', MS diaries 1844–78. 25 vols.

Captain Back's Arctic Journal, 1833–35. SPRI No. 41: 91 (08)

MS 395/71/1 SPRI. Miscellaneous notes written during the First Arctic Land Expedition 1819–22. holograph

MS 395/10/1–2 SPRI. Journal kept during a Tour of the Continent 3 August 1830 to April 1832. 2 vol. holograph

MS 248/278: BJ SPRI. Journal of Occurences at Fort Chipewyan, June 1820–16 April 1821. 1 vol. holograph

MCCORD MUSEUM, MCGILL UNIVERSITY, MONTREAL

George Back Journal 1819–20

John Back Sr. letter to George Back. 14 Oct. 1815 private collection.

Letters of George Back (1833–34)

ARCTIC INSTITUTE OF NORTH AMERICA (AINA)

Bershad – 45 Miscellaneous letters of GB, McClintock, Parry, JF

NATIONAL ARCHIVES OF CANADA (NAC)

Sketch Books. Nat Arch. Canada accession no. 1994–254 Picture Division.

NAC & NATIONAL FILM BOARD OF CANADA (NFBC)

Schoenherr and Wilson. With John Franklin to the Top of the World (extracts from George Back's unpublished journal). Ottawa: PAC & NFBC 1979

NAC & NFBC

2 microfiches of George Back's sketches. Ottawa: PAC Picture Div. 1981.

Index

About the author

A surgeon and mountaineer, Peter Steele was born in England and has lived in Whitehorse since 1975. He ran the Grenfell flying doctor service in Labrador, travelling the coast by snowshoe, dog sled and boat. His first book, *Two and Two Halves to Bhutan* (Hodder & Stoughton, 1970), told the story of his young family's adventures in Nepal. He was the Medical Officer to the ill-fated 1971 International Everest Expedition, an experence recorded in *Doctor On Everest* (Hodder & Stoughton, 1972). He followed this with two books on medical care for climbers and *Atlin's Gold* (Caitlin, 1995), a slice of little-known BC history. His last book, *Eric Shipton: Everest and Beyond* (Mountaineers, 1998), a biography of the great English climber, won the Boardman Tasker Prize for Mountain Literature. In researching *The Man Who Mapped the Arctic*, Peter Steele followed his ebullient hero around Europe and across thousands of kilometres of still-remote barrens in Canada's north country, travelling by plane, boat and on foot.